BY LAW OR IN JUSTICE

By Law or In Justice

The Indian Specific Claims Commission
and the Struggle for Indigenous Justice

JANE DICKSON

PURICH
BOOKS

Purich Books, an imprint of UBC Press
2029 West Mall
Vancouver, BC, V6T 1Z2
www.purichbooks.ca

26 25 24 23 22 21 20 19 18   5 4 3 2 1

Printed in Canada on FSC-certified ancient-forest-free paper
(100% post-consumer recycled) that is processed chlorine- and acid-free.

Library and Archives Canada Cataloguing in Publication

Dickson, Jane (E. Jane), author
By law or in justice: the Indian Specific Claims Commission and the struggle
for indigenous justice / Jane Dickson.

Includes bibliographical references and index.
Issued in print and electronic formats.
ISBN 978-0-7748-8005-3 (hardcover). – ISBN 978-0-7748-8006-0 (softcover).
ISBN 978-0-7748-8007-7 (PDF). – ISBN 978-0-7748-8008-4 (EPUB).
ISBN 978-0-7748-8009-1 (Kindle)

1. Canada. Indian Claims Commission (1991-2009). 2. Native peoples –
Canada – Claims. I. Title.

E98.C6D53 2018   352.8'8508997071   C2018-900325-1
                                                   C2018-900326-X

Canadä

UBC Press gratefully acknowledges the financial support
for our publishing program of the Government of Canada
(through the Canada Book Fund), the Canada Council for the Arts,
and the British Columbia Arts Council.

Printed and bound in Canada by Friesens
Set in Univers Condensed and Minion by Artegraphica Design Co. Ltd.
Copy editor: Deborah Kerr
Proofreader: Judith Earnshaw
Indexer: Pat Buchanan

Contents

Acknowledgments / vii

Acronyms / viii

Introduction / 3

1 Specific Claims in Canada: A Brief History and Policy
Roadmap / 13

2 Dependent on the Good Will of the Sovereign: Background
to the Indian Specific Claims Commission / 38

3 The Indian Specific Claims Commission: Second Sober
Thought / 59

4 Challenges to the Process: Applications for Inquiries and
Constructive Rejections / 82

5 On the Road Again: Planning Conferences, Community
Sessions, and the Integrity of the Process / 108

6 By Law or In Justice: Legal Arguments, Panel Deliberations,
and the Murky Waters of the Mediation Unit / 126

Contents

7 Beyond Lawful Obligation: The Closure of the ICC and
   the Rise of the Specific Claims Tribunal / 148

8 The Legacy of the ICC and Lessons for the Future of Specific
   Claims / 176

   Notes / 187

   Index / 214

Acknowledgments

I would like to acknowledge the great gifts of wisdom and experience shared by all those involved in the inquiry process during my tenure as a commissioner and the support and camaraderie provided by my fellow commissioners, for whom I have the utmost respect and affection. The path to claims justice is not easy or short, and walking it together eased the journey. I believe it brought us a measure closer to reconciliation.

I would like to acknowledge especially my former Indian Claims Commission colleague and close friend Sheila Purdy, who was a patient reader of first drafts and wise counsellor regarding those of our experiences that could, should, and should not be shared. For this, and many other favours, you have my enduring gratitude.

Karen Bolstad and Purich Publishing picked up when I threw up my hands and simply submitted the manuscript; Karen, for your exceptional patience and unwavering faith that the book would actually get finished, I thank you. As a publisher dedicated to Indigenous issues and rooted in a proud treaty province, Purich will be much missed. Thanks to UBC Press for taking up Purich's important work and legacy.

To Taylor, Rachel, and Delaney, my fierce, beautiful daughters, my sincere apologies for all the times my work took me away from you. My pride in your spirit and strength is breathtaking.

And last, but not least, to N.M. You opened the door and made many things possible. My gratitude runs deep.

Acronyms

AFN	Assembly of First Nations
AIM	American Indian Movement
AOKFN	Aundeck Omni Kaning First Nation
DAAND	Department of Aboriginal Affairs and Northern Development
DIAND	Department of Indian Affairs and Northern Development
FNSCC	First Nations Specific Claims Commission
ICC	Indian Specific Claims Commission
ICCP	Indian Claims Commission Proceedings
INAC	Indian and Northern Affairs Canada
JTF	Joint First Nations–Canada Task Force
OIC	Order in Council
ONC	Office of Native Claims
SCB	Specific Claims Branch
SCRA	Specific Claims Resolution Act
SCTA	Specific Claims Tribunal Act

BY LAW OR IN JUSTICE

Introduction

Imagine your new neighbour comes into your backyard and fences off half of it. Then he sells it to someone down the street. This new neighbour tells you he got a good deal but he won't say how much he got. Then, he says he'll take care of the cash – on your behalf, of course.

Maybe he even spends a little on himself.

You complain. He denies he did anything wrong.

What would you do?

Go to the proper authorities? Turns out all the authorities and their agencies work for him.

Sue him? He tells you that none of the lawyers can work for you – he's got everyone in town working for him. When he finally lets a lawyer work for you – it turns out that he can afford five of them for every one you can afford.

Finally he says: Okay, I'm willing to discuss it. But first you have to prove I did something wrong. Oh, and I get to be the judge of whether you've proved it. And, if you do prove it, I get to set the rules about how we'll negotiate. I'll decide when we've reached a deal and I'll even get to determine how I'll pay the settlement out to you. Oh, and I hope you're in no rush because this is going to take about twenty or thirty years to settle.

Sound crazy?

Welcome to the world of Indian Specific Claims.

– CANADA, "NEGOTIATION OR CONFRONTATION: IT'S CANADA'S CHOICE"

On September 30, 2013, a journalist at the Aboriginal Peoples Television Network received a leaked letter written by a group of federal government employees to Bernard Valcourt, the minister of Aboriginal Affairs. It was unsigned, but its authors were staff in the minister's own department – in the Treaties and Aboriginal Government division of its Specific Claims Branch.[1] The letter – or rather, the first page of what was clearly a much longer communication – informed Valcourt of serious concerns about his department's commitment to the timely and just resolution of specific claims.[2] The staffers were greatly distressed about the unreasonable delay in claims resolution at the Specific Claims Branch, a problem that they traced to senior management.[3] As the letter explained,

> delays of several months [are] not unusual for even the simplest and most straightforward matter. Settlement agreements are needlessly delayed over minor and insignificant issues that have already been addressed. Constant and endless reviews come with continual requests for changes. These are not substantive changes ... [They] are needless changes which do not change the substance of agreements but add considerable delays to the process ... Such delays are needless and constant changing also impacts our relationship with the First Nations.[4]

The alleged "micromanaging" and changeability in the approach of senior staff were made worse by an overall intransigence regarding claims.[5] Senior management was charged with refusing to consider the larger context of claims, or being open to broader information about a claim submission that could lead to what staffers saw as a more complete and just outcome. "Bullying" was common and accountability limited,[6] all to the detriment of the claims process itself. Asked to respond to these allegations, the minister dismissed them as nothing more than an "internal human resource management issue"[7] – and both the letter and its contents simply slipped out of the public eye.

For those of us who have a history with the recently renamed Indigenous and Northern Affairs Canada in general and the Specific Claims Branch in particular, there was little in the leaked letter – or the minister's response to it – that was new or terribly surprising. Since the first formal policy statement on specific claims, aptly titled *Outstanding Business,* was released by the department in 1982, the approach to specific claims has been pro-foundly undermined by deep problems in both the policy and the process it informs. Although these problems are numerous and varied, almost all of them stem from a fundamental flaw: the Crown, which is the party against whom a First Nation must make its claim, also determines the claim's validity and controls the process through which it is negotiated and resolved. This conflict of interest permeates every pore of the policy and feeds a climate of control in the Department of Indigenous and Northern Affairs (DIAND) that is probably the driving force behind the micro-management that allegedly plagues the claims process. It also nurtures a certain reticence on the part of the Crown, which has little to gain by a generous interpretation of its lawful obligations to Indigenous people or of its own honour in dealing with them. The result is a specific claims process characterized by woefully inadequate resources, levels of delay bordering on paralysis, and what appears to be profound government ambivalence around claims and their resolution. It is interesting that despite an overhaul of the claims policy in 2007, in a policy document titled "Specific Claims: Justice at Last," the conflict of interest persists, and there is little evidence that the new policy is any better than the old one.[8]

"Justice at Last" is merely the most recent of many attempts to improve the resolution of specific claims. The Indian Specific Claims Commission (ICC), created in 1991 in response to the conflict and violence of the Oka Crisis, was one of the more enduring efforts, lasting until 2009. It earned considerable respect for its oversight of the claims process and its contri-butions to advancing Aboriginal law in Canada. That the commission should rise from the ashes of Oka is not surprising – the crisis itself was a direct consequence of a failed specific claim: the Mohawks of Kahnesatake had submitted a claim to the land known as the Pines on three separate occasions over many years, and all three submissions were rejected by the Department of Indian Affairs, leaving the sacred lands open to development and sowing the seeds for the conflict that erupted in 1990. Few Canadians are likely to remember this fact, and they will be greatly outnumbered by those who recall the more spectacular moments of that nearly seven-month clash: the occupation by the Mohawk protesters of the Pines in March of 1990; the subsequent storming of their encampment by Sureté du Quebec, leading to much gunfire and the death of a police officer; and the later replacement of the Sureté, first by the RCMP and then by the Canadian Forces, at barricades set up at Kahnesatake, Kahnawake, and Akwesasne. The crisis persisted from July 11 to September 26, 1990. By the time the barricades came down and the last remaining protesters were arrested, the fiasco had ignited protests throughout Canada in support of the Mohawks, drawing critical attention to, and international condemnation of, Canada's approach to Indigenous land rights.

Shocked that a rejected claim involving such a small parcel of land could spark a national crisis, Prime Minister Brian Mulroney announced before the House of Commons a set of parallel initiatives to expedite the claims resolution process and, on the advice of the Assembly of First Nations (AFN), to improve public scrutiny of that process.[9] At the core of the latter initiative was an independent review body that would operate at arm's length from the government; it would have the power to inquire into the basis for rejection of claims, facilitate negotiation, and break any impasses that might arise in their negotiation and settlement. Following a rather painful period of consultation, the Indian Specific Claims Commission came into being on July 1, 1991. Its purpose was to conduct public inquiries into claims rejected by the federal government and provide mediation services to the Crown and Aboriginal communities whose claims had been accepted for negotiation. Between 1991 and 2009, when it was decommissioned by the Harper government, it conducted mediations and inquiries in ninety-six claims, produced sixteen annual reports, and completed twenty-six joint studies for First Nations and Canada. This is an impressive record, but one whose efficacy in achieving greater social justice for First Nations and greater accountability in the claims process remains unclear.

As an interim measure, the ICC was certainly never intended to last as long as it did; indeed, commissions of inquiry rarely have a lifespan of more than three or four years. Over its almost eighteen year history, there were numerous calls to replace it with a permanent, independent body that would oversee and adjudicate specific claims. The 1996 Royal Commission on Aboriginal Peoples recommended this measure, and through participation in joint working groups with Indian Affairs, the AFN made similar calls in 1992 and 1997. By 2002, these efforts had acquired a sufficient critical mass to produce Bill C-6, the Specific Claims Resolution Act.

This bill, which was not favourably received by many First Nations, including the Federation of Saskatchewan Indian Nations, the Treaty and Aboriginal Rights Centre of Manitoba, the Union of BC Indian Chiefs,[10] or the AFN, was passed by the House and Senate, and received Royal Assent in 2003. Substantial and ongoing opposition to the bill, much of which was captured by the Standing Senate Committee on Aboriginal Peoples in its "Special Study on the Federal Specific Claims Process,"[11] killed the legislation. The Specific Claims Resolution Act was never proclaimed into force, and rather like the letter that opened this chapter, it simply slipped away. Recognizing failure when directly confronted by it, Indian Affairs withdrew and regrouped.

These events have brought us to the present moment and "Justice at Last." This latest permutation of specific claims policy made bold promises – but not necessarily new ones. These included greater transparency in claims assessment and funding, faster processing of claims pressed by a three-year rule that sets time limits for assessment and negotiation, and a climate wherein "every reasonable effort will be made to achieve negotiated settlements."[12] When Indigenous Affairs and Northern Development fails to meet its three-year rule, or a First Nation's claim is rejected, the claimants may take it to a Specific Claims Tribunal, which provides a final determination.[13] The "permanent body" that answers the historic calls for such by First Nations, their advocates, and the ICC, the tribunal is a central pillar of the Crown's "new approach" to the resolution of specific claims.

And yet, here we are, a decade into the new approach, and it seems that not much has improved.[14] According to the AFN, the department has assumed an adversarial and Machiavellian approach to claims assessment and resolution since 2007, focusing on either hasty rejection of claims or acceptance with an offer of resolution that is partial and grossly out of step with even the most parsimonious interpretation of fairness.[15] Rejection appears to be the preferred mode of "resolution," a practice facilitated by "formalistic quibbling" and rigid and unreasonable adherence to a "minimum standard" for claims submissions.[16] The result is that, whereas history and expert opinion suggest that roughly 70 percent of submitted claims are valid, the "actual rate of validation under Justice at Last, after an initial flurry of offers, is 20 percent or less."[17]

Given this approach, it is hardly surprising that the department can boast remarkable progress in reducing the staggering backlog of claims, as well as high rates of resolution. In its "Progress Report – Specific Claims" for 2012–13, the department stated that it had reduced the backlog by 51 claims out of the 800–900 claims estimated to constitute the backlog in 2007 and 2009, respectively, and settled 95 claims through agreements totalling $1.8 billion.[18] These results are impressive, but as is so often the case, it seems there are many devils dancing among the details. If one looks closely at the numbers for even a slim section of the recent history of the "new approach," it becomes clear that addressing the backlog was primarily achieved on the backs of the Aboriginal claimants. For example, a break-down of "resolved claims" for October 2008 to October 2011 reveals that the vast number were resolved by rejection or through "file closure," which occurs when a First Nation declines the Crown's offer to settle. Such "resolutions" constituted just over *90 percent of the total claims removed from the backlog* during that timeframe. Of the remaining 10 percent, the majority were resolved by "administrative remedy" or through actual settlement.[19] As the AFN, the Union of BC Indian Chiefs, and many other Aboriginal advocacy bodies note, the combined impact of the three-year rule and the increasing focus on closing files and rejecting claims creates the illusion that the Department of Aboriginal Affairs and Northern De-velopment is making "substantive progress in resolving claims and clear-ing up its claims backlog," when in fact, it is merely shifting responsibility for the logjam onto the tribunal.[20] As the AFN observes, "the Tribunal was not created to be the new home of the massive backlog of claims that are considered 'unresolved' by First Nations,"[21] yet this is precisely what has happened.

If this scenario persists, it is unlikely that there will be much justice at last. And though the tribunal has the power to rule decisively on claims and bind both Crown and claimant, the wheels of justice grind slowly – perhaps not as slowly as the Specific Claims Branch, but certainly slowly enough that the backlog has little chance of being reduced any more quickly by simply being passed over to the tribunal. Early indications are that this is indeed the case: the start-up of the tribunal was significantly delayed, in part due to issues regarding the appointment of its judges, so it undertook no real work until nearly three years after its creation by legislation. Once under way, much of its initial work consisted of applications, but this was soon overtaken by the forty-nine decisions it has handed down since 2012, some of which contain strong judicial criticism of the state of affairs at the Specific Claims Branch (SCB).

Between the apparently pugnacious approach of Indigenous Affairs and the SCB, and the independent but necessarily legalistic focus of the Specific Claims Tribunal, there is precious little middle ground for a non-adversarial approach in which law, rights, history, and co-existence can achieve a balance. In its 2012 review of the Justice at Last policy, the AFN cited the elimination of the Indian Claims Commission as a significant loss to that middle ground, as it "was to assume a major role in alternative dispute resolution" in the new claims policy. When the commission closed, its significant experience and history with claims was lost, and "currently, independent mediation through a neutral third party is unavailable."[22]

There is no formal port of entry into the "new approach" of the Justice at Last policy for the knowledge and expertise that the ICC acquired during its eighteen-year journey to assist First Nations and Canada in the resolution of claims. This is regrettable. As an ICC commissioner for seven years, I was fortunate to benefit from the considerable wisdom and expertise of my colleagues and predecessors in juggling the competing interests complicating just claims resolution within the claims policy. I have also seen the difficulties encountered by First Nations, who experience many challenges in mounting a claim. As commissioners, we observed first-hand the egregious levels of delay, the idiosyncrasies of the specific claims process, and the myriad problems arising from the inherent conflict of interest in the Crown's approach to claims. We met with claimant communities, took testimony, perused volumes of historical research, and engaged the thrust and parry of the fields of law that intersected with our duties as commissioners – Aboriginal law, administrative law, constitutional law. We confronted the limitations of both claims policy and our oversight of it as a body empowered solely to recommend, not order, necessary change. It was an interesting, frustrating, inspiring, and highly educational journey, and given the increasingly apparent problems with the Justice at Last policy, both within Indigenous Affairs and outside it, I feel it is time to bring our experience and expertise into the current conversation about claims.

The pages that follow will trace the origins of claims policy and the ICC. Readers will be invited into the inquiry process and behind the scenes of a select sample of our inquiries and into some of our most bedevilling struggles. Opening with a brief outline of the history and development of specific claims policy, the initial chapter chronicles the early approach to Indigenous nations and lands, and briefly touches upon the resulting treaties, surrenders, and jurisprudence. From this limited discussion, the chapter explores the development of Canadian claims policies and specifically the repeated calls for a claims commission like that which emerged in the United States. It concludes with an examination of the US Court of Claims and the history of American treaties, claims, and claims processes, revealing the influence and impact of US approaches on the evolution of a Canadian claims process.

Chapter 2 shifts the focus directly to the Canadian experience, describing the development of specific claims policy and the conflict of interest that lies at its heart. The flaws of the policy laid bare, the chapter shows how the 1990 Oka Crisis was the inevitable result. Oka's implications for state policies in relation to Indigenous people provide the opening discussion of Chapter 3, which examines the events and interests that sparked the creation of the Indian Specific Claims Commission. The early commission is described, as is the process that the first commissioners created, which persisted largely unchanged throughout the ICC's eighteen-year tenure.

From here, the book concentrates on the last seven years of the ICC, during which I sat as a commissioner (from 2002 to 2009). Chapter 4 discusses the specific claims process, as well as its associated difficulties and their impacts on claims resolution. Chief among these difficulties is shocking delay: claims languishing for an average of thirteen years, awaiting a determination of acceptance or rejection. In some cases, the process can take even longer: consider the example of the Peepeekisis people, who waited fifteen years for the SCB to complete its review of their claim, or the seventeen-year wait of the Siksika First Nation to hear the outcome of its submission.[23]

Though remarkable in its magnitude and ubiquity, delay was not the only problem with the claims process, but it was a central factor in the development of the ICC's "constructive rejection policy." This evolved over time in response to the entreaties of First Nations whose claims were stuck in limbo at the SCB, thus undermining the integrity of the process and any assertions regarding its fairness or efficiency. In Chapter 4, I explain the origins and details of our constructive rejection policy and discuss our efforts to implement it in the Alexis First Nation and Red Earth and Shoal Lake Cree First Nations inquiries.[24] Although such inquiries were technically outside our mandate because they involved claims that had not yet been formally rejected by the minister, constructive rejection claims reflected important truths about the claims process and the honour of the Crown in its dealings with First Nations.

The fifth chapter begins the discussion of our process and my experiences with it, which continues through Chapter 6. These chapters detail the strengths and weaknesses of our process, including the unique challenges of planning conferences and community sessions, as well as some of our more controversial rules of procedure, such as the rule against cross-examination of elders. These chapters focus on the "orals," the session in which the parties' legal counsel presented their arguments, the forum of panel deliberations, and the never dull, and often surprising, relationship between commissioners and ICC lawyers. As the story draws to a close, the penultimate chapter dedicates attention to the rise of "Justice at Last" – the "new approach" to claims – and the Specific Claims Tribunal's role in that new approach. The book concludes with a brief statement about the legacy of the ICC and what lessons this may hold for the future.

Readers who are familiar with the ICC will notice that its mediation function receives a limited treatment here. Throughout its lifetime, the commission provided mediation services free of charge to claimants and Canada, and in that context also funded and oversaw a number of studies, pilot projects, and negotiation support services.[25] Mediations that reached a successful conclusion are detailed in fourteen reports, published in our *Indian Claims Commission Proceedings*. I discuss these services only briefly because, quite frankly, I know very little about them. Although as commissioners we received extensive mediation training, and some of us were quite proficient in that skillset, we had virtually no involvement with the mediation aspect of the commission. As a result, though the Mediation Unit appears to have performed a fair amount of work, I have little to say on the subject.

A final word about this book before we begin. It is important to understand that my goal in sharing my experiences of the ICC is not to speak for or critique the commission, the Crown, or First Nations, but rather to help foster understanding of the strengths and weaknesses of the key players and policies in specific claims, and in so doing, to assist in achieving better outcomes in the future. Like any organization, the ICC manifested significant strengths and weaknesses. I will refer to many of both in this book but must admit that much cannot and should not be shared. Our work often required us to balance many difficult and delicate issues and situations; much of that work was confidential and, in respect for the parties, must remain so. That said, the members of the ICC have remained largely silent on our experiences since the commission closed in 2009. After careful consideration, it seems the right time to break the silence and share the rich experience and education implicit in the story of the Indian Specific Claims Commission.

1

Specific Claims in Canada
A Brief History and Policy Roadmap

Although legal and policy responses to Indigenous claims are complex and can be challenging to navigate, the bald reality is actually quite simple: claims exist because promises were not kept. Most of those promises are contained in the historic treaties between Indigenous nations and the Crown, but they also reside in the federal Indian Act and within the larger set of legal and ethical obligations that flow from the Crown to First Nations.[1] To understand claims, then, we must start with the treaties. To understand treaties and the treaty relationship, we must recognize that treaties owe their mere existence to two dominant facts – the pre-existence of Indigenous nations in what would become Canada and the recognition of Indigenous rights to land, which lay at the heart of British imperial policy in the "New World."[2]

In the earliest days of contact between Indigenous people and newcomers, when the latter depended on the good will of the former to survive and prosper, treaties focused not on land, but on confirming "friendship" and peaceable co-existence. The explorers, merchants, and missionaries who led the penetration of Indigenous territories were preoccupied with harvesting the wealth of fish, fur, and souls, and agreements struck between their respective governments reflected this reality. The resulting treaties spoke of "amity and commerce," and confirmed emerging alliances that melded Indigenous interests with those of the French and British, and drew them into each other's communities, cultures, and conflicts.[3] As long as newcomer dependency on Indigenous people as trading partners, military allies, and mentors persisted, Indigenous nations were respected, and the relationship maintained equilibrium. When trade declined and military alliance became less important, the balance began to tip in favour of the newcomers, with now notorious long-term impacts on Indigenous people, communities, and cultures.

Early Approaches to Indigenous Nations and Lands:
From Dependence to Dispossession

When Britain defeated New France on the Plains of Abraham in 1760, leading to the French handover of New France to Britain in 1763, the treaty relationship shifted radically. Now that the threat of colonial war had passed, the Indigenous-newcomer conjunction required recalibration. The new relationship was defined, not by trade or the courting of military and commercial allies, but by the need to deftly balance state interests in expanding settlement with ongoing Indigenous rights and interests in land. As Indigenous and newcomer fortunes had shifted, the former were now seen as impediments, especially to settlement. The result was the rise of "great Frauds and Abuses" in "purchasing Lands of the Indians," raising Indigenous ire and the potential for uprisings. In the interests of avoiding further conflict, the Royal Proclamation of 1763 inserted the state into the purchase of Indigenous lands, in a passage that is now firmly etched into Canadian history:

> We do, with the Advice of our Privy Council strictly enjoin and require, that no private Person do presume to make any purchase from the said Indians of any Lands reserved to the said Indians, within those part of our Colonies where, We have thought proper to allow Settlement; but that, if at any Time any of the Said Indians should be inclined to dispose of the said Lands, the same shall be Purchased only for Us, in our Name, at some public Meeting or Assembly of the said Indians, to be held for that purpose by the Governor or Commander in Chief of our Colony Respectively within which they shall lie; and in case they shall lie within the limits of any Proprietary Government, they shall be purchased only for the Use and in the name of such Proprietaries, conformable to such Directions and Instructions as We or they shall think proper to give for that purpose.[4]

In setting out a process for securing Indigenous title to land, the Royal Proclamation recognized not only Indigenous land rights, but the sovereignty and right of First Nations to negotiate with the Crown for the release of those rights. In this regard, the proclamation has been referred to as "the Charter of Indian Rights," which, "like so many great Charters ... does not create rights but rather affirms old rights."[5]

The approach spelled out in the Royal Proclamation guided the treating process both before and after Confederation – more or less. Between 1763 and 1850, the Crown entered into more than thirty treaties in the Great Lakes basin, and the prairies were secured and settled primarily through the eleven "numbered treaties" negotiated between 1871 and 1921. Large parts of British Columbia were not covered by these treaties.[6] Nor were the Yukon and the Northwest Territories, though Indigenous claims were substantially resolved in the Yukon in 1993 and with the creation of Nunavut in 1999.[7] British Columbia, however, remains predominantly unceded territory.[8]

Although the Royal Proclamation created a process for securing Indigenous title and aspired to restricting frauds and abuses, the treaty process remained fraught. On many occasions, it was subject to disingenuousness on the part of government. If we focus on the numbered treaties, which dominated treaty activity after Confederation and unsurprisingly comprised much of the ICC caseload, we see that the seeds of the modern state approach to rights, treaties, and claims were sowed early on.

First Nations were not fools and were quick to see that their lands would require some protection from the settler influx. Many sought treaties at the first sign of newcomers and were unwilling to be bought off with a few trinkets or token payments. Confronted with rapid and compelling change, Indigenous leaders took treaties to protect their land base and way of life, and in some cases to become agriculturalists as an "economic alternative or adjunct to the fur trade."[9] As Ray, Miller, and Tough note, "Indians used the treaty negotiations to advance their own economic and social program, which sought to diversify their own economy."[10]

Non-Indigenous government also understood the need to secure title to Indigenous lands, especially in the face of reports from Indian agents that a failure to act on claims could lead to violence against settlers.[11]

Indeed, state disregard of Metis land claims was at least partially responsible for the Red River uprising in 1869–70 and the Riel Rebellion of 1885,[12] which saw Metis and Indigenous people fighting alongside each other in defence of their lands and rights.

In 1870, Secretary of State for the Provinces Joseph Howe expressed the importance of early settlement of the rights or claims of Indian tribes. A number of treaty commissioners were appointed – all from the ranks of the Indian Department – a choice that, on its surface, made some sense.[13] After all, the department was the primary mechanism through which the Crown discharged its treaty and statutory obligations to Indigenous people. Indeed, and as such, it was required to do so, consistent with the Crown's fiduciary relationship with Indigenous people and its own honour. The latter held – and continues to hold – department officials to a high standard in their dealings with Indigenous people, and thus the selection of commissioners should have ensured that the treaty process would be conducted with fairness and respect. Regrettably, however, when faced with tensions between its legal and ethical obligations to Indigenous people, a government deeply committed to westward expansion and settlement, and in some cases, the self-interest of officials themselves, the department soon abandoned its fiduciary role.

When one of the first treaty commissioners was sent out to treat with the Fort Frances First Nation in 1871, Howe instructed him to "endeavour to secure the session [cession] of the lands upon terms as favourable as possible to the Government."[14] This became the essential mandate for the treaty process. Treaties were sometimes presented as ultimatums to Indigenous leaders, who were told they had no land rights that could be enforced in the absence of a treaty, the terms of which were only minimally negotiable.[15] When leaders resisted, commissioners were not above playing upon communities' fears of settler encroachment and conflict, or enlisting the assistance of missionaries or traders, to influence reluctant chiefs to accept the terms. Once signed, the treaties were not placed before Parliament; instead, they were presented to Cabinet in the commissioners' reports and ratified by Order in Council.[16]

Most of the eleven numbered treaties struck between 1871 and 1921 were remarkably consistent in their form and content, reflecting a pattern established in the Robinson-Superior and Robinson-Huron Treaties signed in Upper Canada in 1850.[17] They secured Indigenous title to lands in exchange for the payment of annuities, the establishment of reserves, and the preservation of hunting and fishing rights. Thus, for example, Treaties 1 and 2, struck with the Ojibway and Crees of southern Manitoba and Saskatchewan, originally provided reserve lands of up to 160 acres per family of five, annuities of three dollars per person, a gratuity of three dollars per person, and a school on each reserve.[18] As a general rule, the government preferred uniformity and economy in the treaties, and it strongly opposed attempts by Indigenous negotiators to deviate from this. In some instances, negotiators did succeed: the central Saskatchewan and Alberta Crees convinced the Crown to provide for a "medicine chest" and relief in times of famine or pestilence, within the terms of Treaty 6.[19] More common than these gains, however, were "outside promises" that were very much part of treaty negotiations, but often did not find their way into the text of a treaty.[20] These unwritten promises often raised annuities or offered additional non-monetary compensation, such as clothing for chiefs and headmen, livestock, and farming and other implements.[21] In many cases, these verbal undertakings were only belatedly recognized and appended to treaties, and only after much Indigenous protest. In the case of Treaty 1, noted above, the outside promises had been recorded in a memorandum by officials who were present at the negotiations. Although it was fixed to the treaty, these promises were not included in the version of the treaty later approved by the Privy Council.[22] The Treaty 1 signatories were successful in pressing their case. The government later accepted the terms of the memorandum, and included them in the treaty.[23] Other treaty nations had less success, and modern treaty claims are often marred by allegations by many First Nations that such promises never appeared anywhere in the written texts of their treaties and that Crown obligations to them are thus far more extensive than has been acknowledged.[24]

Once in place and despite the best intentions of many of those involved in treaty negotiations, the treaties proved of limited value in protecting the lands of Indigenous nations. In many instances, the treaties freed up lands, which were then taken by the Crown to appease non-Indigenous interests, often without Indigenous knowledge or consent.[25] There was also widespread squatting of settlers on reserve lands, to which governments routinely turned a blind eye. The problem of encroachment on Indigenous land became sufficiently compelling that a parliamentary commission was struck in 1884 to inquire into it. The chair of the commission was Sir Charles Bagot, whose final report chastised provincial governments for ignoring rampant theft of Indigenous land by settlers and trespassers, and recommended that all provincial control of this land should be handed over to the Crown. It is interesting that legislation to protect Indigenous land from theft and trespass existed as early as 1830, but the Crown seemed disinclined to enforce it. In this way, the treaty process, which should have laid the foundation for the mutually prosperous and peaceful co-existence of Indigenous people and newcomers, instead paved the way for dispossession and a deeply conflicted relationship between Indigenous people and the department that should have championed their interests.

Almost without exception, the end result of the treaty process was the crowding of Indigenous people onto insufficient and scattered reserves, where, after 1876 and the passage of the first Indian Act, the state defined and regulated virtually every aspect of their lives. Once established on reserves, many communities endured compelling want. The Crown, which seems to have taken an ambivalent and lackadaisical approach to honouring treaties, did little to alleviate the problem.[26] As the strictures of reserve life and Indian Act regulations began to weigh upon communities, discontent arose. Confronted with unfulfilled treaties and concerned over the mismanagement of their lands and assets, many Indigenous groups began to press the government with claims for redress and compensation. Their battle would prove lengthy and uphill, fought largely alone and for many years without the assistance of legal counsel or the Crown. In fact, one of the first and most important legal decisions regarding Indigenous land rights in Canada was fought over the heads of the Indigenous rights holders and without any direct input or involvement from them.[27] That case was *St. Catherine's Milling and Lumber Co. v. R.*, and it is worth discussing in some length.

In the 1880s, the federal government issued a permit to the St. Catherine's Milling and Lumber Company to harvest 1 million feet of timber in southeastern Ontario. The timber was to be taken from a parcel of roughly thirty-two thousand square miles, which lay in the traditional territory of the Saulteaux. In 1873, however, the Saulteaux had ceded the land to the

Crown through Treaty 3, though they retained a "qualified privilege of hunting and fishing," subject to periodic limitations imposed by "settlement, mining, lumbering or other purposes."[28] Arguing that the Saulteaux had surrendered their title, the Crown asserted that it retained the "entire beneficial interest in the lands" and was thus well within its rights to grant the logging permit. The Ontario government disagreed and fought the permit, insisting that the lands were part of the province and thus it alone had the right to dispose of them. Central to this argument was the contention that the title secured by the Crown was a fiction: Indigenous title was not a "creature in law." In fact, it had no *legal* substance at all. Three levels of court agreed with this reasoning. In 1888, the British Judicial Committee of the Privy Council ruled in favour of the Province, ending the dispute and declaring that Aboriginal title was not a legal right but only a "mere burden" on the Crown. The practical effect of this decision was to place ownership of the Saulteaux lands in the Province of Ontario, with the result that Ottawa was left with no jurisdiction or authority to fulfill the treaty promises it had made to the Saulteaux, including the selection and setting aside of reserves. As Michael Coyle explains,

> In the end, it took 41 years for the Ontario government and the federal government to agree on the reserve selection, by which time third parties had taken much of the more valuable lands agreed on by the federal government and the First Nations. One First Nation, which lived on land particularly desired by the province, lost its entire reserve, apparently at the insistence of the province.[29]

The importance of *St. Catherine's Milling and Lumber* for Indigenous land rights is difficult to overstate. The decision reduced the sacred connection between Indigenous nations and their land to no more than a "personal and usufructuary interest," one that originated not in their ancient relationship to the land, but in the Royal Proclamation of 1763.[30] In the complete absence of any consultation with or involvement by Indigenous peoples, the court wiped out centuries of occupation and stewardship of lands that Indigenous people saw as living things immune to ownership. The court reframed Indigenous title as originating in settler law and as limited simply to use of the land.

Nearly a century would pass before the courts stepped back from this position. In 1973, the Supreme Court decision in the *Calder* case confirmed that Indigenous rights to the land resided in historic occupation rather than in the Royal Proclamation. In *Guerin,* a 1984 decision, the court defined that title as "sui generis," or "unique in law."[31] In its 1998 *Delgamuukw* decision, which was informed by the extensive and intricate oral histories of the Gitksan and Wet'suwet'en people, Aboriginal title received its most wide-ranging elaboration. *Delgamuukw* set out the general features of Aboriginal title, its content, and the criteria for proving its existence, the latter including occupation prior to the assertion of British sovereignty and continuity and exclusivity in the possession of the lands.[32] In 2014, the Supreme Court built upon these and related decisions in *Tsilhqot'in,* which dealt with the duty of provincial and federal governments to consult with Indigenous people over the use and exploitation of their territory. Declaring that the Tsilhqot'in possessed Aboriginal title to their lands, the court stated,

> Aboriginal title confers ownership rights similar to those associated with fee simple, including: the right to decide how the land will be used; the right of enjoyment and occupancy of the land; the right to possess the land; the right to the economic benefit of the land; and the right to proactively use and manage the land.[33]

Tsilhqot'in preserved the restriction that Indigenous title can be alienated only to the Crown and confirmed that decisions about Aboriginal title lands must respect the collective ownership of the lands over successive generations.[34] The deep involvement of the Tsilhqot'in people in the case, and the court's decision, which essentially framed Aboriginal title as equivalent to the settler concept of fee simple ownership, reveals how far we have come from the tight-fisted process and position of the Privy Council in *St. Catherine's Milling and Lumber.* That said, the path to *Tsilhqot'in* was long and difficult, and it remains to be seen just how significantly the decision will affect the land rights and futures of Indigenous people.

In the aftermath of *St. Catherine's Milling and Lumber,* Indigenous people who either had no treaty or who were facing non-fulfillment of their treaty had only two options through which to seek redress. They could go to court and hope that the judiciary would protect their rights, or they could focus their energies on getting the federal government to respect Indigenous rights and title, and provincial governments to respect those rights within provincial policy.[35] Going to court presented risks, certainly, but courts were less likely to be influenced by the political considerations that often undermined the Crown's apparent commitment to its fiduciary responsibilities. For its part, Ottawa had little interest in dealing with claims and, at the time, no policy or procedure for doing so.[36] Any claims that came its way and that could not be ignored were dealt with in an ad hoc manner. This approach became untenable over the long run, as the number of claims and Indigenous activism grew.

Crunching Claims: A Canadian Claims Policy Begins to Emerge

In 1927, Parliament decided that the time had come to deal with Indigenous claims. Rather than developing a workable policy, however, it chose to push back against Indigenous activism. It passed a series of amendments to the 1876 Indian Act that were designed to squash Indigenous claims: Indigenous people were prohibited from gathering in meetings and denied the right to raise funds to retain legal counsel or to advance claims against the government.[37] This prohibition, which remained in place until 1951, effectively barred Indigenous people from using the courts to vindicate their rights and force the government to deal with claims.[38]

That Parliament should take such a heavy hand is not surprising. The negotiation of claims leading to the creation of reserves and the provision of resources, albeit meagre ones, to support Indigenous communities was inconsistent with Canada's more general approach to Indigenous people. In the nineteenth century, Canadian "Indian policy" was premised on two fundamental assumptions: that Indigenous people were a dying race resistant to progress and doomed to disappear, and that those who did survive should be "civilized" and assimilated into Canadian society.[39] Civilization was to be accomplished through education and exposure to the benefits of settler culture; Indigenous people were to abandon traditional pursuits and become farmers, aided by the Crown, who used the proceeds from the sale of their lands to fund the creation of model villages, farming instructors, and Indian agents.[40] Indigenous children were to be educated, a task notoriously left to the churches and residential and industrial schools, the devastating and long-term impacts of which are well documented.[41] Civilizing and assimilating Indigenous people provided no space for land or treaty claims, which by their very nature spoke to the persistence of Indigenous communities and cultures. The 1927 amendments to the Indian Act were thus as much about the government's desire for assimilation as they were about stifling claims by undermining Indigenous organizations and cutting off their access to advocacy.[42] This tactic was simply part of a larger set of policy responses to an "Indian problem" that refused to dissipate and a people who refused to disappear.

From 1927 until the Second World War, Parliament's commitment to assimilation and denial of treaty claims obviated the need to develop any coherent response to those claims. The war, however, changed many things. Canadian soldiers fought alongside Indigenous warriors, who volunteered at remarkable rates, and Canadians generally awoke to the idea and importance of human rights. At the same time, Indigenous activism had accelerated and fostered the creation of a series of regional organizations that were increasingly effective advocates for their people. The Indian Association of Alberta, the Native Brotherhood of British Columbia, the Federation of Saskatchewan Indian Nations, and the North American Indian Brotherhood challenged an ambivalent Canadian public and polity to address the dire conditions in which the growing on-reserve population lived and to respect Indigenous rights.[43] In 1943 and 1944, the government met with Indigenous leaders and activist groups in Ottawa to discuss the abysmal conditions on most reserves, as well as the broader issue of Indigenous rights.

As Christa Scholtz suggests, these meetings achieved little in the way of concrete policy change but went some distance to solidifying the foundation of national Indigenous rights organizations, including the North American Indian Brotherhood.[44] It was the activism of this and regional Indigenous groups that, when added to the post-war social changes, moved the Mackenzie King government to strike a special Senate-Commons joint committee to study the "Indian Act and other Indian Affairs matters" in 1946.[45] The committee undertook a series of hearings over the year, listening to testimony from a wide range of policy wonks, parliamentarians, and bureaucrats, many of whom promoted the policies of assimilation. Most importantly, however, it heard from Indigenous people directly, who spoke powerfully against the assimilation policies endorsed by the government representatives and urged action to investigate and address treaty- and title-based grievances.[46] They proposed the creation of a commission that could inquire into such complaints, and though the committee recommended this measure, neither Parliament nor the Indian Affairs Branch had much stomach for it. The recommendation seems to have been ignored.[47]

The committee's proposal for an independent commission to deal with treaty and land claims was probably influenced by the US government formation of an Indian Claims Commission in 1946, the year before the committee itself began its work. That Canadians should have looked to the south for guidance was hardly surprising. Although the Americans had been far bloodier in their relations with Indigenous nations, there were many similarities in the two federal governments' approach to claims. Both began their claims journey from a historic standpoint that recognized a basic fact of title, and both took steps to secure that title through treaty negotiations, leading to compacts that were often flawed, incomplete, and in some cases, fraudulent.[48] American courts had also similarly acknowledged a "right of occupancy" and "Aboriginal title," which could be pressed against all but the government.[49] And when Indigenous Americans began to agitate for their rights, Congress displayed no greater scruples than its Canadian counterpart, using the law as a blunt instrument to thwart claims and undermine Indigenous rights.

Canada and the United States worked assiduously to narrow the possible routes to successful resolution of Indigenous claims arising from treaties, title, and the taking of lands without treaty. They staged elaborate dances around courts and commissions, and did much to appear amenable to claims without actually opening meaningful negotiations or, in the end, their wallets. Where their paths diverge is in their recent history. The US government got out of the claims business pretty much completely when it shut down its Indian Claims Commission in 1978 and concluded its last case in 2006. Canada persists but has proven remarkably attached to the American way of doing business. Whereas the United States initially directed Indigenous claimants to a Court of Claims and then moved to an admittedly very court-like claims commission, Canada chose a similar course, but in reverse: Ottawa founded a commission and then moved to a very court-like tribunal, created largely to divest Indian Affairs of much of its claims business. And though it may seem a bit tangential to our discussion of Canada's path to a claims commission, it is important to look at our southern neighbour's route to the same end. Tracking the American experience with courts, commissions, and back to courts offers insights into the choices made by Canada regarding claims and is worth a short segue.

Lessons from Our American Cousins: Following the Trail of Tears North

As early as 1855, the US Congress had created a Court of Claims that had as its sole purpose the adjudication of citizens' claims against their government. Despite the fact that Indigenous Americans had at least theoretical claims to citizenship (actual citizenship was forced upon them in 1924) and should have been able to rely on the protection of the Constitution and access to the courts, both failed them.[50] Through an 1863 act of Congress, Indigenous nations were barred from the Court of Claims,[51] a ban that would remain in place until 1946. However, there was a loophole – of sorts. Congress could pass a special jurisdictional act waiving the sovereign immunity of the United States and allowing a "Tribe" to bring a suit in the Court of Claims.[52] These acts, which were neither easily nor quickly secured, limited Indigenous nations to seeking money damages for a Fifth Amendment taking of recognized (or reservation) title to particular lands or for the cession of land to the federal government for supposedly inadequate compensation.[53] Not surprisingly, few court actions for claims against the American government occurred between 1863 and 1924. Fewer than four cases were filed with the court in any given year, and it ordered more than a single award per year just once.[54] Most tribes that successfully argued their case before the court received "only about one percent of what they considered due to them."[55] Reflecting on the experience of tribes that accessed the court through special jurisdictional acts, a congressman later remarked that "those tribes ... really got taken."[56]

To further reduce the potential for treaty-based claims, Congress enacted legislation in 1871 to terminate the treaty process.[57] The relevant law declared that "no Indian nation or tribe shall be acknowledged or recognized as an independent nation, tribe or power with whom the United States may contract by treaty."[58] Stripped of their status as nations and not yet legally defined as citizens, Indigenous Americans were unable to negotiate with Congress either as nations or American citizens for more than fifty years.[59]

Establishing a distinct body or court to deal with Indian claims was mooted as early as 1905, when Commissioner of Indian Affairs Francis E. Leupp recommended that either a special court or a special branch of the Court of Claims be created to deal exclusively with Indian claims.[60] In 1913, the assistant commissioner of Indian Affairs suggested that an "investigatory commission" be founded to elucidate claims and provide information and support to Congress to deal with claims "for all time."[61] Nothing came of this chatter, but a turning point of sorts was reached in 1928, when the influential Meriam Report was published and endorsed the creation of the Indian Claims Commission. These calls were echoed in the 1930 hearings before the Senate Subcommittee on Indian Affairs and were picked up by key progressive Indian Department officials after 1935. In that year, a bill to create an Indian Claims Commission was presented before Congress; it was debated but led to nothing, as did subsequent bills in 1937, 1940, 1944, and 1946.[62]

In 1946, certain factors and historical forces combined to support the creation of a commission. The number of claims pressed by Indigenous nations had been growing exponentially since 1924, and Congress was becoming seized with the need for final resolution of the issue. Its newly found commitment was partly moral – Harvey Rosenthal and others acknowledge that Congress struggled with the smear on American democracy presented by claims – but was also rooted in a perceived need to reorganize Indian administration and get out of the expensive and increasingly fractious "Indian business."[63] Diversifying Indian administration across a number of departments, and thus governing Indians in the same manner that non-Indians were, was both fiscally attractive and justified as a way to encourage greater Indigenous independence. It was also an important step towards assimilating Indigenous people into American society, a long-time goal of the US government, as it was with its Canadian counterpart. An added incentive was the potential for a commission to deal definitively with claims, which created uncertainty in the marketplace and took a troublesome measure of time and energy from Congress, the courts, and the bureaucracy.[64]

The bill creating the commission was championed by Henry M. Jackson, a young congressman from Washington State who was also chair of the House Committee on Indian Affairs. Jackson explained the bill as a mechanism that would "dispose of all those random claims and let the Commission decide what the obligation is of this Government to the Indians."[65] He envisaged an Indian Claims Commission equipped with "a jurisdiction broad enough to deal with the entire problem as it now exists," including moral claims based on "unconscionable consideration, mutual or unilateral mistake or other equitable consideration."[66] Indigenous tribes would be required to "present their claims within 5 years or forever hold their peace."[67]

In arguing for a commission, Congress also briefly considered setting up an Indian Court of Claims, such as that proposed by Leupp in 1905. This option was rejected out of hand, however, due largely to the demonstrated failure of the Court of Claims to deal with the Indian cases that had come before it. By 1946, nearly two hundred claims had been filed with the court via special jurisdictional acts, but it had resolved only twenty-nine through the awarding of damages and had dismissed the greater part of the remainder due to "technicalities."[68] Dissatisfaction with the convoluted processes of the court and its limited effectiveness in concluding Indian claims "once and for all" was a major factor in the decision to create a claims commission:

> That process is enormously costly and unsatisfactory to everyone. It means that Government clerks and attorneys in the Interior Department, the Department of Justice and the General Accounting Office spend years and years examining and re-examining Indian claims in an effort to determine whether the Indians should have a day in court ... And of course, when a special jurisdictional bill is enacted, the process starts all over again. Then, only too often, the Court of Claims or the Supreme Court finds some fault with the language of the jurisdictional act, and the Indians come back for an amended jurisdictional act, and the merry-go-round starts up again. In the last 20 years the General Accounting Office alone spent over a million dollars ($1,000,000.) in reporting on Indian claims bills. And not one cent of that went to any Indian to settle any claim.[69]

The Indian Claims Commission Act passed easily and was signed into law by President Truman in August of 1946.[70]

Ironically, though Congress had rejected a claims court in favour of a claims commission, the actual construction of the latter borrowed much from the processes and structures of the former. As Harvey Rosenthal observes, the Court of Claims had been the arbiter of all Indian tribal cases since 1881, and "it was to this body of precedent that the new Commission looked. Its procedures and theories were largely adopted by the Commission, in effect making it a court."[71] Other factors were reportedly also at work. Congress supported the court-like approach of the commission due to its fear that a more informal, less constrained body would lead a "raid on the treasury." Indigenous people preferred an adversarial process that enabled their participation in decision making, and their lawyers supported any approach that would not render them redundant.[72] Rosenthal opines, "The commission concept, then, was meant to avoid the inefficient litigatory process and the evils of the past, but even if this goal were feasible, it was not destined to be achieved."[73]

The resulting Indian Claims Commission was given a broad mandate and a clear timetable for dealing with claims. The original commission, which consisted of a chief commissioner and two associate commissioners (later expanded to five), had the authority to

> hear and determine all claims against the United States on behalf of any "tribe, band, or other identifiable group of American Indians residing within the territorial limits of the United States or Alaska." It includes all claims at law or equity arising under the Constitution, laws or treaties of the United States, Executive Orders of the President, and all claims which the claimant would have been able to sue if the United States were subject to suit. It also includes all claims which arise if treaties, contracts, or agreements between the claimants and the United States were revised on the ground of fraud, duress, unconscionable consideration, mutual or unilateral mistake, or other equitable consideration. It further extends to all claims arising from the United States' taking of land owned by the claimant without the payment of compensation. Finally, the Commission's jurisdiction extends to all claims based "upon fair and honourable dealings which are not recognized by any existing rule of law or equity."[74]

In a staggering display of optimism, the commission was expected to address all claims arising under this jurisdiction within ten years. It was supported in this ambition by a strict cut-off date, after which it would accept no further claims. Under section 12 of the act, any claim not filed before August 13, 1951, was to be "forever barred by operation of law."[75]

Claims that came before the commission were heard in a three-stage process consisting of "title, value-liability, and off-sets." The first of these was often the most difficult and protracted, as it entailed determining the "definable territory" that had been exclusively occupied by the claimant tribe. This determination required the involvement of numerous experts and witnesses, and much time researching in archives and the field; it could easily consume years of both the claimant's and the government's time. Once the territory of the claim was established, the next phase was occupied with placing a value on the lands taken and the requisite government liability, which was followed by determining the "allowable offsets."[76] That constituted yet another time-consuming task, in which the commission analysed the relationship between the tribe and the government to determine if an offset were warranted.[77] Each stage required two interlocutory judgments and a final judgment by the commission, which were almost inevitably followed by motions from the parties for rehearings of controversial matters.[78] The final judgment could be appealed to the Court of Claims and to the Supreme Court of the United States through a writ of certiorari.[79]

Proponents of the commission hoped that it would provide tribes with "their day in court." In the end, however, most were given far more than a day, spending months and even years before the commission and, in many cases, before a court on appeal.[80] The drawn-out nature of the commission's process and the resulting delays became a focus of criticism from virtually all onlookers.[81] Less than a decade after the creation of the commission, experts gathered at a meeting in Detroit to discuss and address the delay, laying the bulk of the blame on the commission's cumbersome processes. Although these were certainly part of the problem, other factors were at play. Thomas Le Duc documents that the approach of the attorney general to claims was "leisurely" at best and that claims placed before the commission could easily wait in excess of three years for any response from the government:

The Justice Department not only resorts to delaying tactics in its fight against the Indians, but refuses to settle out of court even the most meritorious claims. In all other civil proceedings the government habitually relies on out-of-court settlements, but in Indian claims cases it requires the tribe to engage costly counsel and investigators to establish even the most elementary and undeniable facts. In the premises one could say that official chicanery at the expense of the Indians has merely been transferred from the Indian Bureau and the Army to the Justice Department.[82]

Robert C. Bell, an "Indian attorney" who logged over thirty years of work on claims, put the matter even more baldly, asserting that the commission failed to do justice to Indian claims "because the government's lawyers did not like to lose, even in a just cause, and what was supposed to be an 'expeditious inquiry or investigation and settlement of just claims' turned into a very slow-moving adversary proceeding."[83]

The commission never managed to overcome the challenges of delay or those presented by its own processes, and it proved unable to complete its dockets within its initial lifespan of ten years. In the end, its demise was postponed three times, for the last time in March 1976, when Congress extended its life to September 30, 1978, and provided for the transfer of any unresolved claims to the United States Court of Federal Claims.[84] Despite the extension of its original mandate by more than twenty years and its termination in 1978, its last case – *Pueblo of San Ildefonso v. United States* – was not resolved until October 2006.[85]

During its existence, the commission dealt with over 1,200 claims and petitions, and awarded more than $8 million in compensation, all in an effort to secure "a full discharge of the United States of all claims and demands touching any of the matters in the controversy."[86] Whether the Indigenous nations agree with that finality is unlikely, and indeed, Rosenthal and others are convinced that many hard questions and unresolved claims remain, which continue to beg some meaningful response by Congress and the American people:

Did the Indians gain "their day in court?" Technically the answer is yes. The commission was a court, complete with appellant bodies. The tribes, represented by some of the best legal talent in the country, pressed 484 claims and won awards on 58 percent of them. However, the commission was created for the express purpose of circumventing the "technical" letter of the law and allowing moral claims heretofore "not recognized by any existing rule of law or equity." This is how the Indians understood and expressed most of their claims, but the commission and the attorneys "refined" them into language for a presentation that had long been recognized by existing rules of law or equity – money damages for injuries against property and breach of contract. In this sense the Indians did not have their day in court. It might be said the Indian had his hour in court, and it should be added that he will be back.[87]

Negotiation, Adjudication, or Reconciliation? Canadian Claims Policies Emerge

As will be seen, although there are important distinctions in the structure and processes of the American and Canadian Indian Claims Commissions, they shared much in the inevitable intrusion of law over morality, the challenges of delay, and the disingenuous attitude of the government and many, if not all, of their legal counsel. By the time Canada turned its mind to the creation of a commission, most of these problems were readily apparent, so its decision to emulate the deeply flawed US model is that much more remarkable. That said, given the synchronicity characterizing the Indian policies of both countries, perhaps there is less reason for surprise than one would suppose. Their general agreement regarding how to deal with the "Indian problem" and the tendency of governments to favour established policies and practices, however imperfect or morally questionable, render atrophy in social policy virtually inevitable. These factors may go some distance to explain why Canada chose a commission, then a court, as acceptable options in dealing with Indigenous claims.

The 1947 joint committee proposal endorsing the creation of an Indian Claims Commission in Canada failed to capture government attention; three years later, the question of a commission was revisited and again in 1958–60. In that juncture, the Diefenbaker government established a parliamentary committee, co-chaired by the first Indigenous senator, James Gladstone, to study Indian policy.[88] Gladstone's committee met for two years and heard from a number of stakeholders on a range of issues, including land rights and Indigenous engagement with Canadian society. The discussion generated by the hearings indicated a shift in the tide with regard to Indigenous rights to reserved lands, which moved towards a vision of title vested in individual Indigenous persons and held in trust by the government, as opposed to remaining in the Crown. This was a significant development that, according to Christa Scholtz,

> shows the beginning of a changing causal thought process among Indian policy watchers that links Indian control of land to furthering social development, rather than impeding it. This and the cautious acceptance by non-natives that Indian integration need not be achieved through Indian deculturation showed an acceptance not of native rights per se, but of the growing salience of cultural pluralism in the national post-war dialogue on Canadian citizenship.[89]

Equally significant was the committee's endorsement of a land claims commission to inquire into the British Columbia and, in an interesting portent, Oka land questions, which received fairly robust support from the Department of Indian Affairs.[90]

Apparently immune to the turning tides in Indigenous policy, the department's response to the commission question had little to do with altruism and much more to do with the purely instrumentalist ends a commission was deemed likely to serve. Claims were – and are – a difficult business, one that the department (like the government) was eager to hand off to a commission. If a commission were set up, the responsibility for failing to address Indigenous land grievances would be transferred to it. The director of Indian Affairs reportedly believed that much of his department's burden would be alleviated if it were able to "say that we no longer had anything to do with such claims, that the Indians should take them to the Claims Commission, a body separate from the branch."[91] Thus, the "support of the bureaucracy for the creation of an independent arbitrator was based on a self-interested analysis about what made its job easier, rather than a principled acceptance of the validity of Indian land rights."[92]

Nonetheless, departmental support was pivotal, and when added to that of Diefenbaker and key ministers, it won the day. In 1962, the government put forth legislation to support the creation of a claims commission. The bill visualized a three-person commission that would have a broad mandate to inquire into and recommend monetary compensation in treaty and title claims, and "other claims that might have no foundation in law ... but which might merit consideration on grounds of honourable dealings and fairness and good conscience."[93] A series of hearings were held to discuss the bill, and three issues quickly dominated the debates. These included the question of Metis claims and whether the commission would have jurisdiction over them, given that the Metis were not then included within federal jurisdiction and were thus technically outside the commission's mandate. There was also the sticky issue of whether the commission should decide on claims or simply make recommendations and leave the decisions to the government. In the end, Parliament excluded Metis claims and chose to retain final say on claims resolution; the commission would be limited to making recommendations. The final issue was one of politics and timing. A federal election was looming – how would the voting public react to legislation that established a claims commission? The Diefenbaker Conservatives were poised to win, and though polls indicated that Canadians were broadly supportive of greater state attention to claims, it was decided to wait until after the election to announce the legislation.[94] The Tories were returned to power but only briefly; another election was called in 1963, resulting in a Liberal minority government, and the claims commission legislation was not passed.

In the days following the election, the promotion of a commission appears to have fallen to the Department of Indian Affairs, which, as noted earlier, saw the commission as a way of easing its own workload. A 1963 departmental memo explained the problems:

The conviction in the mind of any Indian group that justice is being denied makes it extremely difficult to obtain the necessary cooperation between them and government that is so necessary in every field of endeavour that may be undertaken to improve their lot ... If a claim is good, then it should be settled. Equally important, if a claim is bad, the Indians should know it so they can put it aside.[95]

The department submitted a proposal for a commission to Cabinet, which appears not to have taken either the commission or land claims themselves terribly seriously. Dismissing the former as a mechanism with no power to decide and the latter as no more than "contractual obligations," Cabinet approved the bill creating the commission but with no apparent intention of seeing it through to the end of the legislative process.[96] Rather, the bill was floated out to gauge Indigenous reaction, which was largely negative. Two years after its approval, the bill was unenthusiastically presented to the House, which promptly killed it.

The question of a claims commission would not re-emerge until June of 1969, when Minister of Indian Affairs Jean Chrétien inserted the establishment of a commission into his notorious White Paper as a possible lure to attract otherwise elusive Indigenous support for the paper's goals. Prime Minister Pierre Trudeau reportedly disagreed with the idea of a commission, which offended his liberal values of equality. A standoff ensued, and a compromise of sorts was reached: the government would propose the appointment of a claims commissioner who would investigate treaty-based claims only and solely for the purpose of advising Cabinet on their settlement.[97] The commissioner would have no jurisdiction over Indigenous title claims, which, guided by the *St. Catherine's Milling and Lumber* decision, the Department of Justice saw as having no basis in law.

On December 19, 1969, Trudeau appointed Lloyd Barber, then vice-president of the University of Saskatchewan, as the first Indian claims commissioner. Barber was an interesting choice. He was both "outside the Indian community and outside government," and was thus deemed a neutral party in the claims arena.[98] Educated primarily in economics and business, Barber was new to claims but not to Indigenous issues. A long-time proponent of Indigenous rights and education, he later founded the Saskatchewan Federated Indian College, which would become First Nations University. He would also be an effective and respected advocate for Indigenous people and their rights.

However much Indigenous support existed for a commission, it proved a small and woefully inadequate recompense for the larger policy goals of the White Paper, which included the end of the Indian Act, Indian status, and reserves – in effect, the assimilation of Indigenous people into Canadian society. Not surprisingly, Indigenous protest arose almost immediately on the heels of the paper's release. Among its best-known opponents was Harold Cardinal, a Cree from Sucker Creek First Nation in Alberta and a lawyer who was also head of the Indian Association of Alberta. In 1969, Cardinal authored *The Unjust Society*, a passionate and effective evisceration of the White Paper; it was soon followed by the Red Paper, a meticulous Indigenous reply to the Liberals' white counterpart, which was placed before Parliament in the summer of 1970.[99] Sally Weaver notes that the response of the government to the "forthright and constructive" Red Paper was surprising; Trudeau reportedly demonstrated some contrition and admitted that

> we were very naïve in some of the statements we made in this paper. We had the prejudices of small "l" liberals and white men at that who thought that equality meant the same law for everybody, and that's why as a result of this we said, "well, let's abolish the Indian Act and make Indians citizens of Canada like everyone else. And let's let Indians dispose of their lands just like every other Canadian. And let's make sure that Indians can get their rights, education and health and so on, from the governments like every other Canadian." But we have learnt in the process that perhaps we were a bit too theoretical, we were a bit too abstract, we were not, as Mr. Cardinal suggests, pragmatic enough or understanding enough.[100]

The federal government formally abandoned the White Paper on March 17, 1971.

The appointment of Lloyd Barber as claims commissioner was one of the few White Paper initiatives to survive the controversy, though the association of the commissioner with the paper would dog Barber's early days in the position. Indigenous groups protested his appointment, and his office at the University of Saskatchewan was occupied for a time. Barber dealt with the situation by quietly but clearly distancing himself from Ottawa. He continued to work from his university office and set about pressing the government to expand his mandate beyond specific claims arising from treaties to include Aboriginal title claims. His achievements in this regard earned him the respect of Indigenous leaders, but the intransigence of the Department of Justice and its highly legalistic, narrow approach to claims curtailed his success in resolving treaty or title claims.[101]

Although he may have had limited sway with government lawyers, Barber has been credited with moving Ottawa to a more progressive and "sympathetic" approach to claims.[102] He managed to secure federal government funding for Indigenous rights and treaty research to regional Indigenous organizations, and his relentless pressure on Ottawa to step away from arbitration or litigation in favour of negotiation also bore fruit. Although these accomplishments owe much to his skill and persistence, it is also important to recognize the context that informed his work. The embarrassment of the White Paper, the subsequent mobilization of Indigenous activism, and its effective education of the non-Indigenous population all conspired to push government towards a new approach that emphasized negotiation and resolution of outstanding claims.[103]

In All Fairness and Outstanding Business: Canada Chooses Negotiation

The rising tide of Indigenous activism in Canada greatly unnerved the state, as did what appeared to be increasing judicial intervention regarding Indigenous rights. This disquiet reached new heights in 1973, when a well-organized group of Oglala Sioux, led by the American Indian Movement (AIM), mounted a strategic and violent defence of their land rights at Wounded Knee in South Dakota.[104] The spectacle of armed Indigenous protesters in open conflict with federal agents over land claims was not lost on the Canadian government. Indigenous activists in Canada had learned much from their successful attack on the White Paper, and Ottawa must have assumed that they would find AIM's methods equally educational. Spurred by fears of violent protest and by the Supreme Court's 1973 *Calder* decision, wherein a clear majority of the court acknowledged the existence of Aboriginal title,[105] Ottawa set to work on the first of what would be two new claims policies.

In August of 1973, and in a clear response to *Calder,* the federal government announced that it was prepared to negotiate "comprehensive claims" with Indigenous nations, "where their traditional and continuing interest in the lands concerned could be established."[106] This approach provided mechanisms for modern treaty negotiation in regions, such as British Columbia, where the Crown had not obtained title by treaty or other legal means prior to colonization and settlement. Since 1973, comprehensive claims negotiations have led to a number of agreements, including the 1975 James Bay and Northern Quebec Agreement, the related Northeastern Quebec Agreement of 1978, and the 2000 Nisga'a Final Agreement, which is British Columbia's first modern treaty.[107]

Ottawa's new claims policy was to be administered by DIAND, through the newly established Office of Native Claims (ONC), created in 1974, and empowered with a "dual role of reviewing Indian claims arising from governmental failure to discharge 'lawful obligations' and representing the government in negotiations with First Nations groups" regarding claims that were deemed valid.[108] The conflict of interest implicit in the ONC mandate was not lost on Indigenous people or policy-watchers: DIAND was to be both the arbiter of claims and a party to them. This deep and disturbing conflict, which undermined the legitimacy of the entire claims process, persists to the present day, as will be seen. Chapter 2 discusses it in greater detail, and it will resurface repeatedly throughout our conversation about claims, the Crown, and the commission.

Whereas the government had committed to a formal policy on comprehensive claims, its approach to specific claims remained ad hoc and true to the principles of the White Paper.[109] In 1979, DIAND commissioned Gérard La Forest, a University of Ottawa professor who would later take up a position on the Supreme Court of Canada, to review its approach to specific claims. In the resulting report, La Forest was deeply critical of the ONC for the absence of a clear policy and independence in the department's management of specific claims; he called for the creation of an "Independent claims body."[110] In a pattern that would reoccur many times, the government largely ignored the report, simply ordering another review of claims policy in 1980.

The 1980 review gained some traction with government and seems to have informed its 1982 specific claims policy, which was outlined in *Outstanding Business: A Native Claims Policy*. This document delineated specific claims as arising through "actions and omissions of government as they relate to obligations taken under treaty, and requirements spelled out in legislation and responsibilities regarding the management of Indian assets."[111] Thus, the business of specific claims included non-fulfillment of a treaty or agreement between the Crown and Indigenous people; breaches of obligations under the Indian Act, treaties, and surrenders; and breaches arising from government administration of Indigenous monies and assets or from the illegal disposition of Indian land.[112] Although there has been tinkering around the edges of this policy since 1982, the alterations have been minimal, and *Outstanding Business* embodies the Canadian government's current approach to specific claims.

2

Dependent on the Good Will of the Sovereign
Background to the
Indian Specific Claims Commission

The claims business is not less than the task of redefining
and redetermining the place of Indian people in Canadian
society. They themselves are adamant that this shall be done,
not unilaterally as in the past, but with them as the major
partner in the enterprise.

– LLOYD BARBER, *A REPORT: STATEMENTS AND SUBMISSION*

Although *Outstanding Business* committed Canada to a formal policy on
specific claims – a significant step forward, given its historically inadequate
ad hoc approach – Indian Affairs (DIAND) and the Specific Claims Branch
of the Office of Native Claims quickly came under fire on the heels of its
release. Opponents of the policy included Aboriginal communities and
organizations, academics, policy-watchers, and activists, and their criticisms were directed at both the policy itself and the processes it created.
Indigenous people perceived both as unfair and plagued with delay,
conflict of interest, and the inconsistent and obstructionist practices of
the Specific Claims Branch and Justice. For one community, the process
would prove frustrating beyond its capacity to endure and would lead
to the first "Indian uprising" since the Riel Rebellion – that community
was the Mohawk Nation at Oka, Quebec.

In a distinction that is fuzzy and somewhat arbitrary, *Outstanding
Business* deals with claims that are not based on outstanding title, which,
as noted in the previous chapter, fall under *In All Fairness* as comprehensive

claims. Because treaties are largely about land and deal with such questions as reserve allocation, treaty land entitlement, surrenders, and so on, specific claims are as much about land as are comprehensive claims. This irony is not lost on Aboriginal claimants, who have a much more holistic understanding of their relationship to land, one not clouded by the legal niceties of claims policy. More than once, they have challenged claims processes that require them to navigate complicated government criteria, created without Aboriginal consultation and based entirely upon Western concepts of land use and ownership. To date, however, those concerns have largely been ignored, and as will be seen, modern claims policies seem less about Indigenous lands than how best to divest Aboriginal communities of these fully and finally.[1]

Outstanding Business: The Policy and Its Processes

As introduced in the previous chapter, the Outstanding Business policy focuses exclusively on Crown actions or inactions and is very much rooted in non-Aboriginal understandings of rights and claims. As such, it provides for government recognition of claims that disclose an "outstanding lawful obligation" arising from

i) the non-fulfilment of a treaty or agreement between Indians and the Crown.
ii) a breach of an obligation arising out of the Indian Act or other statutes pertaining to Indians and the regulations thereunder.
iii) a breach of an obligation arising out of government administration of Indian funds or other assets.
iv) an illegal disposition of Indian land.[2]

These contrast with claims that are deemed as "beyond lawful obligation," which arise from the government's failure to provide compensation for lands taken or damaged by the Crown or any of its agencies. Also on this list are claims associated with clearly demonstrated acts of fraud on the part of Crown officials in their dealings with Indigenous people.[3]

On the surface, making a claim appears quite simple and straightforward: the Indigenous group submits its claim and all supporting documentary and legal materials to the Specific Claims Branch (SCB), which determines its completeness and prima facie validity. Next, the Department of Justice decides whether the claim reflects an outstanding lawful obligation on the part of the Crown. If the lawyers at Justice feel that it does, the SCB notifies the Indigenous group and negotiation begins. If the claim is deemed invalid, the SCB informs the band of its rejection.[4] This decision cannot be appealed, though bands can seek judicial review of their rejected claim through the courts. Presumably in lieu of review, the policy states that rejected claims "may be presented again at a later date for further review, should new evidence be located or additional legal arguments produced which may throw a different light on the claim."[5]

Acknowledging "general Indian dissatisfaction with the specific claims policy," *Outstanding Business* asserted that DIAND had "sought the views of Indian organizations" and reviewed "numerous reports and other submissions."[6] However, Aboriginal leaders felt that they had not been meaningfully consulted; nor had their views been captured in the resulting policy. Rather, as is so often the case, the government was highly selective both in terms of which leaders were consulted and what submissions were actually heard and incorporated into the policy. A section of *Outstanding Business,* entitled "Indian Views," lists Indigenous leaders' long-standing complaints about the narrow focus of specific claims. Claims based on moral or equitable grounds were not admissible, and treaty-related rights, such as self-government or the right to hunt, fish, or trap, were not considered. All "Indian representatives" demanded genuine consultation and expressed grave concern about the Crown's inherent conflict of interest in connection with claims – a clear indictment of DIAND's consultation process. Not surprisingly, the policy does not appear to have heeded a single one of these points. In fact, the sole concession made by the "new approach" was an agreement by the Crown not to prohibit Indigenous groups from pursuing claims on the basis of laches, which bars action on injuries due to the passage of time. Instead, *Outstanding Business* boasts that "the government has decided to negotiate each claim on the basis of the issues involved. Bands with longstanding grievances will not have their claims rejected before they are even heard because of the technicalities provided under the statutes of limitations or under the doctrine of laches."[7]

Only in the realm of Indigenous claims would a government proudly state its intention of actually considering the issues in trying to resolve a problem, thus tacitly admitting that it had not previously troubled to explore this avenue. Yet, even here the policy took a large step back, negating the small forward one. Although DIAND agreed to set aside limitations and laches, it warned claimants that if the parties ended up in court, the Crown reserved the right to use laches and limitations to fight the claim in that realm.[8] The underlying message to Indigenous claimants was clear: accept a flawed policy and process that does not reflect your input or interests, and take what we offer you – because if you go to court, the gloves will come off. We will use any and all means at our disposal to negate your claim. This is a serious threat, and one that seems at odds with the Crown's fiduciary role or the honour that should inform its dealings with Indigenous people.

Oh Brother Where Art Thou?
The Fiduciary Obligation and the Crown Conflict of Interest

The federal government's fiduciary obligation to Indigenous people means that it is required to act in their best interests and to be fair and honourable in its dealings with them. Although the concept of the fiduciary remains undeveloped on some fronts,[9] there is sufficient judicial interpretation of the term in the context of Crown-Aboriginal relations to establish the standard for Crown behaviour. For example, in *Guerin,* the Supreme Court of Canada recognized that the Crown had a judicially enforceable fiduciary obligation towards "Indians."[10] In *Sparrow,* the court asserted that "the honour of the Crown is at stake in all its dealings with aboriginal peoples. The special trust relationship and the responsibility of the government vis-à-vis aboriginals must be the first consideration in determining whether the legislation or action in question can be justified."[11]

The centrality of this trust relationship and the honour of the Crown in the management of claims would seem incontrovertible, yet nothing in *Outstanding Business* "acknowledge[s], or even contemplate[s] the concept of fiduciary obligation which, since Guerin, goes to the heart of every stated basis for a claim."[12] Although *Guerin* postdated the release of *Outstanding Business* by two years, there is no question that the federal Crown was already seized of these obligations before the court turned its mind to the subject. And yet *Outstanding Business,* both at its incipience and since, and as a policy and process, has often appeared utterly devoid of the fiduciary or the honour of the Crown. Nowhere is the absence of the trust relationship more apparent than in the Crown's deep conflict of interest in specific claims, wherein it is both a party to and arbiter of such claims. As a 1990 discussion paper by the Indian Commission of Ontario states,

> On the one hand the federal government has a fiduciary or trust-like responsibility towards aboriginal peoples to act in their best interest, while at the same time it seeks to act in its own best interests. Clearly the interests of the two parties are not the same and often directly conflict. Therefore, how can one party to resulting disputes control the resolution process and expect the others to perceive that the process results in fair and just settlements?[13]

The federal government is implicated in every aspect of the claims assessment process through the Specific Claims Branch. When prospective claimants apply for funds to support their claims research, it is the SCB that vets their application and determines whether and how much funding they will receive. Once a claim is submitted, the same SCB assesses it and, together with the Department of Justice, decides whether to reject or accept it. If it is denied, the SCB informs the band and is not required to provide reasons for the rejection. If the claim is accepted, the SCB shifts from adjudication to negotiation, representing the government and its interests. Due to its previous role as assessor of the claim, it is in full possession of all the claimant's research, documentation, and legal arguments, which immeasurably strengthens its hand in negotiations. By contrast, it is not required to share its own legal arguments.[14] How such a process would *not* violate Canada's fiduciary obligations is difficult to see. Essentially, the claims process is one in which "the fiduciary of today assesses the conduct of fiduciaries of the past and determines, in secrecy, the validity of every claim submitted."[15] The conclusion of the Assembly of First Nations on the claims process is apt: "In the democratic world there are few examples of such a grievance procedure being so totally controlled by one party to a dispute."[16] In the minds of Indigenous claimants, many academics and activists, and, it must be said, most Indian claims commissioners, this conflict of interest and the complete absence of "any sense of neutrality ...

condemns this policy and process to be viewed as biased, arbitrary, and unfair."[17]

The failure of *Outstanding Business* to address this long-standing conflict of interest was not surprising. Despite Lloyd Barber's efforts to usher in an era of greater government sympathy and progress on claims, *Outstanding Business* was conceived and created through a unilateral process that was utterly devoid of meaningful consultation with Indigenous people and that lacked their consent. As a result, the ongoing conflict of interest was only one of several problems with the policy, which include vague terminology, narrow conceptions of rights and obligations, delay and disingenuous government practices, and a focus on termination and extinguishment of Aboriginal rights.

Implementing *Outstanding Business,* or, When Is an Indian Band Not an Indian Band?

As policy statements go, *Outstanding Business* is actually quite simple; it explains its position succinctly and in plain, if somewhat creative, language. Cradled by the government's fiduciary obligations and the honour of the Crown, the new policy should have provided a clear path to the resolution of claims. However, as is so often the case, the wording of the policy proved to be less of a problem than the approach taken by the Crown to that language. Even a brief review reveals that Canada's attitude towards claims, Indigenous communities, and Indian commissions remains very much focused on assimilation and an end game that has much in common with that of our American cousins.

In fairness to the government, I have been told that a major challenge in drafting good policy and law revolves around fashioning language that is both precise and flexible: it must afford clear directions about what to do and how to do it but must also permit the law to adapt and capture the full breadth of the problem to be addressed. I don't know if this is true or simply aspirational – certainly, there is much in the law to indicate the magnitude of the challenge (think about the many permutations of the word "reasonable" across a range of fields of law and policy). However, it is clear that we rely on courts and lawyers to interpret and argue legal wording, thus translating the law in theory to the law in practice. Not unexpectedly then, much of what happens in courts, commissions, and tribunals consists of battles over interpretation, with the respective parties hoping to convince decision-makers that their understanding of keywords or phrases is the correct one. Of course, in specific claims policies, the parties are hardly equal: one of them has created the policy, funds the process, and will also have the final say on whose arguments and evidence win the day. Given this, it is surprising that Indigenous claimants *ever* win the day – though accepting and resolving some claims is certainly good policy on the part of the Crown because accepting the odd victory requires that claimants also accept the far more frequent losses. That Indigenous nations continue to fight the good fight speaks to their resilience and strong determination to see the treaties respected and Indigenous rights vindicated.

The approach taken by the federal government to specific claims is perhaps most obvious in "lawful obligation," the linchpin of its specific claims policy, a phrase that DIAND appears to have plucked from the ashes of the White Paper and dusted off for later use.[18] As outlined above, Ottawa defines these obligations narrowly and restrictively, providing no space to address such treaty-related matters as self-government, education, and hunting, fishing, or trapping rights.[19] Similarly, land-connected and cultural values that often arise within specific claims are not encompassed by the term. For example, when the Mohawks of Kahnesatake (Oka) submitted a claim in 1977 to the lands they had claimed consistently since 1780, DIAND's focus was not on the dubious counterclaims of the French Sulpicians who had founded a mission at Oka,[20] but on whether any part of the historic land conflict between the missionaries and the Mohawks implicated an outstanding lawful obligation on the part of the Crown. Nearly a decade later, the government formally rejected the Kahnesatake claim.[21] As it informed the Mohawks, the government "recognized that there is an historical basis for Mohawk claims related to land grants in the 18th century,"[22] but it could find nothing in its own actions that encumbered it with an outstanding lawful obligation.

In essence, the Crown found that, though the Mohawks had a historic claim, they did not have a specific claim – a thin hair to split. Specific claims *are* historic claims – they are rooted in a series of historic encounters in which treaties were struck, promises were made, lands were taken, and other lands kept. The historical record comprises the greater part of virtually all claims submissions, and DIAND's acceptance that the Mohawks had a historically valid claim though not a specific one is an interesting act of solipsism. The narrow construction of lawful obligation permitted the Crown to distinguish its actions from those of the French sovereign, who had negated Indigenous title when he granted Oka to the Sulpicians. Their title later fell to Canada, who then claimed that the loss of the Mohawk land was due to French error, not to any action by the Canadian government. Leaving to one side the Crown's purchase of some of the Oka land both before and after the crisis of 1990, it appears that Canada's predominant role in the Mohawk loss of title was one of inaction rather than action. This amounted primarily to failing to respect its fiduciary obligations to the people of Kahnesatake either before or after the advent of *Outstanding Business*. Had *Outstanding Business* included the failure to discharge fiduciary obligations among its bases for claims, the Mohawk case would have been greatly strengthened. Had it provided for consideration of the deep cultural significance of the lands at Oka, especially the Pines, the Oka Crisis might well have been avoided altogether.

Degree of Doubt, Discounting, and Delay: Paving the Path to the Summer of 1990

The mealy-mouthed approach of the Crown to its lawful obligations is echoed in its creative construction of many other terms in *Outstanding Business*. Two good examples are "degree of doubt" and "special value to the owner." The former can determine the amount of compensation that a successful claim will receive. This has less to do with the strength of the evidence and arguments presented by the claimants than with the degree of doubt that the Crown harbours regarding the claim. Take, for example, a claim in which a band argues a wrongful taking of reserve lands. Despite an agreement that lands were taken and that some compensation is owed to the band, the Crown may reduce the amount of the compensation in direct proportion to its "degree of doubt" that all the claimed lands were, in fact, part of the reserve. The greater the Crown's doubt, the lower the compensation it will pay to the band.[23] Almost every written record related to a claim is the work of federal bureaucrats and a bureaucracy with the power not only to define reserves but also to adjudicate on claims, so the insertion of "degree of doubt" enables the Crown to assume the moral and legal high ground by accepting a claim but then lowballing the amount of compensation. Indeed, the practice of arbitrarily discounting settlements became quite commonplace. Discounting was – and is – a truly remarkable practice in which Indian Affairs in conjunction with the Department of Justice reduce

> the amount of compensation to be offered on claim by a percentage equal to the federal government's assessment of the chances for success a claim would have if submitted to the courts. Therefore, if a claim was assessed as having a fifty percent chance of being successfully litigated, the government would cut the compensation by fifty percent.[24]

The fate of the Mississaugas of the New Credit First Nation is an apt exemplar here: After their claim was accepted, they sat down with SCB representatives to begin negotiations. At that point, the SCB told them that DIAND had a 50 percent degree of doubt regarding their claim and that they should expect a commensurate reduction in compensation. Not surprisingly, things deteriorated badly after that, and the Crown subsequently walked away from the negotiations.[25]

It is important to recognize that the discount figure appears simply to be pulled out of, well, let's say thin air, based on federal lawyers' assessments of the likelihood of winning or losing should the claim be litigated. Whereas one could certainly argue that such guesstimates by (ideally) senior claims litigators may have some basis in experience, it is also clear that discounts are simply that – guesses – hardly a respectful or honourable approach to compensation nor one worthy of a fiduciary. And yet as part of *Outstanding Business*'s new and more "rigorous" approach to claims negotiation, discounting is a common and disturbing practice. In a 1990 analysis of DIAND claim practices, the Assembly of First Nations (AFN) documented that the Department of Justice routinely discounted claims by 50 percent.[26] DIAND does not disclose how this figure is obtained; nor is there any direct linkage made to the factual basis of the claim.[27] In the absence of an explanation, we are left to surmise that Justice discounts claims based upon a view that pretty much any case will have a fifty-fifty chance of succeeding or failing in court. This seems as valid an assumption as the practice itself.

The dubious habit of discounting is similar to the Crown's very narrow understanding of the value of lands to Indigenous peoples. *Outstanding Business* is clear that the only value the Crown will entertain is one calculated in dollars: "Compensation shall not include any additional amount based on a 'special value to owner' unless it can be established that the land in question had a special economic value to the claimant band, over and above its market value."[28]

As the AFN points out, this position stands in stark contrast to the spiritual, cultural, and subsistence value accorded to the land by the majority of Aboriginal nations. It also utterly fails to respect the deep significance of reserve lands. "Given current land acquisition practices," reclaiming wrongfully taken land is virtually impossible, and land abutting reserve boundaries is often in the hands of a third party or unavailable to the community for other reasons.[29]

There are lands that hold special meaning for Indigenous people, such as burial and ceremonial sites, or places of historical significance, such as buffalo jumps on the prairies or caribou migration routes in the north. All land is of cultural importance to Indigenous peoples, but some is so integral to cultural beliefs and practices that its appropriation amounts also to an assault on culture. Of course, it is technically possible to valuate these areas as mere real estate, but the resulting dollar figure cannot capture their integrity. Nor can it respect the reality that many such areas are so important that they cannot simply be exchanged for alternative lands. The failure of *Outstanding Business* to recognize this reveals that the term "lawful obligation" is not the only vestige of the White Paper to find its way into current claims policy.

If, like discounting, the rejection of "special value to owner" was intended to limit Canada's financial vulnerability to claims, subsequent history reveals that it failed spectacularly in this regard. Again, Oka provides an excellent illustration. Central to the Kahnesatake Mohawks' 1977 specific claim was the burial ground and spiritual meeting place at the Pines. Ottawa had innumerable opportunities to address this claim but utterly failed to do so. Throughout, the Mohawks continued to assert title to the lands, even as the Municipality of Oka sold them to condominium developers and for an extension to the Oka Golf Club. In 1990, when the development proceeded, and the Mohawks' repeated entreaties for protection of the Pines was ignored at the federal level, the result was the violent standoff that lasted from July 11 until September 26 (discussed in greater detail below).

Unwilling to deal head-on with the Mohawk claim and apparently unable to arrest the escalating crisis, DIAND offered to pay the Municipality $3.8 million for seventy acres of the Pines, plus one dollar for the Mohawk burial ground. It offered a further $1.4 million to the condominium developers for the thirty acres they had purchased. The offer was rejected by everyone involved, including the Mohawks, who failed to see how the Crown could purchase and give them land that they already owned. Had the Crown chosen to deal with their claim, it would probably have ended up paying $5.2 million at most for the Pines (not including the dollar for the burial ground, which presumably would have been discounted to fifty cents). In the event, the final tally for the failure to resolve the Oka claim was much, much more. As the *Edmonton Journal* observed in the immediate wake of the crisis,

Public Security Minister Claude Ryan told the Quebec legislature recently the standoff at Oka between police and Mohawk Indians cost the province's taxpayers more than $112 million. Most of this, about $71 million, was in overtime costs for police who set up round-the-clock surveillance during the 77-day confrontation. About $20 million more was paid in compensation to nearby residents whose lives were disrupted.

These costs are separate from the $83 million spent by the Canadian Armed Forces after Quebec Premier Robert Bourassa requested that the army come in and deal with the blockade by armed Mohawks. The costs also don't include the estimated $50,000 a day the Quebec police say it costs to patrol around the Kahnawake and Akwesasne reserves even now. Far from resolving the crisis, the police and army action merely created a lasting animosity. The police patrols go on.

These figures total more than $200 million and are rising. To put the cost of the crisis in some sort of context, it is about 10 times what the federal government budgets for land claims settlements each year. It is more than half the $355 million that Prime Minister Mulroney grandly promised recently to spend over five years to speed up the land claims settlements.[30]

In the end, it is estimated that the Oka claim cost the federal and provincial governments in excess of $350 million – "special value to the owners" indeed.

The tendency of DIAND, the SCB, and the Department of Justice to construe the terminology of the specific claims policy as narrowly as possible extends to their approach to Indigenous people and their claims more generally. Consider, for example, "Indian Band," a term that is entirely of the government's making. It first appears in federal Indian legislation in 1876, when the Indian Act defined an Indian band as follows:

> The term "band" means any tribe, band or body of Indians who own or are interested in a reserve or in Indian lands in common, of which the legal title is vested in the Crown, or who share alike in the distribution of any annuities or interest moneys for which the Government of Canada is responsible; the term "the band" means the band to which the context relates; and the term "band," when action is being taken by the band as such, means the band in council.[31]

Today, we refer more generally to Indian bands as "a group of people for whom lands have been set apart and money is held by the Crown."[32] Despite the fact that "Indian band" utterly fails to capture or respect the remarkably rich and diverse Indigenous cultures of Canada, the term and its meaning are both straightforward creatures of government. I state this obvious fact only because, when it comes to the administration of its specific claims policy, DIAND seems quite befuddled about what constitutes an Indian band. Consider the plight of the Michel Band, whose historic reserve, Michel Indian Reserve No. 132, lay northwest of Edmonton, Alberta. The band entered into a treaty with Canada in 1878, when Chief Michael Callihoo signed an adhesion to Treaty 6. Two years later, a forty-square-mile reserve was set apart for the Michel Band and confirmed by an Order in Council on May 17, 1889.[33]

The band soon fell afoul of Canadian legislation. After 1857, the enfranchisement of Indigenous people was an official goal of the Canadian state. A key component of the Crown policies pressing Aboriginal assimilation into the "white mainstream," enfranchisement essentially gave Aboriginal individuals the right to vote in exchange for renouncing their

Indian status. They ceased to be recognized legally as "Indians" and lost any rights or status associated with that recognition. Under the Gradual Civilization Act of 1857 and the 1869 Gradual Enfranchisement Act, enfranchisement was voluntary. However, the Indian Act of 1876 included clauses for *involuntary* enfranchisement. Under section 86 of the act, Indians who became doctors, lawyers, or members of the clergy, or who obtained a university degree, were automatically enfranchised and lost their Indian status, band membership, and right to live on their reserve. Similarly, section 93 enabled the Indian Department to forcibly enfranchise entire bands, and related clauses had the same effect for Aboriginal women who married non-Indians. This approach was preserved through successive versions of the Indian Act until Bill C-31 was passed in 1985. Under its provisions, women who married out were no longer involuntarily enfranchised, and nor were their children. Voluntary enfranchisees and those who were automatically enfranchised owing to educational or professional accomplishments regained their Indian status. There is nothing in the current act, however, that expressly provides for individuals who were involuntarily enfranchised when their band was enfranchised to regain their status.[34]

Over the course of its history, the Michel Band was eroded of members almost entirely through the involuntary loss of status due to marrying out and through the enfranchisement of members who simply grew too prosperous to meet Ottawa's inherently racist and reductionist definitions of "Indians." By 1962, all the reserve lands and assets of the band had been distributed to the enfranchised individuals, which included everyone except a small group that was denied enfranchisement because its members were deemed "unable to support themselves."[35] Thus, Michel Indian Reserve No. 132 ceased to exist, rendered redundant by the assimilation of the band through compulsory enfranchisement. In effect, the entire band was "administratively assimilated" in less than three generations.

In the wake of Bill C-31, approximately 660 former members or descendants of the Michel Band regained Indian status and reconstituted themselves as the Friends of the Michel Society. In 1985, the Friends brought a specific claim against the Crown, challenging the loss of the reserve through the involuntary enfranchisement of band members between 1928 and 1958, and stating that Canada had violated its fiduciary and statutory obligations by permitting the loss of the land.[36] In what can only be described as a cruel and ironic twist of fate, the same government that had forced the enfranchisement and assimilation of the Michel Band now rejected its claim on the grounds that it was not a "recognized Indian band." In short, because the government had rendered them so, the Friends of the Michel were not "Indians" and thus had no standing to submit a claim. In an effort to wriggle out of the ensuing controversy, DIAND agreed to review all the enfranchisements to determine whether the Friends of the Michel Band could be recognized as an Indian band and thus gain standing. Predictably, the answer was no, and efforts by the Friends to have the band reconstituted by the minister of Indian Affairs did not succeed.[37] The government's treatment of this band is rooted in the perversity and unfairness of much Indian policy, including and especially the manner in which DIAND has chosen to understand and administer *Outstanding Business*. The case of the Michel is also an excellent illustration of how assimilation policies benefit the Crown – if there are no Indians, there can be no Indian claims.

The use of vague wording in claims policy, the practice of discounting, and the narrow understanding of the relationship between Indigenous communities and their traditional lands are exacerbated by what is perhaps the most devastating tactic of the Crown in its handling of claims – namely, delay: delays in assessing submissions; delays in the Justice Department review of submissions; delays due to meetings cancelled by both parties; delays caused by DIAND's failure to deliver on its undertakings; and, perhaps most bizarrely, delays that the SCB justifies as part and parcel of its quest for a "mandate to settle" – something that, according to *Outstanding Business*, comes into play as soon as a claim is accepted for negotiation. After working assiduously to research and compile their claim submission, communities routinely wait for more than five years until the SCB accepts or rejects it. The Mohawks at Oka waited just short of a decade, only to have their claim denied. After a similar span of time, the Friends of the Michel gave up and sought the assistance of the Indian Claims Commission. These periods are dwarfed by the fifteen years that the Peepeekisis waited for a response to their claim or the almost seventeen-year wait endured by the Siksika First Nation.[38] These lulls in the process constitute more than mere inconveniences. As stressed above, claims rely on historical evidence. Although both claimant and Crown can rely on a common corpus of written records, almost all of which were generated by Indian agents, treaty commissioners, and various federal government officials, the band often has other records of its own. Many of these are living records – the memories of elders who were present at treaty signings or surrender votes, or who remember hearing their parents, grandparents, and community members talk about them. Such oral histories are fragile, and efforts by young community members to record them rarely capture all the knowledge. Some of it is never recorded – the fast pace of modern life rarely permits the hours required to sit with elders to hear full stories or receive their wisdom. An elder who is sixty or seventy years old can hardly wait ten or fifteen years to provide her evidence to Crown officials. When she dies, her wisdom dies with her, and important historical and community resources are lost. Delay thus damages the band's ability to mount a full claim, putting the Crown in a position like that of notorious company lawyers who fight liability claims simply by waiting for the victim's life or resources to run out. Delay may be a useful, if unintentional, consequence of the Crown's policies and thus something there is little incentive to change. Certainly, it appears to be the latter, as the queue of nations waiting for a seat at the claims table is long and well established, and delaying has become a standard way of doing business at the SCB. We will talk about delay extensively in Chapter 4, when we wade into the unedifying waters of SCB claims processing and the rise of the Indian Claims Commission's deemed rejection policies.

Specific Claims and the Oka Crisis: The Realization of the Inevitable

Few Canadians seem to know that the summer-long crisis at Oka in 1990 was the direct result of a failure of Canadian claims policy and a reflection of the Crown's problematic approach to Aboriginal title. Indigenous people have lived at Oka for more than a thousand years – archaeologists have established that Mohawk Iroquois culture developed in northeastern America and that the Mohawks have used the Kahnawake, Kahnesatake, and Akwesasne region for at least four hundred years.[39] The first Indigenous people to use the lands at Oka were the St. Lawrence Iroquoians, who inhabited much of the St. Lawrence River region until the latter part of the sixteenth century, when they abandoned it to the Algonquins.[40] The Mohawks who have historically resided in the area of Oka and Lac des

Deux Montagnes originally belonged to the community that would become Kahnawake, but they branched off from their brethren around 1676 to reside at Mount Royal with the Sulpician priests who were also the seigneurs of Montreal. They remained there until 1721, when the entire village relocated to Lac des Deux Montagnes and was later joined by Nipissings from Île aux Tourtes and Algonquins from Sainte-Anne-de-Bout-de-l'Île.[41] By 1763, about 150 warriors and their families were living at Oka.[42]

Although there had been a consistent Indigenous presence in the Oka region, it was not an area of settlement until the Mohawks and Sulpicians took up residence there after 1721. When they did, there was little talk of who owned the land – the Mohawks had no doubt that it was theirs. After all, their Iroquoian ancestors had hunted there, and oral history confirmed that as early as the seventeenth century the Iroquois Confederacy "took the land from the French in retaliation for Champlain's raid on their territory."[43] The Sulpicians knew better than to test Mohawk friendship with boasts of French title to the area, which was both good policy and good politics, as the French were outnumbered and their claim to title was thin. However, French concepts of "divine-right kingship entailed a belief in the crown's ownership of all lands in New France" and rejected any notion of Indigenous title. Thus, not bothering with treaties or negotiations, the French granted the lands at Oka to the Sulpicians. Their title, however, was never secure:

> Title to the lands to which the mixture of Mohawks and Algonkians repaired on Lake of Two Mountains was never free from challenge. Neither the terms of the Capitulation of Montreal nor the Royal Proclamation provided much protection to the Indian occupants. The Capitulation promisingly stated that the "Indian allies of his most Christian Majesty [the French king], shall be maintained in the Lands they inhabit; if they chuse to remain there; they shall not be molested on any pretence whatsoever, for having carried arms, and served his most Christian Majesty; they shall have, as well as the French, liberty of religion, and shall keep their missionaries." The Royal Proclamation of 1763, whose definition of "Hunting Grounds" reserved for Indians did not include the area around Lake of Two Mountains because it lay in Quebec, also contained provisions regulating the purchase of Indian lands within

existing colonies. However, this protection did not apply to the Oka lands either, because they were held by Europeans to have been allocated by seigneurial grant.[44]

The issue of title surfaced despite the Sulpicians' reluctance to discuss it, owing largely to conflicts over the grazing of cattle and the cutting of wood on the granted land. The church believed that the land belonged to it and wanted a cut of any revenue realized on it, but the Mohawks and other Indigenous people at Oka disagreed with this view and declined to share their profits. When the conflict found its way to the British authorities, which it did at least three times between 1781 and 1795, the Indigenous community had strong grounds on which to stake its claim. This included a document in which the church granted the Oka lands to the Indigenous residents. Unfortunately, this record was held by the church, which denied any knowledge or possession of it.[45] In addition, a wampum belt confirmed the grant, and oral history documented that the British had repeatedly accepted Indigenous title to the land. For example, during the American Revolutionary War, the British had promised that if the Mohawks sided with them, they would "fight for your [the Mohawks'] Land and when the War is over you shall have it."[46] This evidence easily overpowered the Sulpician claim, which suffered from a significant technical problem:

> The original seigneurial grant of 1717–18 (expanded by an additional grant of 1733–35) had been made to the Sulpicians of Paris, who transferred their rights to the Sulpicians of Montreal in 1784. But since the Canadian missionary body had no legal existence – that is, it was not legally incorporated by positive law – the Order was legally barred from possessing estates in mortmain, or inalienable tenure.[47]

Despite this fundamental defect in the Sulpician title, repeated efforts by the Mohawks to clarify their claim to the Oka lands met with defeat. Neither the British nor the French were prepared to disturb the flawed status quo. In 1839, the Sulpicians tried to regularize their claim, proposing to the Mohawks and other Indigenous residents that their right to use and dispose of specific plots of land be confirmed. No doubt weary of the endless squabble, the Mohawks agreed. The result was the passage of legislation in 1840 that confirmed the Sulpician title to the "Fief and Seigneury of the Lake of Two Mountains" and other properties.[48] Although this reinforced the priests' claim, it did nothing to dissuade the Mohawks, Algonquins, or Nipissings at Oka, who continued to press their title and the rights associated with it. From that point onward, there emerged "a well-established governmental tradition of trying to solve the Oka problem by either or both means: relocating the Indians or resolving the dispute by litigation."[49] Throughout, the Mohawks and others stood steadfast in their belief that they held title to the land, notwithstanding the decision of courts or the Crown.[50]

Eventually, the Sulpicians fell on hard times and into the habit of selling off their real estate at Oka. In 1933, unable to pay a debt to the Province, they sold a hundred lots to the Quebec government for one dollar and later sold a huge parcel to a Belgian company, which promptly enforced its proprietary rights against the Indigenous people living on the purchased land. The Mohawks and others vehemently proteseted the sales, both to the Sulpicians and Ottawa, which did nothing. In 1945, when the Sulpicians were almost bankrupt and the Mohawks had reached the point of insurrection, Ottawa finally acted, only to sidestep the issue. Without consulting the Mohawks, it purchased all the remaining Sulpician lands at Oka for the use of the Indigenous residents. In the end, the original sixty-four square miles that were once held by the Oka community were reduced to a tiny set of scattered lots comprising barely two and a half square miles. Technically, this area now belonged to the federal government, which promptly failed to set it aside as a reserve.[51]

In 1959, the Municipality of Oka granted a permit for the construction of a golf course on land claimed by the Mohawks, assured by DIAND in 1958 that it did "not comprise an Indian Reserve." The land fell within the Quebec premier's constituency, and the Municipality was able to obtain a private member's bill to seize it and build the golf course. The Mohawks were not informed or consulted about either the bill or the golf course, and when both became obvious, they mounted the strongest of protests and sought the assistance of DIAND to confirm their rights and stop the development. None of this made any difference, with the result that "what was once reserved for Indian use and profit is now reserved for golf."[52]

In 1975, together with their brethren at Kahnawake and Akwesasne, the Mohawks of Oka, or Kahnesatake, as they were now known, launched a comprehensive claim against the federal government to a large parcel of land stretching across southwestern Quebec. Reacting with unexpected speed, DIAND rejected it in only a few months. The department explained that, for this particular claim, Aboriginal title was a non-starter:

> If the claimants ever did have aboriginal title to the lands in question, this title has long been extinguished by the dispositions made of the land under the French regime, by the decision of the Sovereign, after the cession [Conquest], to open the territory to settlement and by the grants made over the years pursuant to this policy.[53]

In effect, this rejection confirmed a French claim based entirely on the original divine right of the sovereign, which provided no space for Indigenous title, despite the fact that the British in Canada had always accepted it. DIAND's stance completely negated the treaties. It also controverted its own ongoing efforts to address Indigenous title in most of British Columbia, as a result of the *Calder* decision, and its negotiations in northern Quebec to address Cree rights and hydroelectric development in James Bay. Essentially, DIAND assumed that such rights did not exist in southern Quebec or among the Mohawks. As is its habit, it offered a sop: the rejection of the comprehensive claim did "not extend to any specific claims which the Mohawks of Oka, St. Regis, and Caughnawaga may have with respect to lands contiguous or near their existing reserves."[54] Of course, the "Mohawks of Oka" had no reserve at the time.

Continuing to fight the good fight, the Kahnesatake Mohawks launched a specific claim to their land at Oka in 1977. As mentioned above, this languished in the bowels of the SCB for nearly a decade before being rejected in 1986 because it had not established an outstanding lawful obligation on the part of the Crown. The failure of the claim had little to do with the merits of the Mohawks' evidence or arguments. Instead, it was probably rejected because it arose from a series of events that reached back into the early 1700s. DIAND had a policy of not considering claims that were based on events that predated Confederation in 1867. As far as the department was concerned, the Oka claim lay beyond the pale, and there was no basis upon which to accept or consider it.

With both the comprehensive and specific claims denied, and the Mohawk lands unprotected by reserve status, the Municipality of Oka began to contemplate the Pines as the location for an extension of the Oka Golf Club and a condominium development. When the Mohawks learned of this, they expressed their concerns to the relevant governments, raising what they perceived as the unresolved land claim and asserting an ongoing right to the territory. Undeterred, the Municipality proceeded with its plans, inciting a small group of mostly Mohawk women and children to occupy the site in protest against the development and to protect the Pines.

When the Municipality began to move in heavy equipment, a few warriors joined the women and barricaded the roads into the Pines, effectively thwarting efforts to initiate construction of the golf course extension. A flurry of injunctions ensued, and on July 11, the Municipality's patience with the protesters and their "spurious claims" was exhausted – it ordered the provincial police to remove the protesters, forcibly if necessary. Just before dawn, heavily armed police officers in full SWAT gear, supported from above by helicopters brandishing blinding searchlights, swarmed the Pines. Their attempt to intimidate and expel the protesters was a spectacular failure: the Mohawks had anticipated the attack, and the men rallied to protect their claim and the families occupying the Pines. When the police fired on the camp, the Mohawks shot back, and a young police officer was killed by a bullet whose origin remains unclear.

As word spread of the daybreak raid, other Mohawks in Quebec and Ontario erected barricades around their communities in support of Kahnesatake. Kahnawake, criss-crossed with major commuter highways and bridges, blocked all thoroughfares; Akwesasne did the same. Within a matter of days, Indigenous people across Canada barricaded their borders, highways, and railways in support of the Mohawks or picketed and staged protests against the larger denial of Aboriginal land rights and claims, of which Oka was merely one example. What had begun as a simple administrative stroke of the pen, rebuffing a relatively modest claim, had exploded into a nation-wide "Indian crisis" of unprecedented proportions. Canadians and their governments, lulled into complacency by an Indigenous reticence to take up arms in defence of their rights, experienced a rude awakening and one that threatened Canada's carefully constructed reputation as a place of tolerance and social justice. The crisis persisted from July 11 to September 26, 1990, igniting an international furore and drawing attention to Canada's questionable Indian policies and attitude regarding the land and treaty rights of Indigenous people.

Shocked by the crisis and the associated bad publicity, Ottawa acted. On September 25, Prime Minister Brian Mulroney rose before the House of Commons and announced a set of parallel initiatives to deal with claims. The first aimed to accelerate the resolution of specific claims; the second was a commitment to finally respect legal undertakings made regarding land transfers to treaty Indians, many of which were over a century old.[55]

As a third wave of reforms, the federal government struck an independent Chiefs Committee on Claims to study the specific claims process and conduct nation-wide consultations with Aboriginal groups and stakeholders. In the fall of 1990, after forty days of cross-Canada consultations, the committee released its report – a ringing indictment of Ottawa's approach to claims:

> The current process provides for no independent review of decisions as to the validity of claims or the amount of compensation to be paid for claims. The justification for the rejection of claims is rarely given. Thus, the Government of Canada acts as defendant, trustee charged with protecting First Nations' interests, as well as judge and jury on all claims made against it.[56]

The report envisaged the creation of a much wider, more accessible, and independent authority to respond to claims, one that would embrace mediation as a mechanism for engaging and settling them. Central to the new approach was an independent review body that would operate at arm's length from the government and be empowered to inquire into the rejection of claims, to facilitate negotiation of claims, and to break any impasses that might arise in their negotiation and settlement. This body was to be the Indian Specific Claims Commission.

3

The Indian Specific Claims Commission
Second Sober Thought

This is a very limited Indian Claims Commission with very little power. It is also restricted in its decision-making by an Order in Council which fully embraces the current policy that we say needs to be changed ... A process that is fair and equitable must be established. Respect for our inherent Aboriginal and treaty rights must guide the governments in the future. We know that the people of Canada support First Nations in their struggle for justice and we ask you, as parliamentarians, to assist us in this effort.

– OVIDE MERCREDI TO THE STANDING COMMITTEE ON
ABORIGINAL AFFAIRS, 1991

What is lacking at this point is the sense among all the parties that this commission is going to be able to do the job everybody wanted it to do at the outset. That's our biggest fear. That's what we, as a commission, want to and have to address at this time, before we can go forward.

– HARRY LaFORME, INDIAN CLAIMS COMMISSION, TO THE
STANDING COMMITTEE ON ABORIGINAL AFFAIRS, 1991

The Oka Crisis had served notice on Canada that the current approach to claims was neither fair nor effective and that Aboriginal patience was wearing thin. Both the Crown and Aboriginal leadership knew that change was necessary, and much of the latter's concerns coalesced around the deep biases that characterized claims policy and processes. The tight grip of the Departments of Indian Affairs (DIAND) and Justice on almost every aspect of claims review and outcomes was untenable. The commission as visualized by the Chiefs Committee on Claims would prise open that hold, provide greater Aboriginal involvement in the claims process, and bring balance and fairness to claims resolution. As will be seen, however, loosening the grasp of the Crown would not come quickly or easily. Aboriginal people, their governments, and advocates would have to work hard to secure a truly independent commission and be vigilant to ensure that it remained so.

This activism in pursuit of fairness in both claims and the review of rejected claims would persist both outside and within the commission during its seventeen-year existence, and it was evidenced early on. Less than six months into its mandate, the first commissioner appointed to the Indian Specific Claims Commission (ICC) announced that it would be known as the *Indian Claims Commission*, reflecting resistance against DIAND's spurious distinction between comprehensive and specific claims.[1] This was a small but important step in the subtle activism that would come to define much of the ICC's work.

Challenging the Culture of Control at DIAND: The ICC Takes Shape

From the earliest moments, it was clear that the Crown and Aboriginal communities had very different understandings of what constituted an "independent" commission. The Chiefs Committee on Claims stressed that the new commission must operate at arm's length from government and should be empowered to review and require governments to act on rejected claims. However, the Order in Council (OIC) of July 15, 1991, that created the ICC conferred neither autonomy nor teeth. Indeed, it bound the commission to the current claims policy, an act easily construed as an attempt by DIAND to retain its control. Thus, the commission was to have jurisdiction, upon request by a claimant band, over claims formally rejected by the government, where an Indian band disagrees with the Minister of Indian Affairs and Northern Development's (the Minister) rejection of a claim for negotiation by examining in particular any band alleged,

1.1 non-fulfilment of a treaty or agreement between Indians and the Crown;

1.2 breach of an obligation arising from the Indian Act or any other statutes concerning Indians or the regulations thereunder;

1.3 breach of an obligation arising from the Government of Canada's administration of Indian funds or other assets;

1.4 illegal disposition of Indian land;

1.5 failure to provide compensation for reserve lands taken or damaged by the Government of Canada or any of its agencies; and

1.6 fraud in connection with the acquisition or disposition of Indian reserve land by employees or agents of the Government of Canada, in cases where such fraud can be clearly demonstrated.[2]

The commission was also given the power to inquire and make recommendations regarding the appropriate compensation criteria to be applied to a claim in those cases where the band and the minister disagreed on criteria.[3]

The core of specific claims policy had simply been cut and pasted into the OIC. It went on to detail precisely those qualifiers that Indigenous people and policy-watchers condemned, including the infamous special value to owner, which had been directly implicated in the Oka Crisis, and the dubious practices of discounting and degree of doubt. To make matters worse, the OIC did not remedy the deeply one-sided nature of the claims review process, which was simply replicated and reinforced by ensuring that the ICC was constrained at every turn. This was hardly the independent commission envisaged by the Chiefs Committee on Claims or promised to Indigenous communities by the Mulroney government in the wake of the Oka Crisis. As well, though the commission could provide mediation services to assist in the resolution of claims accepted for negotiation, it was not given the powers the committee had hoped for. In reviewing rejected claims, its ability to "break impasses" consisted solely of making recommendations to government regarding whether a claim had been wrongly (or rightly) denied. The Crown was at liberty to ignore the recommendations and pursue its own interests, which meant that its historic claims practices would simply remain in place.

Indigenous people were quick to express their dismay. The failure of the government to consult with Indigenous leadership regarding the form and structure of the commission, and what was perceived as its uncomfortably close ties to the flawed claims process, formed the crux of their concerns.[4] The charge against the ICC was led by the Assembly of First Nations (AFN) and its grand chief, Ovide Mercredi. A strongly traditionalist chief, he was reportedly seen by the Prime Minister's Office and many in the Conservative government as a difficult and, on some issues, intransigent leader. For many of those whom he represented, however, Mercredi stood for strength and resistance against a self-interested and dishonourable Crown. All these sentiments were probably reinforced by his reaction to the ICC mandate. Invited to speak to the Standing Committee on Aboriginal Affairs in December of 1991, Mercredi was clear and unrelenting in his criticism of the OIC, the commission it created, and the Crown that was responsible for both:

> We find the terms of reference as set out in the Order in Council completely unacceptable. There are several primary problems with the Order in Council. One, there was no consultation with us. Two, the terms of reference and limitations on compensation are not consistent with legal principles. They violate the concept of equality guaranteed under the Charter of Rights and Freedoms. Three, the terms of reference and limitations represent a serious breach of the federal government's fiduciary obligations to First Nations. Four, these limitations tie the hands of the commission and negate its independence. And five, the restrictions imposed upon the commission are inconsistent with the Prime Minister's promise that his government is prepared "to go far beyond the status quo" ... We have found the existing Order in Council to be illegal and intend to challenge it in the courts if it is not changed substantially.[5]

A critic of the OIC with a different approach was the first commissioner and chairman of the ICC, Harry S. LaForme. An Osgoode Hall–educated lawyer with a distinguished legal career and previous experience as a commissioner with the Indian Commission of Ontario, LaForme was a member of the Mississauga First Nation and well regarded among legal and Indigenous communities.[6] He had no illusions about the limitations imposed by the commission's mandate but had struggled to get the organization up and running while pressing the government to amend the OIC. By the time he was called to speak before the Standing Committee on Aboriginal Affairs, LaForme had established fledgling commission offices in Toronto and Ottawa, and had begun to gather a modest staff of researchers, lawyers, and support personnel. He had also received requests from a few bands that were interested in testing the inquiry process. However, as resistance against the commission and the OIC intensified, the construction of the commission slowed to a snail's pace. LaForme understood that the flaws of the OIC must be addressed before the ICC could truly get under way, as he explained to the standing committee:

> If the chiefs and the First Nations do not have confidence in our independence as a commission or in our ability to deal with questions of this policy without being directed and having our hands shackled by an Order in Council, they raise those as problems and say it is not worthy of getting into that process.[7]

He added that the new commission shared the concerns of Indigenous people about the OIC. Fully aware of their views regarding the ICC, LaForme impressed upon the standing committee that

> I am not certain everybody fully appreciates what the language in that Order in Council is creating, but I do believe people want the commission to be at arm's length ... There is suspicion that it is not at arm's length because it repeats the policy of the Government of Canada ... Some people, and not just chiefs, are saying that your hands are bound by criteria before you even get started. They are saying that if it is, and all you are going to do is be a mouthpiece to reinforce the policy, then what good does it do us? ... As I've said over and over, if we're going to have the confidence of all the parties, they have to believe that we have the mandate to address these issues the way they want them addressed, the vast majority of which are suggesting we don't.[8]

Although they presented the problem differently, Mercredi and LaForme agreed on the same fundamental flaw underlying the commission: the OIC's strong reliance on the existing claims policy. LaForme understood only too well that the ICC could not stand if Aboriginal people had no faith in its independence. For his part, Mercredi viewed that lack of independence as a deliberate attempt by DIAND to control the ICC:

> We know one thing: that the bureaucracy is benefitting from this initiative. The reality is that unless there is fundamental change, the vast majority of outstanding claims will not be resolved. The manipulation of the negotiating process by federal officials cannot be allowed to continue ... A process that is fair and equitable must be established.[9]

The resistance to the terms of the ICC's creation led to a stalemate. Until the OIC was amended, Mercredi and the AFN refused to participate in appointing the additional six commissioners. The selection process was to be a joint government-AFN undertaking, so Mercredi's stand effectively halted both the appointments and the establishment of the commission. Lacking a full complement of commissioners, LaForme could not continue building the ICC and could not proceed with inquiries. He informed the government that "we're not in a position to hear complaints from the bands. We're not in a position to have any hearings. We're not even in a position to seek what we believe are necessary changes to the Order in Council. That's where we are at."[10]

In December of 1991, as Mercredi and LaForme struggled to communicate the depth of Aboriginal antipathy regarding the claims policy and its impact on the ICC, DIAND approached the AFN with a proposal for the creation of a joint working group. Tasked with thoroughly reviewing the specific claims policy, it would consist of representatives from the AFN and the federal government. A working group was duly formed, and its first duty, assigned to it by the AFN's Chiefs Committee on Claims, was to turn its mind to the ICC and the flawed OIC.[11] The result of its work was a new OIC, dated July 27, 1992, that not only appointed the six additional ICC commissioners, but also deleted all the parts of the original OIC that invoked the claims policy. The result was a far more succinct mandate for the ICC: it would conduct public inquiries into rejected claims and would provide mediation services to the Crown and to Aboriginal communities whose claims had been accepted for negotiation. These services were to be tied to, but not defined by, the claims policy, and the commission was limited in these tasks to issues or disputes submitted to it by either party to a claim. Specifically, its job was "to inquire into and report on"

a) whether a claimant has a valid claim for negotiation under the Policy where that claim has already been rejected by the Minister, and
b) which compensation criteria apply in negotiation of a settlement, where a claimant disagrees with the Minister's determination of the applicable criteria.[12]

Extricated from the constraints of the claims policy, the ICC was now acceptably tasked and supported by sufficient members to conduct inquiries. The Indian Claims Commission was finally fully ready to begin its work.

Defining Independence: The Indian Claims Commissioners

ICC commissioners were Governor in Council appointees who were initially selected through consultation between the AFN and Ottawa. They faced a rather robust vetting process that scrutinized their backgrounds, political activity and philosophy, and perceived integrity among both Aboriginal and non-Aboriginal constituencies. Achieving acceptance in both communities was no small feat: though many recoil at the tangled web that is Canadian federal politics, it pales in comparison with the Aboriginal political world. There, truly desperate needs and issues must compete for attention and redress, the pool of players is smaller, and their relationships are strained by diverse loyalties to communities, nations, and issues. Those who rise to the top of Aboriginal society must overcome far more daunting odds than most non-Aboriginal elites will ever encounter and will discover that the winds blow strong at high political altitudes. They can be torn between traditional values stressing non-directive leadership and the collective good, and a Canadian political culture that can dismiss such approaches. Aboriginal leaders often face deeper scrutiny both from their own people, who hold them to very high standards, and the Canadian public, many of whom struggle to overcome conscious and unconscious racism.

The first six appointments to the ICC were made in July of 1992 through the joint AFN-DIAND process and were apportioned equally across Aboriginal and non-Aboriginal communities. The former included Dan Bellegarde, an Assiniboine-Cree member of the Little Black Bear First Nation from Saskatchewan; Carole Corcoran, a Dene from the Fort Nelson First Nation in northern British Columbia; and Roger Augustine, a Mi'kmaq and chief of the Eel Ground First Nation in New Brunswick. All three were highly accomplished. Bellegarde had been vice-chief of the Federation of Saskatchewan Indian Nations and had a well-established record in promoting socioeconomic development on Saskatchewan reserves through his work with the Meadow Lake District Chiefs Venture. Carole Corcoran was a practising lawyer who had extensive experience in Aboriginal government and politics. She had served on the British Columbia Treaty Commission and had sat for a time as co-chair of the First Nations Summit.[13] Roger Augustine had been elected as president of the Union of New Brunswick-Prince Edward Island First Nations and had been pivotal in bringing alcohol and drug treatment services to communities, an accomplishment that earned him a Medal of Distinction from the Canadian Centre for Substance Abuse. I was not appointed until 2002 but would have the great pleasure to sit alongside Dan Bellegarde and, for a short time, Roger Augustine, who later took up a position with the AFN. Bellegarde was a well-respected and important member of the ICC for its entire lifespan, and working with him was an honour and a privilege. Carole Corcoran was with the commission for approximately eight years, from 1992 to 2001, at which time she passed away suddenly, a great loss to the ICC, her family, and community.

These commissioners were joined by three non-Aboriginal individuals: Carol Dutcheshen, Charles-André Hamelin, and James Prentice. Dutcheshen was a lawyer from Winnipeg who served on the Manitoba and Canadian Bar Associations. After two years, she left the ICC to work for Ontario Hydro. Hamelin had been an MP for the riding of Charleboix, Quebec, from 1984 to 1988 and a member of the National Parole Board. He suffered a fatal heart attack in 1993 at the age of forty-six and was thus only briefly a member of the ICC. Prentice, a Calgary lawyer, had extensive experience in land claims matters and had provided legal advice and negotiation services to the Alberta government on claims. When Harry LaForme left the ICC in February 1994 to take up a position on the bench of the Ontario Court of Justice, it was Jim Prentice who assumed the role of ICC co-chair with Dan Bellegarde.

LaForme's departure, combined with the losses of Hamelin and Dutcheshen, left the commission with only four members. In May of that year, Aurélien Gill, a Montagnais from Pointe-Bleu, Quebec, founding president of the Conseil Atikamekw et Montagnais and founding member of the National Indian Brotherhood, was appointed to the commission. He sat on the ICC for four years, until his departure in 1998 when he was appointed to the Senate by Jean Chrétien; Gill remains an active member of the Senate. In 1999, Sheila Purdy was appointed to the ICC by Chrétien, as was Elijah Harper. A practising lawyer, Purdy had served as a senior adviser to the minister of justice and the attorney general on Aboriginal issues, human rights, and violence against women, and was a well-respected activist and advocate. She remained on the ICC until its decommissioning in 2009 and was one of its most dedicated and hard-working commissioners. Elijah Harper, who stayed with the commission for only a year, is perhaps best known for his role in the Meech Lake Accord debates of 1990, when he was a Manitoba MLA. Opposed to the accord on grounds that First Nations had not been consulted, Harper, an Ojibwa-Cree, initiated a series of procedural delays that resulted in Manitoba's failure to ratify the accord before its expiry on June 23, 1990. His actions, in tandem with the refusal of Newfoundland to vote on the accord, ensured its collapse.[14] A strong and vocal advocate for Aboriginal people and rights, Harper left the ICC in 2000.

A year later, Jim Prentice also departed. He achieved prominence in federal Conservative politics and after 2006 was a rising star in the Stephen Harper government. When he became Indian Affairs minister in February 2006, those who had had the apparently significant pleasure of knowing him at the ICC expressed the hope that he would compel DIAND to mend its ways. To some extent, their optimism was justified: although Prentice was criticized for his government's abandonment of the Kelowna Accord, he was praised for his work in finalizing and implementing the Indian Residential Schools Settlement Agreement. Regrettably, his approach to specific claims left a great deal to be desired. Because his evolution from ICC chief commissioner to minister of Indian Affairs illustrates much about the tension between the ICC and DIAND, it is worth a brief digression to tell this piece of the story.

Prentice was Indian Affairs minister from February 6, 2006, to August 13, 2007, as the sun was setting on the ICC, which the Harper government decommissioned in 2009. In the last two or three years of the commission's life, we struggled to complete as many reports as possible, most of which the various Indian Affairs ministers simply ignored. During Prentice's roughly year-and-a-half tenure as minister, our records indicate that we completed eleven inquiry reports. The minister responded to only two: on the Peepeekisis First Nation inquiry, completed and submitted to his predecessor in 2001; and on the Canupawakpa Dakota First Nation inquiry, completed and submitted in 2003. Both reports had met with no response from the minister until Prentice took up the office in 2006. Nothing in ICC records indicates that Prentice replied to a single report submitted to him during his tenure as minister of Indian Affairs.

Peepeekisis was a long and difficult inquiry; the claim was submitted to the Specific Claims Branch (SCB) in 1986, where it languished for more than fifteen years with no response from the minister. In the spring of 2001, tired of the delay and lack of response to its claim, the Peepeekisis Band requested that the ICC deem its claim to be "constructively rejected" and accept it for inquiry. The ICC agreed to do so. Canada initially challenged its jurisdiction to hold the inquiry, then formally rejected the claim in December of 2001, and the inquiry proceeded.

In 1874, the Peepeekisis First Nation had signed Treaty 4, through which it received reserve lands and other considerations in exchange for surrendering the bulk of its traditional territories. In 1898, with the clear blessing of the department, the local Indian agent created and imposed a large farming project at the reserve called the File Hills Colony. The best lands were subdivided and given to Aboriginal graduates of local industrial schools, which, along with residential schools, were a key instrument in Ottawa's program of cultural conversion and assimilation. None of the graduates belonged to the Peepeekisis Band, and thus, according to the Indian Act, they had no rights to reside on the reserve or to receive the benefits of membership. Nor did Ottawa have a right to appropriate the reserve land for the colony. Indian Affairs circumvented this difficulty and furthered its grand experiment in assimilation simply by making the graduates members of the band, which was later folded into the File Hills Colony.[15] Within less than a decade, the graduates outnumbered the band members, who were crowded onto a small corner of the reserve and left with little arable land or prospects.

The original members of the Peepeekisis Nation consistently protested the File Hills Colony experiment and their marginalization on their own land and within their own band. As early as 1955, an independent inquiry found that the Indian agent and Indian Affairs had breached the terms of Treaty 4 and the Indian Act by taking Peepeekisis land without the consent of the band and by granting band membership to the graduates. Rejecting this finding, the Indian Affairs registrar confirmed the legitimacy of both, and a subsequent judicial review found in the department's favour. When the Peepeekisis Band submitted a specific claim seeking compensation for the harms done by the File Hills Colony experiment, the minister rejected it on the basis of *res judicata* – that the claim was based on questions already asked and answered, and was thus without foundation. When the band appealed to the ICC, our inquiry found that res judicata did not cover all aspects of the claim. We held that Canada had breached its treaty, Indian Act, and fiduciary obligations to the Peepeekisis Nation and was thus encumbered by outstanding lawful obligations to the band. We recommended that the claim be accepted and negotiated.

Nevertheless, Minister Prentice rejected these recommendations in 2006, noting that "several years of inquiries and hearings into the claim" had dealt with all its aspects and that the matter was closed.[16] Focusing on the *management* of the claim, as opposed to the *substance* of the claim, the Crown did not address its own wrongdoing or that of the Indian agent in the File Hills Colony scheme. As far as it was concerned, the issues had been considered and concluded. Relying on res judicata, the Crown was able to secure an outcome that, technically, was legally correct but also entirely unjust to the Peepeekisis Band. Without question, the ICC finding was legally correct and in keeping with the spirit and principles established in Aboriginal and treaty law to this time. However, the Crown chose to focus on a narrowly construed legal principle rather than on what was just or right. Predictably, given its role as both party and judge in this claim, it won the day.

The Canupawakpa First Nation inquiry arose from the department's 1995 rejection of the band's claim that a portion of its reserve known as Turtle Mountain, the site of an ancestral burial ground, had been wrongfully surrendered. Although the ICC found that Canada had acted as a "reasonable and prudent trustee" and had met its fiduciary obligations in completing the surrender, it nonetheless urged the government to partner with the First Nation to secure and preserve the lands as a significant cultural and historical site.[17] Prentice and DIAND chose to reject this "equitable and moral" course. In his response to the ICC report, Prentice wrote, "while the Indian Specific Claims Commission is free to state its views regarding fairness, however, Canada does not have the authority to accept claims based on these views."[18] This reply is telling. If a claim presents outstanding lawful obligations, the Crown has limited room to refuse to accept it and negotiate a resolution (although the preceding chapter revealed how much latitude the Specific Claims Branch manages to find in that limited space). Confronted by a clear lawful obligation and thus backed against the wall, the Crown accepts and negotiates claims because it has no reasonable alternative. However, its true honour is revealed in claims where it is not subject to a lawful obligation but where unfairness or injustice have nonetheless occurred. In contexts such as those of Canupawakpa, where the only force moving for acceptance and resolution of a claim is moral, we see clearly how the Crown views its fiduciary obligations to First Nations. To do what is legal is mandatory; to do what is right is often simply, powerfully, a matter of choice and character. When the Crown turned its back on Canupawakpa and invoked a narrow legal argument to reject the Peepeekisis claim, its true character was laid utterly, and disappointingly, open.

What is important about these responses is not what they say about Jim Prentice. By all accounts, when he was with the ICC, he was highly regarded as diligent, affable, and committed to the timely and fair resolution of claims. Indeed, had he been viewed otherwise, my ICC colleagues would probably not have greeted his DIAND appointment with optimism. However, what is suggested in his replies to both Peepeekisis and Canupawakpa is that he proved either unable or unwilling to bring the spirit and approach to claims that informed his time at the ICC to his role as minister. This is hardly surprising, given the Crown's traditional approach to claims and the difficult political situation in which Prentice must have found himself. At the same time, however, the role of Indian Affairs minister must also be shaped by his fiduciary responsibilities to Aboriginal people, whose rights and interests must be protected against those of the rest of Canada. In this way, the minister has a difficult line to walk, as he is bound by his obligations to both Aboriginal and non-Aboriginal citizens. However, given that every other federal government department has no special duty to Aboriginal people and may focus all its energies on furthering the interests of non-Aboriginal people, we could certainly encourage and perhaps forgive the minister of Indian Affairs were he – or she – to emphasize the Crown's honour, fiduciary obligations, and fairness in all dealings with Aboriginal people. In this regard, the better barometer for assessing outcomes in claims negotiation should perhaps not be whether they can be justified in law, but whether they are just.

But I digress. The departures of Elijah Harper and Jim Prentice in 2000 and 2001, respectively, left the ICC in need of at least two more commissioners; they also signalled an end to the era of the co-chair. These deficits were soon addressed. In 2001, Alan Holman, a former journalist who had been both Atlantic parliamentary correspondent and later parliamentary bureau chief for the CBC, as well as principal secretary to PEI premier Catherine Callbeck, was appointed to the ICC. He remained a fixture until it was dissolved. In the same year, former AFN national chief Phil Fontaine became chief commissioner of the ICC. He sat on the commission for a relatively brief period from 2001 until June 2003, when he returned to his first love: politics. He was victorious in the 2003 and 2006 AFN elections for national chief, making him the first person to serve three terms in this position. While in office, he achieved significant change for Aboriginal people, negotiating the Kelowna Accord with Canadian political leaders and spearheading the drive to redress the wrongs of Indian residential schools through the settlement agreement and the Truth and Reconciliation Commission.[19]

Renée Dupuis replaced Fontaine as chief commissioner after 2003 and stayed with the commission until the end. A former human rights lawyer, she had a long record of work with First Nations in Quebec and had served two terms as a commissioner with the Canadian Human Rights Commission. As will be seen, she instigated a series of measures to professionalize ICC operations and led the decommissioning process and creation of the ICC legacy.

As a humble academic and grassroots activist, I had probably the lowest profile among ICC commissioners. Being appointed to a body whose roots lay in the 1990 Oka Crisis was serendipitous. At the height of the crisis, I had been present behind the barricades at Kahnawake, a community where I lived for a time, and had witnessed the government's failure to attend to claims, as well as the devastating extent to which all parties would go to secure the land. As I reflected upon the great privilege and responsibility of the appointment, I recalled my experiences in the summer of 1990 and one particular event that became a defining moment in my understanding of the Indigenous-government relationship in Canada. After spending only a few hours behind the barricades at Kahnawake, I was taken on a short drive to check in with the people manning the entry points onto the reserve. At one such place, I was greeted by a very small group of mostly (much) older Mohawk men, who were sitting around a campfire and brewing tea. Despite the chronic reports of "heavily armed warriors," there was only one weapon in sight – an ancient hunting rifle that had obviously seen far better days. I was offered a cup of tea and sat down with the men for a break and a chat. Within minutes, we heard a low rumbling, and I noticed what appeared to be Jurassic Park–style impact tremors rippling the surface of my tea. The sound and shaking intensified. I stood up and as I turned to face the bushes and low trees behind me, the leaves parted, and I found myself looking down the gun barrel of a tank. My first day in Kahnawake had coincided with the replacement of the police at the barricades by armed forces personnel. Had the moment not seemed so surreal, I probably would have had the sense to be deeply intimidated. As it was, I felt only sadness that the government's inability to deal ethically and respectfully with Aboriginal claims had brought us all to this place of violence, conflict, and repression. I believed, and continue to believe, strongly in the rights and claims that we were all defending throughout that crisis. If the ICC could provide a measured, balanced, and ethical response to claims, if it could assist us to avoid another Oka and achieve a measure of justice in claims resolution, I would be honoured to join its work.

My October 2002 appointment by Prime Minister Jean Chrétien was the last one made to the ICC. The commission would close seven years later, to make way for yet another "new approach" to claims, this time in the form of yet more promises of improvements and the creation of the Specific Claims Tribunal (discussed more fully below). Except for two years working under Phil Fontaine as chief commissioner, my seven years on the ICC were spent in the company of Sheila Purdy, Dan Bellegarde, Al Holman, and Renée Dupuis. Afterward, I went back to my teaching and research at Carleton University in Ottawa; Sheila Purdy resumed her work as an Ottawa-based consultant and adviser; Dan Bellegarde returned to Saskatchewan, where he works as director of treaty governance with the Federation of Sovereign Indigenous Nations and serves as chief of the Board of Police Commissioners of the File Hills First Nations Police Service. Al Holman went back to Prince Edward Island and freelance journalism; he writes a regular Sunday column for the *Charlottetown Guardian*. Renée Dupuis was recently appointed to the Canadian Senate.

Staking a Claim to Communication: Defining the ICC Process

The basis upon which the ICC made its ruling in Canupawakpa was a "supplementary mandate," which had evolved in 1993. As discussed above, the ICC mandate originally encompassed two primary tasks: conducting inquiries into rejected claims and into the compensation criteria for negotiations in accepted claims.[20] In both, the ICC was bound by DIAND's view of legitimate claims as founded on an outstanding lawful obligation – that is, legitimacy was defined very much in purely, and often narrow, legal terms. Of course, claims are necessarily bound up with law and legal argument, but what of claims in which lawful actions led to injustice? What of cases such as Canupawakpa, where everyone did what was legally correct, and thus no lawful obligation existed, but where the lawful acts had resulted in poverty, despair, and a strong moral claim to assistance from the Crown? Too often, the Crown's ostensibly legal actions had produced immoral consequences – what would become of bands whose claims arose from this situation?

In 1993, the commissioners found an unexpected route to accommodating such claims in a letter written by Minister of Indian Affairs Tom Siddon to Ovide Mercredi in 1991. Remarking on the ICC and its proposed mandate, Siddon stated, "I expect to accept the Commission's recommendations where they fall within the Specific Claims Policy. If, in carrying out its review, the Commission concludes that the *policy was implemented correctly but the outcome is nonetheless unfair,* I would again welcome recommendations on how to proceed."[21] The ICC construed this comment as an invitation to attend not only to the legal status of a claim, but also to the achievement of fairness in the management of rejected claims. Thus was born what the ICC referred to as its "supplementary mandate." This enabled the commission to bring the government's attention to claims situations that were unfair and worthy of redress, even though the Crown had no ongoing lawful obligation to the claimants. Although we did not use the supplementary mandate on many occasions, pushing the boundaries of our mandate was important. It opened the Crown to the possibility that it might be held accountable for lawful actions that led to unfair, unethical, or improper outcomes. It could simply choose to ignore our recommendations, as the Canupawakpa claim demonstrates, but articulating its moral as well as legal failings lent a certain transparency to its actions and intentions in responding to both claims and claimants.

When I joined the commission, it consisted of five divisions under the auspices of the chief commissioner and the commissioners. Following the appointment of Renée Dupuis as chief commissioner, the divisions were coordinated and overseen by an executive director. The Legal and Research Units, which housed lawyers and articling students, and researchers, respectively, came under the direction of the commission counsel. The Liaison Unit, under the authority of a director, was key to the commission's work. It connected with claimants, secured locations and accommodations for such events as the hearing of legal arguments, which commonly occurred in the urban centre closest to the claimant, and it organized the community session. Liaison also generated "community profiles" to inform the commissioners of the band, its traditional and current culture, and its language preferences. The director of Liaison usually travelled with the panel of commissioners to hearings and community sessions, and was an invaluable source of information and support without whom our work would have been much more difficult. The ICC was also greatly aided by the Corporate Services Unit, which kept it on track through the provision of library, financial, and IT services, as well as basic supplies and services.

Finally, as its name indicates, the Mediation Unit handled mediation services. Consisting of up to four mediators under the supervision of a director, it provided mediation services to the parties to a claim, most commonly to assist in the negotiation process. Although the commissioners received mediation training and were qualified to undertake mediation with the parties, efforts in this regard were short-lived, and most ICC mediation services were supplied by the unit. The relationship between the Mediation Unit and the commissioners will be discussed in some detail in Chapter 6.

Under the mandate outlined in the 1992 Order in Council, the commissioners were authorized to "adopt such methods ... as they may consider expedient for the proper conduct of the inquiry and to sit at such times, and in such places as they may decide."[22] Determined to provide for balance, the first commissioners decided that Canada's representatives and legal counsel would be brought together with those of the Aboriginal claimant early in the inquiry process. This was a significant break with the past: a claimant nation could easily proceed from funding application to rejection of its claim without ever meeting the Crown's representatives. The ICC wished to break this bureaucratic anonymity and ensure that claimants and Crown met in person to discuss the claim and its rejection. As a result, the inquiry process saw repeated interactions between the two parties, at planning conferences, legal arguments, and most important of all, the community session. This seemed to function well, although it was not without its problems. The following sketch of the process sets the stage for the discussion of some of these problems in later chapters.

The inquiry process was initiated by a request from the party to a claim. Following what was, in most cases, the rejection of its claim, a band would write to the ICC, asking for an inquiry. This letter was accompanied by a band council resolution that authorized the ICC to undertake the inquiry and to obtain all relevant documents. Central to the request were copies of the original submission and the letter in which the minister had rejected it. These documents were received and reviewed by the commission's head legal counsel (called commission counsel), who ensured that the application was complete. If the request were in order, counsel forwarded the file to the Research Unit, which prepared a claim assessment report. This was returned to commission counsel, who reviewed it and compiled a recommendation to commissioners regarding whether to accept or reject the request for an inquiry. In advance of the regular commissioner meetings, the Legal Department would send all the commissioners a dossier for each request, which contained commission counsel's assessment and recommendation, the documents included in the initial request, and the claim assessment report. Weighing up these files was a central item of business at commissioner meetings. During my tenure on the ICC, our meetings commonly dealt with two or three, and debates over whether to accept a request were usually relatively brief and uncomplicated. An exception to this trend emerged after 1996, when increasing numbers of bands sought an inquiry even though their claim had not yet been formally rejected by the government. In some instances, the claim had been submitted more than a decade earlier. In response to these requests, the ICC developed a policy on "deemed" or "constructive rejections," which we will consider in the next chapter.

In my experience, the commissioners denied few requests for an inquiry. Those that we did turn away typically involved claims that had not been formally rejected and did not meet our criteria for constructive rejections. In these cases, our legal administrative assistant prepared a letter to inform the band and explain the grounds for rejection. The chief commissioner signed the letter, which was sent to the First Nation. If a request was accepted, the assistant prepared letters for both Canada and the First Nation, notifying them that an inquiry would take place and asking that they share all relevant documents. The Crown was also asked to inform the ICC of the name and contact information for the legal counsel it had assigned to the claim. The letters were sent to the chief and legal counsel of the band and also to the Indian Affairs and Justice ministers.

Once a claim had been accepted, the ICC struck a panel that normally consisted of three commissioners and an alternate, who could step in if one of the three were unable to continue. If an inquiry was especially complex, a case manager might also be appointed. This person, who was not an active member of the panel and who had no direct involvement with the substance of the inquiry, oversaw the process, liaised with the parties, and ensured that everything progressed smoothly. In the history of the ICC, only a very few inquiries enlisted a case manager. In one of these, which involved the Betsiamites Band,[23] Renée Dupuis was the case manager, helping to facilitate an inquiry in which French, English, and Montagnais were the primary languages.

In each case, the panel was assisted by the legal counsel, or associate, who had been assigned to the inquiry, as well as a research officer and a research technician, who ensured oversight and co-ordination of the file. These individuals were vitally important to the ICC's work, and we were fortunate to have the services of a number of well-qualified historians, lawyers, and articling students over the years. One of the most important initial tasks of the researcher was reviewing the documentation provided by the parties and determining whether the record was complete. In many cases, he or she conducted additional research, which was added to that of the parties to create as complete a historical record of the claim as possible. This was preserved on a CD-ROM as a central element of the often substantial documentation that the panel reviewed. The opening task of the associate was to secure statements from the Crown and the claimant, outlining the key issues in the inquiry. The associate and commission counsel reviewed these, confirmed with the parties, and presented them to the panel. The issues were crucial to the inquiry, as they guided the process and structured its arguments and outcome.

The first stage of the inquiry consisted of a planning conference, which was overseen by the Liaison director and the associate and researcher. Commissioners were not involved in the conferences, which were "convened by Commission staff as soon as possible after an inquiry begins. Representatives of the parties, who usually include legal counsel, meet informally with representatives of the Commission to review and discuss the claim, identify the issues it raises, and plan the inquiry on a cooperative basis."[24] An important step in the process, conferences usually transpired about twelve weeks after the request for an inquiry was accepted. They brought the parties together, often for the first time in the history of the claim, to introduce themselves and to secure their commitment to the ICC process and its underlying principles. Conferences also handled a number of practical issues, including document collection, discussion of the issues, if needed, and establishing a rough schedule for the inquiry. As a general rule, they were held in a neutral location near the claimant community. The preference was for a single meeting, and in the early days most inquiries proceeded in this manner. However, a general recognition by ICC staff that the planning conference was sometimes an ongoing process could generate additional meetings. After 1999–2000, the frequency of multiple conferences seemed to increase, sometimes to as many as eight, nine, or ten per inquiry. By the time I joined the ICC in 2002, concern was growing about the resulting delays, and a brief experiment was launched to arrest this trend. The conferences would be run by the panel in hopes that this would impart some discipline and reduce their number. This approach was tested in the Vancouver, Victoria and Eastern Railway right-of-way inquiry, I believe for the first and only time.

The experiment in commissioner-run conferences was short-lived. These meetings were often preoccupied with hashing out a statement of issues that both the claimant and the Crown could accept, and apparently it was felt that involving commissioners at that point could jeopardize their neutrality. By participating in such discussions, they could potentially become biased or at least appear to be biased, which could undermine the impartiality of the inquiry. Thus, responsibility for handling conferences was returned to the Liaison Unit and other staff.

The collection of documentation and research on the claim, which also included the community session, was central to inquiries. The community session was a unique aspect of the ICC process, one that earned considerable praise from bands and, in a number of cases, Crown representatives. Its purpose was to bring the panel and the parties together in the claimant community to hear oral testimony from band members about the claim and the events behind it. As noted earlier, this event was organized in large measure by the Liaison Unit, which managed logistics and protocol. With the help of commission counsel and/or the associate, the unit also secured an agenda for the session. This was achieved largely through the collection of "will says" – summaries of the testimony that would be given during the session. Once everything was in place, the panel travelled to the community and sat for as many days as was necessary to hear from the witnesses. These sessions were important. They brought the Crown and the panel into the First Nation, where we experienced first-hand the conditions, culture, and impact of the claim for community members. In general, we were received graciously and with respect, and we learned a great deal through the sessions.

At the same time, we also visited the site that was the focus of the claim; such visits were often pivotal in our understanding of the significance of the land to the community and thus provided important contextual information. They also revealed additional details about the claim, the Crown, and the band. In the case of the Red Earth and Shoal Lake Cree Nations inquiry (discussed below), they exposed the sometimes significant gaps between the Crown and the claimant in understanding the importance of land and history.

Following the completion of the session and the finalization of the history of the claim, the evidentiary record would be closed, and the parties would move towards making their oral and written submissions. If the Crown or a claimant wished to involve an expert witness, the ICC had a process in place. The party applied to the panel for permission to submit its expert report. If this was granted, the report was distributed to the panel and the opposing party, and everyone had a chance to examine both the report and its author in an expert session. If the opposing party wished to submit its own expert report in reply, it had thirty days following receipt of the original report to apply for permission, after which a second expert session would ensue. In some instances, the panel simply accepted the report(s) and dispensed with the session, in which case either party could request an opportunity to question the expert and the report.

Whether or not expert reports and testimony were involved, the gathering of all evidence in a draft final history of the claim signalled that the inquiry was moving to closure of the evidentiary record. Once the Research manager had approved the draft, which included all the evidence, additional research completed by the ICC researchers, and the results of the community session, the formal record of the inquiry would be closed, and the oral session would begin.

This was typically held in the urban centre closest to the First Nation, and it enabled the Crown and the claimant to present their legal arguments to the panel. By the time of the "orals," the parties had exchanged arguments and rebuttals with the panel and each other. This stage in the process was initiated by the presentation of the claimant's written submissions to the panel and the Crown within six to eight weeks after closure of the evidentiary record. The Crown then had six to eight weeks to provide responding submissions, which were followed in another two weeks by the claimant's reply. This schedule was firm but not inflexible, and parties could apply to the panel for extra time. As a general rule, we accommodated these requests, but only if they did not create undue delay or unfairness to the opposing party. Whenever a party sought special considerations or accommodations, the panel had to ensure that granting these would not introduce bias or unfairness, which would undermine the inquiry and endanger the neutrality and credibility of its final report.

The orals concluded, the panel embarked on deliberations, which were based on the entire record of the inquiry. This stage could take a fair bit of time, and the panel members met on a number of occasions to share their views with each other, the associate and possibly commission counsel, and the researcher. Not all meetings included the lawyers or the researcher, however, as panel members needed to reach their own conclusions about the evidence and arguments. Most commissioners had some legal education and/or direct knowledge of treaties and First Nations realities and issues, and were more than capable of forming their own opinions about the validity of a claim. Debates often arose among them, and disputes sometimes occurred, which was to be expected. Both could be appropriate and helpful if they are managed well and respectfully. Debates and tensions between legal counsel and the commissioners proved more problematic. As mentioned above, the ICC could assess claims on the grounds of justice, fairness, and *what was right,* not solely in terms of their legal validity. It was often possible for commissioners and counsel to be both legally correct and yet in disagreement about the proper outcome of an inquiry. In such cases, the appropriate course was to hear each other out and choose the wiser alternative, but I will not prevaricate – in my view, commissioners were appointed to the ICC not because they knew the law, but because they brought experiences, knowledge, and perspectives that could provide a broader context and justice to the law. In many instances, this experience and knowledge meant that their view of claims differed from those of counsel, and in such situations the proper role of counsel was to defer to those views. In most inquiries of which I have direct knowledge, panel and counsel were in accord, but this was not always the case, and the outcome was not good.

Once the inquiry concluded, the last step was to compile the final report. It is my understanding that, in the early years of the commission, this task was handled by the lawyer who was assigned to the inquiry. The panel then reviewed the draft, often making extensive comments requiring repeated revisions, until the report accurately represented its views. By the time I was appointed, however, this practice was discouraged, and the commissioners themselves did most of the writing. I wrote part or all of some reports, including the supplementary mandate statement in the Red Earth and Shoal Lake inquiry, which will be discussed in later chapters.

When the inquiry report reached its final form, it was circulated to the parties, including the chief of the claimant First Nation, the minister of Indian Affairs, and the minister of Justice, through the Privy Council Office. Because the ICC was a standing royal commission, it was directed to report its inquiry results to Parliament through the Privy Council Office.[25] This was appropriate, given its role as a neutral body operating at arm's length from government – and especially from Indian Affairs. There would be times during its lifespan when that distance felt more illusory than real, but we will return to that sticky issue later.

4

Challenges to the Process
Applications for
Inquiries and Constructive Rejections

There is an old adage in politics to the effect that, when a government has no idea of how to tackle a problem, it establishes a royal commission, which is then tasked with working hard to achieve nothing. Because most commissions are limited to reporting and/or making recommendations, the government determines how much real change they can accomplish. If government wishes merely to look as if it's taking action, it can set up a commission, hand it a mandate and the necessary funding, and then simply ignore its recommendations. The end result is the illusion of supporting change without ever having to effect it.

In the case of the Indian Claims Commission (ICC), our successes and failures were probably more balanced than the popular wisdom around commissions would suggest. Established as an interim measure to inject greater justice and fairness into the specific claims process, the ICC persisted for almost eighteen years.[1] During this time, it completed 88 inquiries with reports – not a bad record, given that most commissions focus on a single inquiry and produce just one, albeit often lengthy, report.[2] We actually accepted 129 claims for inquiries out of 143 requests; 14 requests were denied. Of the 129 accepted requests, a total of 41 inquiries were ended prior to completion: 6 ended at the request of the First Nation, 11 were closed due to a lack of activity on the file, and a further 24 were closed by the ending of the commission.[3]

More telling of our legacy and the government's commitment to real change are the outcomes of the inquiries that were completed and reported with recommendations to the Crown. Of the 88 inquiry reports completed, the ICC found an outstanding lawful obligation in 41 claims and recommended acceptance of those claims for negotiation; in 18, the ICC found no lawful obligation and made no recommendation for acceptance of the claim.[4] A further 19 claims were accepted by Canada without a full inquiry, and another 10 met with unspecified outcomes.[5] The government accepted our recommendations in 19 inquiries and rejected them in another 19, and there was no known response to 24 of our reports as of the closure of the commission in 2009.[6] To be fair, a number of those 24 reports were produced in December of 2008, and the commission closed on March 31, 2009. Unless Indian Affairs (DIAND) and the minister were prepared to work at an uncharacteristically speedy pace to review and decide upon the recommendations in those reports, there would have been no commission to inform of their decision.

Deciding whether to accept a request and conduct an inquiry was a central task of our regular commissioner meetings. As a general rule, applications for inquiries were quite straightforward, and choosing whether to accept them proceeded similarly. Commissioners sometimes differed on this front, and debates occasionally arose between them and legal counsel, but for the most part, if a claim had been formally rejected and there appeared to be prima facie grounds for conducting an inquiry, we were prepared to accept the application. However, debate could edge into disagreement when the claim had not been formally denied, but the Specific Claims Branch (SCB) had dragged its feet for so long that the delay amounted to a "constructive rejection." We considered many issues in deciding whether to declare a claim constructively rejected, but delay was a primary, though not sufficient, factor in virtually all of these requests.

How Long Can Business Be Outstanding?
Delay in the Claims Process

Delay was, and remains, a crucial issue in the SCB approach to claims review. During my tenure as a commissioner, bands often mentioned the deep problems with delay, and there is no doubt that their complaints were justified. In 2007, acting in his capacity as Indian Affairs minister, former ICC commissioner Jim Prentice released "Justice at Last," Canada's rebooted specific claims policy, and acknowledged that "there are currently nearly 800 outstanding claims in Canada, with roughly 630 of these stuck in bottlenecks at the front end of the system. Since 1973, about 282 specific claims have been resolved through negotiated settlements."[7]

The bottleneck exists almost entirely at the entry point of the claims process and in claims assessment. Assessment entails three steps, including an initial review by Canada of the First Nation's research to ensure that it meets the "minimum standard for claims submissions." To satisfy this standard, the claim document must include a list of allegations and a clear statement of the legal arguments and facts supporting them, as well as the compensation requested. It must be backed up by a comprehensive list of all authorities and citations, which must be absolutely correct in every way. The historical report of the claim compiled by the band and all supporting documents must also be attached, and there is a "minimum standard for the form and manner" of the submission. For example, all documents must be "legible and complete" – often a problematic requirement for very old material, including correspondence, and the general state of most records relating to Indian affairs. Interestingly, and as will be discussed below, the failure to meet these standards appears to have enabled the SCB to return many claims after 2007, thus removing them from the queue and creating the appearance of a reduction in the backlog.[8]

If a submission meets the minimum standards, the SCB reviews the First Nation's historical research. If this is deemed insufficient, the band will be asked to make revisions and corrections, and to resubmit its claim. Once the history is accepted, the submission is sent to the Department of Justice, which conducts a legal review of the claim. Justice lawyers assess whether it demonstrates an outstanding lawful obligation and will sign off on the department's legal opinion. The paperwork is then returned to the SCB, which decides whether to reject or accept the claim. It communicates this decision to the claimant, at which point the assessment phase draws to a close. Until 2007, rejected claims could be taken to the ICC for review.[9] Accepted claims embark on the long road of negotiation to settlement.

Regularly confronted with the reality that nearly 70 percent of the claims backlog resided in the initial assessment phase, DIAND's usual practice was to throw Justice under the bus by declaring that too few lawyers were being assigned to claims review.[10] There was probably some truth in this, but it cannot excuse the roughly thirteen years that the SCB took to process an average submission.[11] Justice may have had its problems, but blaming its lawyers for the entirety of the backlog simply absolved DIAND of responsibility for its glacial rate of processing. And in fairness to both DIAND and Justice, delays were sometimes caused by the claimants themselves – a change in chief and council or in their legal counsel could often hold up the timetable, as could the death of an elder. Community visits or oral arguments were often postponed in respect for the band's need to grieve and commemorate the life of the elder.

Although lawyers and communities could affect the speed of the process, DIAND's culpability in the historic mismanagement of claims was reinforced by its post-2007 approach. We will talk about this in greater depth near the end of the book, but for now it will suffice to say that the recent behaviour of DIAND and the SCB implicates them directly in the failure to resolve claims in a timely fashion. For example, in 2013, the SCB boasted that the backlog had been "eliminated." The 541 submissions that had been at the assessment stage in October 2008 had cleared that hurdle three years later, and the claimants had been informed of the result. That the SCB had achieved such a staggering *volte-face* on its ponderous processes was greeted with slack-jawed astonishment by most observers.

A deeper look at the backlog reveals that its elimination was little more than smoke and mirrors. According to the largely glowing summative evaluation of the *Specific Claims Action Plan* completed in 2013 by DIAND's own Evaluation, Performance Measurement and Review Branch, from 1973 to the end of November 2013, DIAND had concluded 399 claims "with finality" and another 704 "without finality." The former figure refers to the 36 percent of specific claims that were "settled through negotiation or resolved through an administrative remedy." Thirty-three of these claims were resolved through administrative remedy, though what this might entail is never defined. *Outstanding Business* is only slightly more forthcoming, offering an example of such as "return of surrendered but unsold land."[12] The lack of clarity is troubling, and it is impossible to know what happened to the thirty-three administratively resolved claims.

This leaves the 704 claims classified as "concluded without finality," an odd choice of wording – aren't conclusions generally considered to be final? Of these, 396 were deemed to have no outstanding lawful obligation, and the remaining 308 were resolved through "file closure." In a slight improvement on the opaque "administrative remedy," this term has received more elaboration from the department: "the file closure category includes claims that would not fall within the scope of the Specific Claims Policy, a First Nation that would decide to withdraw its claims or to reject an offer made by Canada."[13] To all appearances, these are claims that are not "concluded with finality" because they could potentially return to the SCB queue if the claimants revise and resubmit them. Through file closure, at least some of these claims may simply be shifted to the Specific Claims Tribunal. As a result, such claims are characterized neither by finality nor any real conclusion, as they have either been diverted to the tribunal or "returned to the pre-submission stage in the form of new claims entering the process." Indirectly confirming this outcome, the department urged the SCB to develop a "risk management strategy to manage the large number of claims that are considered 'concluded' by AANDC but which have the potential to be submitted to the Tribunal or submitted as a new claim to the specific claims process."[14] In effect, those 704 claims remain live, as does the backlog, much of which has now been left on the tribunal's doorstep.

According to the Union of BC Indian Chiefs, the reduction of the backlog is largely due to two practices: file closure and claims that are "resolved through administrative remedy." It suggests that, "in actuality, 75% of the backlog remains." As it explains,

> The Assembly of First Nations examined AANDC's publicly available data on concluded claims prior to and after the implementation of Justice at Last. Their review found that the number of concluded claims did not differ significantly between the two periods (543 prior to October 2008 and 572 after October 2008).
>
> However, prior to Justice at Last, 300 claims (55%) were settled through negotiations, compared with only 87 (15%) under Justice at Last; 243 claims (44%) were either rejected or had their files closed prior to Justice at Last, while 485 (85%) of claims were rejected or had their files closed under the Justice at Last policy. Canada has dealt with the backlog of claims by failing to resolve the majority of them.[15]

If this assessment is accurate, it does not speak well of DIAND's approach to claims management or evaluation. Nor does it show much honour in the Crown's oversight of claims or respect for its fiduciary obligations.

When Is a Rejection Not a Rejection?
Constructive Rejections in the ICC Process

As early as 1996, the ICC was confronted head-on by the serious and endemic problem of delay at the SCB. This came in the form of a request from the Mikisew Cree for an inquiry into their claim. They were seeking compensation for economic benefits that should have flowed from their participation in Treaty 8. When they signed the treaty in 1899, they lived primarily by hunting and trapping, and they agreed with the Crown's representatives that the establishment of a reserve could wait until they adopted a sedentary lifestyle and became farmers.[16] In 1922, the band asked that reserve lands be set aside, but there is no indication that the Crown acted until 1986 – more than sixty years after the Cree requested a reserve. In that year, the Cree and Canada reached an agreement on a reserve, associated hunting and harvesting rights, and a cash compensation of $24 million. Although this resolved the issue of reserve lands, it did not release the Crown from its obligations relating to agricultural benefits, known as the "cows and ploughs" clause, which were clearly connected to the 1899 promise of reserve creation.

Because the agreement did not address the cows and ploughs promises of Treaty 8, the Mikisew Cree submitted a claim to the Specific Claims West Branch in 1993,[17] seeking compensation for their loss of use and benefits of Treaty 8's economic provisions. After assessing their submission, the branch informed the Mikisew that it would accept and negotiate their claim, an offer that the Cree accepted. Yet during the next three years, the claim seemed stalled in departmental inertia. The Mikisew repeatedly contacted DIAND to initiate negotiations but were continually rebuffed. Their patience wore out in 1996, when DIAND told them that it had decided to review "the whole issue of entitlement to the economic benefits of Treaty No. 8 and other similar treaties" and was thus placing their claim in abeyance.[18] A resolution of the matter was promised in the following three months, but it does not appear that this ever happened.

Citing delay and lapsed undertakings by the Crown, the Mikisew asked the ICC to conduct an inquiry on the grounds that Canada's management of their claim amounted to a constructive rejection. Their request found a receptive audience in the commission, which as noted above had long been deeply concerned about the Crown's ambivalence, delay, and chronic under-resourcing of claims. Our first constructive rejection inquiry, Mikisew got under way in June of 1996 but was suspended in December when Canada offered to negotiate the claim with the Cree.[19]

Between 1996 and 2009, the commission received twenty-one requests for inquiries into constructively rejected claims.[20] In considering them, we settled on three criteria to determine whether their treatment amounted to a de facto rejection on the part of the Crown. These criteria were delays in processing that lacked any reasonable explanation; lapsed undertakings by Canada; and/or a lack of proportionality between the complexity of the claim and the apparent time taken to review it. As noted above, Mikisew was accepted on the basis of the first two criteria. Eventually, the ICC would conduct ten more, virtually all of which were characterized by delay and at least one, if not both, of the remaining criteria.

Canada reacted swiftly to this development. Arguing that the ICC's jurisdiction was limited only to claims that had been formally rejected by the minister, the government refused to participate in constructive rejection inquiries and withheld the funding that enabled First Nations to do so. In some cases, such as the Treaty 8 Tribal Association's request for a constructive rejection inquiry in August 1998, the denial of funding effectively placed the inquiry in abeyance. In others, such as the Red Earth and Shoal Lake inquiry (discussed below), Canada's refusal to participate prompted the ICC to threaten the use of its subpoena powers to obtain documents from DIAND. Despite Canada's obstinacy, we proceeded with inquiries in all possible circumstances. Our mandate supported this work, as did the Order in Council that had created the commission: it asserted that the ICC's overarching purpose was to "review the application by the Government of Canada of the specific claims policy to individual claims" and to "interpret this mandate as it considers best to achieve that end."[21] In our opinion, it was incumbent upon us to be vigilant in ensuring that the goal of the claims policy – fair and expeditious resolution – was pursued in a manner that upheld the honour of the Crown.[22] Unreasonable and unexplained delays, lapsed undertakings, and the absence of proportionality tarnished the honour of the Crown and directly contradicted the goals of the government's specific claims policy. As a result, if a First Nation asked us to inquire into a claim in which DIAND mismanagement was tantamount to a rejection, our mandate permitted us to proceed.

Canada commonly disagreed with our stance, and its grounds, though weak, were usually threefold. In its view, a claim could not be constructively rejected. ICC inquiries could be launched solely on the basis of a formal rejection – the challenge, of course, was how to define "formal rejection." At the time, there was no jurisprudence and no federal government policy statement that might have guided the ICC in this regard. Its own mandate was silent on the question. And though Canada consistently clung to formal rejection as the sole prerequisite for an ICC inquiry, it generated no authoritative statement regarding exactly what qualified as a formal rejection. It raised this objection in Mikisew and in almost every constructive rejection inquiry thereafter. The ICC dealt with the question at length in the Alexis First Nation inquiry, which it reported in March 2003.[23]

In this claim, the Alexis First Nation sought compensation for the Crown's alleged violations of its fiduciary duties. Specifically, DIAND had granted three rights-of-way to Calgary Power to run electricity lines across the Alexis Indian Reserve No. 133 in 1959, 1967, and 1969. At the time, the Alexis community was vulnerable and dependent on the Crown to guard its interests; few English-speakers lived on the reserve, the level of education was low, and high rates of unemployment made the band susceptible to promises of jobs.[24] Although the band consented to the first two rights-of-way, the third and largest one resulted from its own direct negotiations with Calgary Power, with limited to no knowledge or oversight by DIAND. When the department learned of the deal, it evidently did not review it, and as a result it failed in a number of its fiduciary obligations to the Alexis First Nation.[25]

The 1969 expropriation formed the bulk of the claim that the band submitted to the SCB on October 4, 1995. Because the claim was likely to amount to less than $500,000, the band asked that it be fast-tracked. The assessment process was duly completed in August 1996, when Justice confirmed that DIAND had breached its "lawful and fiduciary obligations to the First Nation." It recommended acceptance of both the claim and the band's request for fast tracking.[26] This was communicated to the band, which understandably expected a swift and positive conclusion to materialize.

Although the assessment had proceeded quickly and efficiently, things fell apart after Justice returned the claim to the SCB. A year went by, and the band heard nothing. Then it received a letter from DIAND, informing it that there would be a "delay of an undetermined amount of time" in processing the claim. In 1998, concerned about protecting its legal position, the band proceeded with an action against DIAND in Federal Court, but it told the department that it would suspend this if the claim were validated and accepted for negotiation. Despite this assurance, DIAND's response to the litigation was to stop any further review of the claim while the litigation was under way, effectively hamstringing the entire process. Recognizing the success of its efforts to encourage the SCB to complete its review, the band withdrew its litigation in 1999, assuming this would free up DIAND to finish the review. This proved no more effective than initiating litigation, and the SCB continued to drag its feet.

In October 1999, after numerous fruitless inquiries by the First Nation to DIAND regarding progress on its claim, and a number of requests to the ICC to deem the claim constructively rejected, the commission agreed to conduct an inquiry. In January of 2000, Canada responded to this by asserting that "the claim has not yet been rejected by the Specific Claims process, and therefore, the Indian Claims Commission is not in a position to review the file."[27] A month later, the Department of Justice informed the ICC of its intention to levy a mandate challenge against the commission, attacking its jurisdiction to accept claims that had not yet been formally rejected. In our response to that challenge, we considered the question of what constituted a formal rejection.[28]

By this time, Canada had already raised the formal rejection issue in four inquiries, involving the Athabaska Denesuline, the Lac La Ronge Band, the Mikisew Cree, and the Sandy Bay First Nation.[29] In all four, the bands had argued that the ICC had a right to review claims in which Canada's conduct effectively amounted to a rejection. The ICC concurred. Taken together, these cases illustrate our position that as neither the government nor the courts had provided guidance regarding what constituted the rejection of a claim, it need not be "confined to an express communication, either written or verbal, but could be the result of certain action, inaction or other conduct." Furthermore, the restriction of the ICC mandate to "a narrow and literal reading of the Specific Claims Policy would prevent First Nations in certain circumstances from having their claims dealt with fairly and efficiently."[30] We stressed that the

Commissioners have confirmed their interpretation of their mandate as being remedial in nature. In our view, it is incumbent upon all participants in the specific claims process to ensure that Canada's final resolution is arrived at without subjecting the First Nation to a myriad of delays. We remain cognizant of the fact that this process was designed to speed up the resolution of specific claims and to provide parties with an alternative to expensive and protracted litigation. As such, the process is required to meet the test of expediency and cost savings. It could not have been the intent of Parliament when it designed the mandate of the Commission to prevent a First Nation from utilizing the ICC in circumstances where Canada has not made a decision on acceptance or rejection within a reasonable time. The ability to intervene in these circumstances is wholly consistent with the remedial nature of the Commission's mandate.[31]

Despite a clear position on the part of the ICC that claims could be rejected by the action or inaction of the Crown, Canada continued to maintain that it had no jurisdiction over constructively rejected claims.

The Crown raised two other objections in attempting to limit the ICC's jurisdiction: By accepting claims that had not yet been formally rejected, the ICC was creating and condoning queue jumping. Furthermore, it was usurping Canada's powers of review and determination of claims.[32] The question of queue jumping initially gave us pause. According to the SCB, its approach to claims had always been "first in, first reviewed." That is, the submission date of a claim determined the order in which it was processed. If this was indeed the case, delays could be as much a consequence of the length of the queue as of SCB mismanagement. If, in fact, an orderly queue system were in place, who were we to challenge it? It was one thing to criticize the SCB for the slow processing of claims that had reached the front of the queue, but where was the fault, if any, in the queue itself?

There was (and is) no doubt that the delays and, in some cases, mismanagement of the claims policy and process were unacceptable. Delay created genuine unfairness; however, as a neutral body, the ICC had to be careful not to counter one unfairness by introducing another. This may have achieved some balance, but balancing wrongs does not necessarily lead to a rightful outcome. We were thus quite cautious about accepting requests for constructive rejections, especially those based solely on delay. Our hesitation was not due to ambivalence about the obvious failings of DIAND in perpetuating delay or the need to send a strong message that this was unacceptable. It was grounded in the reality that delay affected *all claimants*. By the SCB's own admission, its average processing time for claims was a staggering thirteen years – a timeframe that was egregious by almost any standards.[33] And yet, if the delay affected all claimants equally, accepting a claim that had experienced less delay than average risked disrupting a perverse parity.

Our caution and our response were thus premised on an assumption that the queue was real and orderly, and that "some reasonably objective criteria" were "consistently applied to claims and ... thus define[d] a clear and relatively systematic queue."[34] However, as became apparent in connection with the Red Earth and Shoal Lake inquiry, the queue was more illusory than real. Testimony from DIAND officials confirmed that the queue was arbitrary and that the SCB "system" of first in, first reviewed was less systematic than may have been implied. A claim's location in the queue could have little connection to the timing of its submission; instead, a number of factors appeared to influence the queue, most of which resided in the SCB assessment process. These could include "the complexity of the claim, the state of the research file, the nature of the issues in the claim, and the amount of time the First Nation takes to review Canada's research report confirming the information submitted by the First Nation."[35] For its part, Canada conceded the influence of these factors and confirmed that time spent in the queue was highly variable and vulnerable to circumstance.[36] We thus concluded that

> it is difficult to understand Canada's concerns about a First Nation attempting to shift its unknown location in an unsystematic or unverified queue, when Canada itself is apparently unable either to elucidate that queue or monitor the progress of claims through it. In the absence of any evidence by Canada documenting the queue and indicating some means of tracking the various claimants' movements through it (thereby enabling some determination of whether, in fact, the queue has been jumped), arguments of queue-jumping ring decidedly hollow.[37]

We were equally unimpressed with Canada's assertion that, in accepting a constructively rejected claim, we were usurping its right of review and determination of claims.[38] First Nations that sought an inquiry almost invariably did so after their claim had become endlessly mired in the black hole of the assessment process. The Mikisew came to us after three years and many broken promises by Canada, the Red Earth and Shoal Lake Nations waited for eight years, and the Nekaneet and Peepeekisis waited nearly eleven and sixteen years, respectively.[39] Obviously, there were (and are) compelling problems with the assessment process.

Our consideration of whether to conduct an inquiry had nothing to do with the issue of outstanding lawful obligations on the part of the Crown. In fact, it had very little to do with the substance of the claim and a great deal to do with the substance of DIAND's claims process. In deciding whether to proceed, we applied our three criteria: Was there unreasonable, unexplained delay? Were there lapsed undertakings by the Crown? Was there a lack of correspondence between the complexity of the claim and the time taken to process it? At issue here, then, was not the claim itself, but rather Canada's treatment of the claim. If this created unfairness or undue delay in the application of the policy, we were likely to see a claim as constructively rejected. As we observed, this approach had "no impact on the power of the Minister to reach his or her own determination on the merits of the claim and on whether that claim is actually rejected. The latter remains a separate and distinct question that is outside the province of the Commission."[40]

Our approach to constructively rejected claims was rooted in our experience with Canada's policy and with its implications for the fair and expeditious resolution of claims. I and some of my ICC colleagues had no doubt that the fundamental conflict of interest characterizing the policy and its ambivalent application often resulted in blatant unfairness to claimants. Too often the centrality of the fiduciary and the honour of the Crown came a very distant second to priorities that were known only to Canada and that reflected a narrow set of interests. This disappointing reality was laid bare in the Red Earth and Shoal Lake inquiry.

Searching for Higher Ground: Red Earth and Shoal Lake

The Red Earth and Shoal Lake inquiry has remained front of mind for many reasons. Although there was no outstanding lawful obligation in connection with the claim, this was qualified by the presence of deeply compelling moral and ethical factors. We believed that these should induce the Crown to resolve the issues behind the claim. As noted above, this inquiry had the misfortune to conclude during the final moments of the ICC, thus enabling the Crown to simply ignore our report and recommendations. As will be seen, this outcome was probably evident as early as the community session and site visit of the inquiry, in which the behaviour of Canada's representatives suggested that the Crown had little interest in the claims of the Red Earth and Shoal Lake people.

The origins of the claim lie in the 1876 adhesion of Red Earth and Shoal Lake to Treaty 5 through their association with the Pas Band of Manitoba. Treaty 5 had been signed a year earlier by the Saulteaux and Swampy Cree of central Manitoba, but it was greatly expanded in 1876 and 1908 through adhesions that extended its reach as far north as what would become the Nunavut border and west to the Saskatchewan border and beyond. Its eastern edge reached to the shores of Hudson Bay and flowed over provincial boundaries into Ontario. It was through the treaty's penetration into Saskatchewan that the Red Earth and Shoal Lake people were captured within it, owing to their connection with the Pas Band of Manitoba.[41] Like Treaties 1 and 2, Treaty 5 provided for the creation of Indian reserves, but it also made specific reference to setting aside both farming lands and "other reserves." The Crown reportedly had some difficulty with the negotiations for the 1876 adhesions to Treaty 5 owing to the chiefs' awareness of the terms of Treaty 6, which had been signed only a couple of weeks before the commencement of the negotiation of the adhesions. Its terms were far more favourable than those presented to the Saulteaux and Swampy Crees. For example, it offered 640 acres of reserve land per family, whereas Treaty 5 offered only 160 acres per family. Canada argued that the discrepancy reflected the quality of the land being surrendered: the central Saskatchewan farmland given up through Treaty 6 was reportedly superior to that surrendered through Treaty 5, which was "useless to the Queen."[42] Concerned about increasing settler encroachment on their land and apparently eager to take up farming, the people accepted the terms of Treaty 5, but only if they were permitted to select their own reserve lands.

By all reports, the Pas Band was consulted on the location of its reserves, but this proved a less than easy task for the Red Earth and Shoal Lake

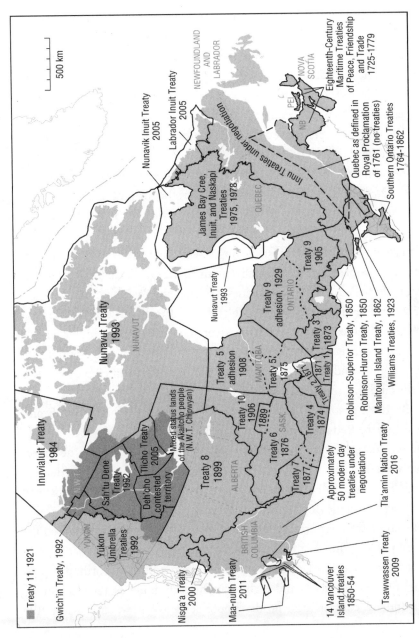

The numbered treaties

Treaty 11, 1921

Gwich'in Treaty, 1992

Inuvialuit Treaty 1984

Nunavut Treaty 1993

Nunavik Inuit Treaty 2005

Labrador Inuit Treaty 2005

Eighteenth-Century Maritime Treaties of Peace, Friendship and Trade 1725-1779

Quebec as defined in Royal Proclamation of 1761 (no treaties)

Southern Ontario Treaties 1764-1862

James Bay Cree, Inuit, and Naskapi Treaties 1975, 1978

Innu Treaties under negotiation

Nunavut Treaty 1993

Treaty 9 adhesion, 1929

Treaty 9 1905

Treaty 3 1873

Treaty 5 adhesion 1908

Treaty 5, 1875

Treaty 2, 1871

Treaty 1 1871

Treaty 10 1906

1889

Treaty 4 1874

Robinson-Superior Treaty, 1850

Robinson-Huron Treaty, 1850

Manitoulin Island Treaty, 1862

Williams Treaties, 1923

Treaty 6 1876

Treaty 8 1899

Deh'cho contested territory

Tlicho Treaty 2005

Mixed status lands of the Akaitcho people (N.W.T. Chipwyan)

Sah'tu Dene Treaty 1992

Yukon Umbrella Treaties 1992

Nisga'a Treaty 2000

Maa-nulth Treaty 2011

Treaty 7 1877

Approximately 50 modern day treaties under negotiation

Tla'amin Nation Treaty 2016

14 Vancouver Island treaties 1850-54

Tsawwassen Treaty 2009

500 km

NEWFOUNDLAND AND LABRADOR

NOVA SCOTIA

PEI

NB

QUEBEC

ONTARIO

NUNAVUT

MANITOBA

SASK.

ALBERTA

BRITISH COLUMBIA

YUKON

people. Very little land at The Pas was suitable for farming, and most, if not all, of the good arable acreage was already under cultivation. As a result, Red Earth and Shoal Lake chose lands that suited their subsistence habits, rather than strictly satisfying the needs of farming. Elders whose parents and grandparents were present at the negotiations informed us that their ancestors had selected reserve land close to hunting grounds. They were also suitable for fishing and trapping, and they included traditional meeting places where the people congregated throughout the year.

The reserves were surveyed in 1882 and were reported to include all the good land that could be found, but almost 3,300 acres apparently remained outstanding. Nothing near The Pas was suitable, so the surveyor suggested that the remainder be provided in the form of reserves for the Red Earth and Shoal Lake people, who were living at the Pas Mountain. The communities agreed, and in January 1884, they petitioned the Crown to make up the shortfall by surveying reserves at the Pas Mountain, also known as Oopasquaya Hill, which contained the only farmable land in the region. In the end, 1,500 acres were set aside at the Pas Mountain, another 1,500 were reserved northwest of the reserve already surveyed at The Pas, and 246.57 acres along the Carrot River were reserved as timber land.[43] Although concerns were expressed about the possibility of flooding in some regions and about the necessity for drainage in swampy pieces, most of the land was considered arable.

By 1885, despite an extremely harsh winter that brought significant hardship, the Red Earth community in particular appeared to be thriving and was described by the resident Indian agent as "probably the finest reserve in the agency."[44] Within five years, Red Earth alone was producing roughly a third of all the potatoes grown in the thousand-member agency and was also achieving significant success with cattle raising. The Shoal Lake crops were reportedly less good, but in 1893 Red Earth shared its excess potato crop, and the Shoal Lake people began to farm farther inland; soon they too realized greater success with agriculture. According to primary reports, "from the mid-eighties to the early-nineties, the Pas Mountain Indians continued to produce potatoes and barley, and raise cattle as well."[45]

Between 1892 and 1926, the Red Earth and Shoal Lake First Nations requested, and received, a number of alterations to their reserves. The first of these, occurring in 1892, concerned an exchange of the land set aside at Flute Creek for reserve lands along the Carrot River at Red Earth, where the people were actually residing, and a timber limit a few miles west of Red Earth along the river.[46] The government approved these changes, as well as a similar adjustment in the mid-1890s, when Shoal Lake's reserve was resurveyed with the goal of exchanging part of it for other land to the east, which was already under cultivation.

In 1900, the inspector of Indian agencies visited Red Earth and Shoal Lake, and though he acknowledged their great success with agriculture and husbandry, he expressed some apprehension about the "damp" and "spongy" nature of much of the Shoal Lake reserve.[47] The high water levels affected its hay fields, and in especially wet years ranchers could not harvest enough hay to support their livestock. As a result, in 1908, both Red Earth and Shoal Lake requested that additional land be attached to their reserves, which would improve the hay yield. Given their prosperity despite the difficulties presented by damp and flooding, and mindful of the meagre Treaty 5 entitlement of only 160 acres per family, the government quickly assented to these requests. The department agreed to set aside a half-section, or 320 acres, but later increased this to a full section and subsequently to 651 acres.[48] The reserves were surveyed to record the additions and the new boundaries. Red Earth Indian Reserve No. 29 was documented as consisting of 3,595.95 acres, reflecting an increase of 884.31 acres, which was more than the band had requested. Shoal Lake was also adjusted, and the final land tally reflected the community's population of eighty-nine souls, which entitled them to 2,848 acres under Treaty 5, and then some. In 1913, the Shoal Lake Indian Reserve No. 28A was approved at a total acreage of 2,888 acres.[49]

In 1914, Red Earth asked for 320 more acres of hay land, and Shoal Lake requested an addition to protect a burial ground. These were denied, as was a 1921 request by Red Earth for 640 acres of hay land to address its ongoing struggle to produce sufficient fodder. Five years later, in 1926, Shoal Lake requested a surrender of 640 acres of reserve land containing a small lake and swamp, in exchange for an equal amount of land northeast of the reserve, which consisted largely of timber and hay land. This request was granted, and the surrender for exchange was approved and taken in 1927. This was reportedly the last alteration to the Red Earth and Shoal

Lake reserves. Although both communities petitioned for expansions of their land in 1946 – Red Earth requesting an addition of three entire townships and Shoal Lake seeking an additional one and a half townships – there is no record that the government responded.[50]

In May of 1996, Red Earth and Shoal Lake submitted a joint claim to Indian Affairs, alleging that Canada had breached the terms of Treaty 5 and the 1876 adhesion by not providing farmlands to them. Their claim seems to have sat untended at the SCB for roughly eight years, at which point they asked the ICC to inquire into it. We agreed in 2004 and held a planning conference in February 2005. Not long afterward, Canada formally brought a motion to challenge our jurisdiction. This was its standard reaction to our constructive rejection inquiries, and we were unsurprised by it. However, the situation became much more interesting when the Treaty 8 First Nations of British Columbia, who had a constructive rejection inquiry of their own, applied for intervenor status in our consideration of Canada's motion. I will examine the Treaty 8 motion first and will then resume our discussion of Canada's challenge to our mandate.

The Treaty 8 First Nations had come to the ICC in August of 2003, seeking an inquiry into their claim, which had been with the SCB for a decade. We agreed to conduct an inquiry, and DIAND had refused to participate or to provide funding to the claimants. As a result, the Treaty 8 inquiry had been delayed for roughly a year. Upon being informed by ICC legal counsel of Canada's motion in the Red Earth and Shoal Lake inquiry, the Treaty 8 First Nations requested involvement in the hearing on the grounds that they had a direct interest in the mandate challenge. If Canada triumphed, it would undoubtedly use this result as ammunition against the Treaty 8 inquiry. The claimants also argued that they could bring a timely and unique perspective to the hearing:

> Treaty 8 points to the fact that currently, they have approximately 15 claims that are in the specific claims process. These claims have not been accepted or rejected for negotiation by Canada. Treaty 8 further asserts that their particular experience with the specific claims process is indicative of the more general experience of British Columbia First Nations that have filed specific claims. Treaty 8 points to the fact that 58% of the claims awaiting a legal opinion by Canada originate in British Columbia.

The Red Earth and Shoal Lake Cree Nation, in comparison, have no claims in the process other then [sic] that which is the subject of Canada's mandate challenge. According to Treaty 8, therefore, Red Earth and Shoal Lake are not in a position to speak to the detrimental effect a successful mandate challenge would have on the claims process in general.[51]

In the end, we denied Treaty 8's application for intervenor status. In our view, the issue of ICC jurisdiction was a legal question, one that would be adequately analyzed and argued by the parties involved. Given this, there was little that Treaty 8 could bring to assist in its resolution. And if Canada's motion did not succeed (which was just as likely as the alternative), Treaty 8 could use this fact as it saw fit. Furthermore, as the ICC would assess Canada's motions individually and on their own merits, it did not necessarily follow that a success for the Crown in the Red Earth and Shoal Lake mandate challenge would affect similar motions.[52]

Canada's motion featured the usual objections to our constructive rejection policy: we were exceeding our mandate and were usurping ministerial authority. Asserting that rejection of a claim was limited to a "ministerial letter following a determination of the claim" and that the ICC had no authority to "inquire into and report on delay in the specific claims process," Canada took its traditional approach one step farther, arguing that "the Commission should not take questions of reasonableness or justice into consideration in interpreting its mandate."[53] This ludicrous statement flew in the face of our Order in Council and negated the remedial nature of our work. It also spoke volumes about Canada's view of its specific claims policy, of treaties, of the fiduciary, and of the honour of the Crown. It overlooked the fact that had the Crown behaved reasonably and fairly towards Indigenous people, constructive rejections would never have arisen, and the ICC would never have developed its policy. We stressed,

> as is clear from the principles expressed by the Minister in *Outstanding Business,* it is precisely justice that the specific claims policy of 1982 promised to provide to First Nations. If there is, in fact, patent unreasonableness in the administration of a specific claims review process that allows relatively simple claims to wait 15 years without any decision, that is an absence of justice that must be remedied. The Commission was given

the responsibility to review the specific claims process and that responsibility will be discharged mindful of the imperatives of "mutual respect
and cooperation" which were intended to characterize the resolution of
specific claims "without further delay."[54]

We had additional, equally important reasons for pressing our jurisdiction. First Nations enter the claims process in good faith, trusting in
Canada's commitment to its stated goals of resolving claims expeditiously
and fairly. However, when submissions remain unanswered for decades or
more, and it becomes obvious that the process is neither expeditious nor
fair, claimants have precious few avenues for redress. Most are reluctant
to embark on litigation; should they choose this route, DIAND immediately
ceases work on their claim, declaring that it does not have the resources
to both review a claim and argue it in court.[55] Having joined the specific
claims queue, many bands are reluctant to exchange it for yet another queue,
which promises to be just as long. This is especially true for bands that
have been in the queue for many years – the longer they wait, the closer
they feel to some sort of resolution. Although this hope may be as illusory
as the queue itself, it cannot be doubted that the longer a claimant is in the
queue, the harder it becomes to abandon it.

It is also the case that, during the ICC's tenure, there was absolutely no
legal or bureaucratic pressure on DIAND to reach a determination on a
claim in a timely manner. Nor was there any legal remedy through which
First Nations could compel the timely review of their claims.[56] As a result,
they were left with limited options – they could simply give up and accept
that their claim would never be resolved, they could head to court, or they
could ask the ICC for a constructive rejection inquiry.

In denying Canada's motion, we weighed DIAND's treatment of the
Red Earth and Shoal Lake claim against the three pillars of our constructive
rejection policy: delay, lapsed undertakings, and lack of proportionality.
Delay was obvious: the claim had sat in the queue for over a decade. During
that time, the SCB took nearly four years to conduct a preliminary assessment and produce an acceptable historical report, and Justice had failed
to generate a legal opinion. And over much of that time, the SCB made
no effort to inform the claimants of the progress on their claim or the

reasons for delay.[57] In and of itself, the delay was unacceptable, but it also seriously undermined the ability of the claimants to mount a complete and cogent case:

> While they wait for the Crown, the First Nations have watched the evidentiary record of their claim be diminished and disadvantaged by the deaths of six elders whose historical evidence is no longer available to assist in establishing the validity of the claim. The First Nations adduced evidence that the Red Earth First Nation has witnessed the passing of Elders Abel Head, John McKay, and Ralph Head, while the Shoal Lake First Nation has lost Elders Jeremiah Whitecap, Joe Bear, and Horace Kitchener. As we stressed in the elucidation of the Commission's mandate earlier in this ruling, as societies whose historical records were, until relatively recently, retained orally in the memories of elders and others who were present at treaty signing or told of the event by their ancestors, such oral evidence is often a First Nation's primary, if not sole, source of evidence. Canada's delay in addressing this claim has prejudiced the Red Earth and Shoal Lake Cree Nations' ability to effectively present their claim and, in the words of the First Nations' counsel, has led to feelings of "frustration, anger, disappointment, depression, loss of hope, and loss of confidence" on the part of the First Nations in the commitment of Canada to the fair and expeditious resolution of specific claims.[58]

The matter of lapsed undertakings also favoured the First Nations. The Crown had made at least three statements that could "be reasonably seen as creating an expectation on the part of the First Nations that review of their claim would be expedited when, in fact, there is no evidence to indicate that this undertaking initiated any shift in the approach of the Specific Claims Branch towards the claim."[59] In addition, though Canada persisted in promising that the claim would "soon" be decided, it seemed unable to offer a firm date or even a ballpark estimate regarding when this might occur.

The delays and lapsed undertakings were exacerbated by the disproportionality between the complexity of the case and the time it spent under review. As will be recalled, the claim was relatively modest, focusing on both the quantity and quality of lands that Red Earth and Shoal Lake had received under Treaty 5. Although Canada had extensive experience with land entitlement under the numbered treaties, it stated that

> the quality of farming land is a novel treaty interpretation issue which may have broad legal significance for other Treaty 5 First Nations. As such, Canada alleges that this aspect of the claim has contributed significantly to the delay in processing the claim. Canada argues that, while the processing of historical claims is by its very nature complex and time consuming, responding to novel treaty interpretations in a Specific Claims Branch characterized by inadequate and highly strained human and financial resources requires considerably more time and effort.[60]

Unsurprisingly, Canada could not show that the claim's complexity had affected the review period, and we were unable to accept its argument. Nor could we permit the egregious and chronic under-resourcing of the claims process to become an excuse for delay or a means for Canada to "avoid its obligations to manage claims in a fair and expeditious fashion."[61] We certainly understood that resource constraints posed a challenge for the process and the players, but we could not allow Canada to shift responsibility for delays or their consequences onto the First Nations:

> The Commission has long held the view that it is the responsibility of the parties to manage their resource constraints as effectively as possible and in a manner that will not have any impact on the fairness of the claims review process. If, in fact, resource constraints are responsible for some portion of the considerable delay characterizing Canada's Specific Claims process in the present case, this fact would go to the question of Canada's ability to effectively manage those resources to ensure that they impair the integrity of the claims process as little as possible.[62]

Thus, we denied Canada's motion and proceeded with the inquiry. As a result, Canada sought a judicial review of our decision in the Federal Court. In an application filed on October 25, 2006, Canada requested that the court quash our finding, declare that we had erred in our interpretation of our Order in Council, and halt the inquiry.[63] A number of us at the commission, including myself, welcomed the opportunity to test our constructive rejection policy in court. We were confident in our understanding of the Order in Council and our power to declare claims constructively rejected. There were also several claimant First Nations who would have been interested in the court's determination of these matters. In the end, however, we were disappointed. Canada withdrew its application when, in December of 2006, the minister formally rejected the Red Earth and Shoal Lake claim.[64]

Although this development removed the possibility of ending the disagreement regarding our mandate, it certainly eased the conduct of the inquiry. Canada now became involved in our process and agreed to fund the First Nations to participate. For our part, we had been so sure of our findings regarding the claim that we had held a planning conference in Regina in February 2005, where together with the claimants we had set a schedule for the inquiry. Now in possession of both parties' documentation, we proceeded to the community session, which was held at Shoal Lake on October 16 and 17, 2007.

As discussed in Chapter 3, the purpose of this session is to obtain the testimony of elders and other community members about the substance and impact of the events captured in the claim. Sessions were significant in many respects and were a unique and important part of the ICC process: they brought together Canada and the claimants in the latter's community, often for the very first time. We believed strongly in the power of dialogue, and the exchange of ideas that occurred in the session enabled both parties to gain a greater understanding of the claim and its implications for the stakeholders. Communities could present their perspectives, and Canada was often confronted with the consequences of its choices for them. For government representatives who journeyed from Ottawa, some of whom had little or no direct experience of Indigenous communities, the session often provided important insights into the impacts of inadequate lands, treaty monies, or claim settlements for all the generations. Our experience at Red Earth and Shoal Lake was no different in this regard.

We spent two days in Shoal Lake. It was reasonably warm for mid-October on the prairies. We stayed in a town not far from the reserves and drove into Shoal Lake each morning, passing a remarkable number of moose grazing in the flooded ditches that paralleled the highway. The community itself was bathed in sunshine and was calm and peaceful. The session took place in the school gymnasium near the centre of the reserve, and it was a bustling and happy place. Teachers and students came and went; sometimes entire classes joined as observers, witnessing their elders sharing stories about the land, the impact of environmental and industrial changes, and the promises made at the time of the treaty and subsequent alterations of the reserve.

The hearings themselves proceeded smoothly and were informative; the elders and others provided compelling and moving testimony in English and Cree. Many made passionate statements about their belief in the commission and our potential to bring some resolution to their claim and justice to their community. I found these submissions deeply engaging but also difficult. In Red Earth and Shoal Lake, as well as in many other communities, it was sometimes hard to look the people in the eye, receive their stories and testimony, and their belief in us. Although I am profoundly grateful for the privilege of serving on the Indian Claims Commission, there were times when I felt ambivalent about my role as a commissioner. Our inquiries often seemed to give communities hope, and I sometimes felt that it was unfounded, given the constraints we faced as a commission. As mentioned above, the ICC completed eighty-eight reports; we recommended that the government accept claims for negotiation in forty-one inquiries and that it reject eighteen.[65] If we take out of the mix the nineteen claims that were accepted by the government mid-inquiry, our legacy seems a bit of a draw: the government accepted nineteen of our recommendations, rejected nineteen, and simply ignored twenty-four of our reports. Even if it is acknowledged that we faced an uphill battle, given that all the inquiries involved rejected claims, our effectiveness in changing the minister's mind seems to have been rather limited. That the government ignored twenty-four of our eighty-eight reports is also revealing. Admittedly, some of those reports were completed following the closure of the ICC in 2009, and thus the government may perhaps be forgiven for assuming that they were as redundant as the commission itself. However, the fact that the ICC was closed did not diminish the extensive work completed between 2007 and 2009 or the potential value to the claims resolution process implicit in the reports. There was nothing to prevent Canada from considering our reports and recommendations, and communicating a position to the claimants, but there is little indication that this occurred.

The time we spent hearing from witnesses at the Shoal Lake school proceeded smoothly. The community was warm and respectful, and the testimony compelling and informative. The truly teachable moments, however, arose during our visit to Red Earth at the end of the day and the site visit on the second day. Once we reached Red Earth, we quickly learned why the session had been held almost entirely in Shoal Lake. Virtually all of Red Earth was under water – the main road was flooded, and we were greeted by what was clearly an ongoing battle by a number of local people to keep the waters at bay. Using earthmovers, shovels, and sheer force of will, the men working on the road had for some time waged war against the rising water levels, but their success appeared modest. The community had always faced some risk of damp, but after 1963 and the building of the E.B. Campbell Dam not far away, flooding had become frequent in both Red Earth and Shoal Lake. By the time we visited in 2007, it was virtually constant. Despite the persistence of community members, the waters would not recede. As we stated in our inquiry report,

> While there was clear evidence of the efforts by these Bands to work with and improve the lands they possess, their efforts cannot help but be undermined by persistently wet conditions. The communities have been riven by the rising waters, so that houses are clustered onto isolated pockets of dry land – even here, however, the basements and foundations are rotting from moisture. The land is no longer cultivated, and stock-raising is impossible due to the lack of pasture land. We observed horses crowded into small enclosures or onto patches of dryer land, where even then they stood in mud. Touring the reserves was made difficult as the roads had clearly been damaged by water and erosion, and it was easy to envisage that they could quickly be rendered impassable even by the slightest additional precipitation.[66]

Community members communicated their predicament cogently and with a liberal dose of cynical wit, but I was deeply affected by the conditions in which they lived. The omnipresence of flooding and damp was oppressive, and I could not imagine the tenacity required to deal with it every day. For every person who seemed determined to take it in stride, there were also those who seemed beaten down. I understood the latter; I had spent only a very brief time in Red Earth but had been unable to avoid the emotional impact of the ever-present, stifling damp.

Nonetheless, our focus was on the treaty and whether Canada had kept its promises to the Red Earth and Shoal Lake people when they adhered to Treaty 5. As we combed through the history of the treaty relationship, we discovered that Canada had, in fact, honoured its promises. In law, then, the Crown had no outstanding obligations to Red Earth and Shoal Lake. At the same time, however, it was clear that life on the reserves had become increasingly untenable due to factors that neither the community nor the government controlled: the construction of the E.B. Campbell Dam had resulted in chronic flooding, which was thought to be exacerbated by climate change. Our visit showed that the reserves were neither habitable nor able to support farming or ranching.

Because Canada had discharged its obligations to the communities, there was no legal burden upon it to remedy the challenges facing Red Earth in particular. Concerned about the justice of leaving the people to struggle with the flooding and dampness, we invoked our supplementary mandate. This enabled us to advocate for fairness in claims that had no outstanding lawful obligation but where the correct legal outcome led to unfairness or injustice. As a result, we urged Canada to rise above the level of legal obligations:

> In spite of the panel's finding that the Crown fulfilled its treaty obliga-
> tions to provide "farming lands" to the Red Earth and Shoal Lake Cree
> Nations, we have seen and the Elders have told us that the reserves are
> no longer viable places to grow crops and raise animals due to the in-
> crease in water levels on the land. In particular, Elders have spoken about
> the fact that since the building of the E.B. Campbell Dam in the 1960's,
> their land is consistently wet not only in the spring but throughout the
> year. From the testimony of the Elders, the panel is struck by the possi-
> bility that the lands have been changed by forces which could not have
> been anticipated by these Bands or the Crown at the time of treaty and
> for several decades afterward. Consequently, the panel urges Canada to
> initiate discussions with the Red Earth and Shoal Lake Cree Nations to

find a long-term solution to the problems caused by the condition of their reserve lands.[67]

We made this recommendation on December 18, 2008. At the time of writing, there is no indication that Canada has taken any heed of it or of the need at Red Earth and Shoal Lake for higher lands that would provide a better future. Admittedly, the government is not legally obliged to do the right thing. Certainly, one could argue that the honour of the Crown is at stake in this as in all of Canada's dealings with First Nations, especially in those cases where honour is the sole force impelling constructive action. To truly resolve claims and move Canada and First Nations towards reconciliation, the Crown must be prepared not only to respect legal justice, but also to pursue and realize social justice. In the case of Red Earth and Shoal Lake, it remains to be seen whether Canada will choose social justice over legal justice and in so doing, make real the honour of the Crown in its dealings with these First Nations.

5

On the Road Again
Planning Conferences, Community Sessions, and the Integrity of the Process

The mandate of the Indian Claims Commission (ICC), as defined by our Order in Council, granted us the power to choose our own process and implement it in a manner consistent with our overarching responsibility to review the application of Canada's specific claims policy. In crafting the inquiry process, the first commissioners were undoubtedly mindful of the deep-seated power imbalances that informed the claims process and the implications of its narrow legal approach for claims and communities. Of especial importance in this context are the fundamental differences between Indigenous and Western cultures with regard to history and the keeping of the stories that comprise our histories. For most Indigenous cultures, history is a living, evolving thing that is fundamentally changed and compromised if written down and frozen in time. Non-Indigenous societies, on the other hand, venerate the written record and tend to discount any statement that cannot be verified by a static document. If, as Jack Kennedy once paraphrased from the Greeks, history is made by those who write it, achieving success in a specific claim would seem equally dependent upon and vulnerable to the written record – a reality that can disadvantage Indigenous cultures who retain their historical records orally.

The inquiry process was designed to reinsert some balance into the consideration of history and to bring together claimants and Canada to share their stories of the events leading to the claim. The community session was a unique and important part of this. It not only humanized the claim, and potentially the claims process, but it also forced the parties to see the claim from a different perspective. By sharing their stories, they were obliged to confront the inconsistencies in their respective versions and to understand that, in most cases, behind each other's positions were real people struggling with real problems and hoping to discover workable solutions. Over my seven years with the ICC, community sessions were among the most rewarding and bedevilling part of our process and often the most illuminating of both claims and the parties' approaches to them.

Getting to Go: Planning Conferences and Community Sessions

As will be recalled from Chapter 2, the community session was the first significant event of the inquiry process. With the limited exception of the planning conference, which included the parties' representatives and legal counsel, it often constituted the first face-to-face meeting between Canada and the claimant. The dates and details of each visit were orchestrated well in advance and under the steady and experienced hand of the commission's liaison. She would have met with the band and communicated extensively with its leadership and with Canada about the session's timing and location; she also had the not insubstantial challenge of juggling the busy schedules of claimants, Canada, a bevy of lawyers and researchers, and the inquiry panel.

Co-ordination often proved difficult. The legal counsel were busy people who were commonly stretched thinly across a number of claims. We ourselves were never more than part-timers and were also active on a number of panels and claims simultaneously. Community schedules also had to be considered, and more than once a carefully planned session was cancelled at the last moment due to the death or illness of an elder or other witness. The loss of elders was especially problematic, as it cut a piece out of both the history of the claim and the community itself. As a token of respect, claims would be set aside while the community came together and mourned its shared loss.

Sessions could also be affected by weather and travel problems, especially in the north. A sudden snowstorm could make air or ground travel impossible, cutting off the community and pushing the session to another day. Even when it was not sufficiently inclement to cause delays, travelling to more remote communities could prove challenging. One flight in particular, from Vancouver to a session in British Columbia's northern interior, stands out in my mind. When we left Vancouver, the weather was beautiful

– bright, sunny, and calm – and the views from the plane were nothing short of spectacular. Nothing hinted that the flight would be anything other than smooth. However, as we headed into the interior, we hit a remarkably fierce snowstorm. Strong winds buffeted the plane to an alarming degree. The small craft was not equipped with sophisticated radar, so the pilot was forced to fly increasingly lower to avoid the cloud cover, which only exacerbated the turbulence. He made a number of attempts to circumvent the storm itself. As we neared our destination, he announced that the storm and low cloud might make it impossible for us to land and that we might have to divert to another airport. He then added that our fuel reserves were very low, that we would get just one chance to land, and that we might have difficulty making the distance to an alternative landing site. The announcement then cut off, which was a tad disconcerting. As it turned out, after a very bumpy and stressful attempt, we landed successfully. Once on the ground with the engines cut, the pilot stepped out of the cockpit, grinned sheepishly, and voiced his relief with, "Well, we made it." I generally avoid air travel whenever possible, so that experience merely reinforced my fear of flying. I was not alone. One of our junior lawyers was terrified by the thought of the flight home, and having located a soulmate, I investigated renting a car for us to drive back to Vancouver. This was not to be, however, as she was told in no uncertain terms that she was expected to take the plane, and I, in solidarity, agreed to abandon ground travel and once more brave the uncertain skies. Of course, our flights back to Vancouver and Ottawa were smooth and steady, though I spent most of the trip gripping the arms of my seat with white knuckles!

That trip was, admittedly, an extreme, and most of our travel was eventful only in the most positive ways. As we journeyed across the country to community sessions and the locations of the legal arguments, we experienced the extraordinary beauty of Canada. Most of my travels were to the prairies, especially Saskatchewan, and to British Columbia. We followed access roads to the farthest reaches of northern British Columbia, encountering black bears en route to the tiny community of Atlin, and spent many hours driving the vast expanse of the prairies and into the north of Saskatchewan, disturbing moose grazing along the roadside.

My first community session occurred in British Columbia through my involvement with the rejected claim of the Lower Similkameen Indian

Band. The Lower Similkameen, or Smelqmix, have historically resided in southcentral British Columbia, and today they live on a cluster of eleven reserves centring upon the small town of Keremeos. Many reserves lie on the banks of the Similkameen River. The band itself consists of 459 people, roughly half of whom currently live on the reserves,[1] which feature lush forest and orchards, and are framed by mountains.

The claim of the Lower Similkameen reached back to events in 1905, when the Vancouver, Victoria and Eastern Railway and Navigation Company requested a right-of-way across the band's land (Indian Reserve Nos. 2, 7, and 8) for a railway line that would primarily transport ore from mines in Hedley and Princeton to the United States, and that would link VVandE with its parent company, the Great Northern Railway.[2] The company offered to pay $25 per acre for 116.84 acres of the reserves, roughly a quarter of what it paid for adjacent land. Despite the already discounted sum, the Indian agent valued the reserve land at $5 an acre, which is what VVandE paid. It also provided a lump sum payment of $2,370 to compensate for improvements made by band members and to cover the removal of buildings in the path of the tracks. In 1906, the chief challenged the compensation paid to the band for the right-of-way, citing the far greater amount that white landowners had received for virtually identical property outside the reserves. His complaint was supported by a local justice of the peace, who had been paid $100 per acre for land that did not differ from that sold by the band. In response to the complaint, the Indian Department sent in a surveyor, who, working closely with the agent, confirmed the $5 valuation and advised against "disturbing the original compensation."[3] Although the Indian Act provided for arbitration in such cases, the department did not offer this service to the band.

The right-of-way secured, the railroad cut through the heart of the reserves, causing unexpected and extreme harm to the land and the First Nation. An entire community was displaced, and farmers and ranchers saw their holdings bisected by the tracks. The company left detritus in both building and later removing the line, the band suffered much injury and loss of livestock due to its construction, and the trains ran through the reserves almost daily for over six decades. In 1972, following the destruction of the bridge spanning the Similkameen River, the trains stopped running through the reserves, and in 1985 the Burlington Northern Railway

Company, which had absorbed the Great Northern Railway and VVandE, legally abandoned the line from Keremeos to the US border. When the Canadian Transport Commission approached the band regarding the abandonment, the council supported it, providing that the right-of-way lands were returned to it. In the end, however, both Canada and Burlington Northern claimed ownership of the right-of-way, leaving the Similkameen caught in the middle and without either the lands or the support of their fiduciary to secure them.

I had been with the commission for less than a year when we were sent out to Vancouver to lead the planning conference in Lower Similkameen. As a part-time commissioner who also taught full-time at Carleton University in Ottawa, I had studied the ICC mandate and process but had limited direct experience of an inquiry. We gathered with the parties' representatives and legal counsel in a hotel meeting room, supported by Liaison staff and the lawyer and researcher on the inquiry, and the business of planning and scheduling the process was soon under way. I was a little nervous; this was my first inquiry, and it was embarking on the unprecedented experiment of having the commissioners run the conference. These seemed deep waters indeed, but I was prepared to do my best to navigate them, even if that meant mostly treading water.

As will be recalled, the purpose of the planning conference was to secure the parties' agreement on the issues that would define the inquiry and to set a timeline for the process. As I would learn, the conference also enabled the parties to gauge each other's arguments, positions, and strategies. Given this, it could require the deft but heavy hand of the Liaison and legal staff to stay on track.

Prior to Lower Similkameen, panel members had no direct role in conferences, though commissioners who were not on the panel sometimes assisted at the request of ICC staff. The drafters of the ICC process had originally anticipated that inquiries would require just one conference, but as mentioned above, their numbers increased over time. After 1999–2000, multiple conferences became more the rule than the exception; in many cases, the rise was modest, whereas in others it seemed extreme. For example, the Sandy Bay Ojibway First Nation inquiry required eight conferences, seven of which were held in Winnipeg between October 1998 and June 2004, with the final conference in Vancouver in September 2004.[4] The five James Smith Cree Nation inquiries, conducted concurrently between 1999 and 2007, necessitated the largest number of conferences. The James Smith Cree Nation Chakastaypasin Indian Reserve 98 inquiry required ten, held variously in Saskatoon, Ottawa, Melfort, and Prince Albert, Saskatchewan, between September 1999 and June 2002.[5] And the James Smith Cree Nation Indian Reserve 100A inquiry required nine.[6] Admittedly, the James Smith inquiries were complex affairs that were presided over by a panel of just two commissioners, and many of the conferences attended to matters pertinent to more than one inquiry. However, the Sandy Bay and James Smith inquiries were merely the most extreme examples of the trend towards multiple conferences.

Bringing the panel in at this early stage was a bold move. Its intention was to provide some coercive oversight at conferences. Whereas the early commissioners had assumed that the parties would take a collaborative approach, conferences were often fraught with contention, as the parties attempted to define and shape the issues that would direct the inquiry. The difficulty of reaching agreement often necessitated repeated meetings. Inserting the panel into the situation would discipline the parties, as it could simply take the matter out of their hands and decide on the issues. At the same time, however, some ICC staff were concerned that this might jeopardize the neutrality of the panel. Through their involvement with conferences, commissioners could be exposed to information or interactions that might raise concerns about bias. This was not a small apprehension: the integrity of the inquiry hinged on the impartiality of the panel – parties who sensed bias or unfairness were unlikely to place much stock in our findings or recommendations. We preserved our neutrality by striving to remain within a "bubble," taking care not to fraternize with the parties, their lawyers, or witnesses and community members. Involving us in refining the legal issues and structuring a timetable risked linking us with the jockeying and skirmishes that sometimes arose at conferences and took us outside our carefully guarded bubble.

Conferences were the province of the Liaison staff and commission counsel, who were well versed in their delicate politics and the lawyer wrangling that was often necessary to get results. As commissioners, we had received tribunal training and education in the legal principles that defined our role as decision-makers within an administrative body. I understood only too well that the integrity of decision making lay in objectivity and fairness, and was always careful to observe the many restrictions and limitations on commissioners that were central to preserving it. All that said, at the time and in retrospect, the bold experiment of the Lower Similkameen conference seems largely to have been doomed.

I had no direct experience of inquiries when we arrived in Vancouver, and neither I nor my fellow panel members, Sheila Purdy and Dan Bellegarde, had previous involvement with the conference process. What Sheila and Dan did have, however, and what set them apart from me, was a broad understanding of the ebb and flow of inquiries, the challenges that the parties could present, and an appreciation of the process that transcended any individual inquiry. In short, they had perspective. Over time, I would acquire this as well, but it was in its very early stages of development when we crossed the threshold of the Lower Similkameen conference. This was unlike anything I had ever encountered – which is saying a lot, as I have considerable experience with that most bizarre of political entities, university administrative work. Even by this standard, however, the conference was wholly baffling. Understandably concerned about protecting our neutrality, ICC staff repeatedly hustled us out of the room, and we loitered in the hallway while staff and parties hashed out matters that were apparently too sensitive for us to hear. Setting the timeframe for the inquiry was also a challenge, as the parties had complex schedules, and locating mutually workable dates was not easy. Again, we were confronted with the delicate dance entailed in preserving our independence and were warned that pressing too hard on both or, worse, either party to commit to a particular date could suggest partiality. Knowing that an allegation of bias could derail the inquiry and its recommendations, we were constantly mindful of the need to appear diligent but distant and to focus on simply getting the inquiry under way. In the end, managing the panel's role in the conference proved too difficult, and the experiment was quickly shelved. To my knowledge, Lower Similkameen was the first and only inquiry in which the panel was involved in a conference.

Nonetheless, it was a fascinating introduction to the dynamic that informed much of the relationship between the commissioners and ICC staff. Though I certainly cannot speak for the other commissioners, I often found the internal politics of the ICC challenging and mystifying. The five commissioners constituted the actual commission, but it seemed to me that we were kept on a rather short leash by ICC staff, which often appeared to have limited faith in our competence. In some cases, of course, we earned their oversight; there were certainly moments when some of us over-stepped our boundaries. In some cases, these were relatively minor internal gaffes, whereas in others the stakes were much higher.

For example, I came to the ICC from an academic background with a strong record of community-based research and fieldwork. As a researcher, when I need the answer to a question, I go directly to the source that is most likely to provide it. This tends to be a book or a journal article, and thus my chances of generating an inter-office conflict or political contro-versy are slim. As I learned at the ICC, this approach was not necessarily a good fit in a federal government bureaucracy. On one occasion, I required clarification of an aspect of the historical record of a claim, so I simply walked into the cubicle of the researcher who was assigned to the inquiry and posed my question. Unbeknownst to me, this was a complete breach of protocol. Researchers worked under the supervision of the legal counsel, who in turn worked under commission counsel, and commissioners did not consult directly with them. I should have submitted my question to commission counsel, preferably in writing, who would pass it on to the lawyer on the inquiry, who would review it and forward it to the researcher, who would research the answer and then send it back up the chain of command until it reached me. Of course, as an academic, I failed to under-stand this process and saw it merely as inefficient. My inexperience with government blinded me to the fact that, like all institutions, the ICC had developed a rational set of processes that met its needs and goals. To say that I was unschooled in the ways of bureaucracy is an understatement. I was baffled by the utter panic displayed by the researcher when I appeared in her cubicle to ask my question and later horrified to discover that I had caused some trouble to her and the inquiry lawyer, who bore the brunt of my flouting of protocol. During my seven years with the commission, I became savvier, though I never really did crack the code of internal politics and protocol. As will be seen in the following chapter, I eventually came to worry less about these sorts of issues and more about completing inquiries appropriately, effectively, and expeditiously. And though staff undoubtedly shared this priority, our respective approaches to pursuing it were not always compatible. Sometimes, this constituted a troublesome and bewildering distraction from the work of commissioners and panels.

My stumbling through the bureaucratic maze undoubtedly created problems and inconveniences for ICC staff, but for the most part these troubles were small and did not hamper our effectiveness as a commission. However, other moments of commissioner stumbling were more problematic. Many of these seemed to crop up during community sessions, often in site visits. In my experience, First Nations often looked to the commission as a source of justice in their efforts to vindicate their claim, and community sessions often involved passionate statements by witnesses of their faith that it would assist them. I found these situations difficult. The strength of our work resided in our ability to analyze claims from a position of neutrality, and that neutrality required us to preserve a measure of distance from the parties. Our role was to conduct a dispassionate assessment of the claim, and our only interest was in facilitating its resolution. Some witnesses seemed not to understand this, which reinforced the importance of keeping a respectful distance and preserving the bubble. Risks to the bubble were highest during pauses in the session and in site visits. During breaks in the taking of testimony, commissioners could mingle with the parties and community members, but there were many reasons to keep the mingling to a minimum. Conversations could stray into the issues or the evidence, and even where this did not occur, onlookers could potentially assume otherwise. Speaking with Canada's representatives or legal counsel could easily engender suspicions of bias in the claimants, and the opposite also held true. It was best, therefore, not to interact too much with either party or with community members.

However, not all commissioners subscribed to this view. Site visits were especially problematic, as commissioners, community members, and witnesses often took long walks to the location of the claim. All discussions that occurred during a site visit presented challenges; there was rarely any way to film or audiotape witnesses as they spoke about the site or answered the questions of commissioners. Thus, we were discouraged from asking questions in that context, lest important information not be included on the record. Any queries inspired by the site visit were normally asked later, during the formal hearings that comprised the greater part of the community session. Beyond the basic directive that we save important questions for the hearing, our behaviour during site visits was subject to only a few guidelines: stick together and don't get into discussions with individual witnesses. The guidelines ensured that all panel members received the same quantity and quality of information. They also protected our appearance of independence. When a panel member talked privately with community members, Canada's representatives and legal counsel could easily become apprehensive about bias and the possibility that the errant panellist was receiving off-the-record information. Conversely, community members were unlikely to look kindly upon similar conversations between a panel member and Canada's representatives.

All commissioners were fully aware of these dangers, but some remained prone to wandering off with local people. That they were confident in their ability to remain neutral and that their conversations might consist solely of innocent remarks was immaterial – sidebar exchanges during site visits created the appearance of bias. As a result, we generally tried to stay together and limited our discussions with community members. This was not always easy; I remember scurrying after itinerant commissioners or watching as legal counsel or Liaison staff deftly intercepted them and returned them to the bubble. To outsiders, this preoccupation with appearances may seem odd or misplaced. However, it is important to remember that the stakes were often very high for the parties to our inquiries, especially for the claimants. As with the courts, so with the commission: justice must not merely be done – it must also be seen to be done. Where parties perceived the panel or process as biased, the justice of our findings was imperilled.

Bearing Witness to Claims

The Lower Similkameen inquiry proceeded despite the failed experiment of the panel-led planning conference, and following the collection of the parties' historical materials, we travelled to Keremeos in mid-April of 2004. The reserve community lay in a south Okanagan valley, which, unlike Ottawa, was already in the full bloom of spring. The reserve was dotted with modest, well-maintained houses and farms, and the people were generous and welcoming. The session consisted of hearings, which took place in a local hall over two days. We heard from thirty-seven witnesses, who spoke to the impact of the railway line, the unfair compensation paid for the right-of-way, and Canada's numerous violations of its fiduciary obligations regarding compensation rates, its failure to arbitrate those rates, and its questionable possession of the right-of-way lands. Accompanied by the parties' lawyers, we were taken on a fascinating tour of the claim site, observing first-hand the legacy of the right-of-way.

As my first inquiry, Lower Similkameen offered a steep learning curve. Now that the planning conference was behind us, I felt a bit more prepared for the community session: I had read all the documents provided by the parties, as well as our own ICC-generated history of the claim; I was conversant with the issues and the relevant legal principles regarding them; and I felt slightly more in sync with the ways of the ICC. However, in what would become the story of this inquiry, the community session gave rise to almost as many controversies as the planning conference before it and the panel deliberations that would follow. The most challenging of these surrounded the testimony of elders.

Long before my appointment, the ICC had adopted a rule against cross-examination of elders during inquiry processes. Although the origins and rationale of this rule were never fully explained to me, it was evidently premised on a few key considerations, including concerns about panel competence in overseeing the inquiry process, the zeal of lawyers in questioning witnesses, and the assumed frailty of elders.

When I joined the commission in 2002, I had a reasonably robust measure of experience with fieldwork. Notable among this was a number of years spent with eastern James Bay communities in northern Quebec and a period of residence in the Mohawk Nation territory at Kahnawake during the completion of my doctoral research. In both contexts, I had been privileged to spend much time in the company of elders. In Kahnawake in particular, I had interviewed a number of elders about traditional law and conflict resolution, recording their stories for future generations. I spent many hours hearing about how life was lived in the past and learning how those lifeways could assist in dealing with many of the problems facing families and communities.

My time with the elders taught me many things, two of which are especially relevant to the question of their frailty and community sessions. First and most importantly, the elders taught me how to listen, in a world where many people see listening as simply waiting for their chance to talk. I learned the value of sitting quietly for long periods and respecting the power of the speaker to share and shape his or her wisdom. This lesson took time to fully root itself, and it has served me well in many areas of my life. The second lesson I learned from the elders is not to be deceived by appearances. Unquestionably, the elders who gifted me their time and wisdom were old; their bodies showed the wear of a lifetime, and some struggled with mobility and the maladies that come with aging. But at the same time, they possessed a deep strength and robust memories of their life path and those of their community and nation. Though it is certainly true that the experience of aging differs from person to person, and that some elders were in better health than others, my time with them showed me the danger of equating age with infirmity in body and mind. Generalizations are dangerous things, regardless of whether they are made about people or anything else.

Confronted with a blanket rule against cross-examining elders, I baulked. I understood that it was grounded in respect, but it also seemed misdirected and based on generalizations, not only about the elderly, but also about the idea of respect. Not all elderly people are frail, and not all of them shrink from the opportunity to tell their stories. The characterization of elders seemed incorrect, and the rule itself reflected a rather strange type of respect, not only for elder witnesses, but also for the inquiry process and those who were central to it, including the panel, legal counsel, and the parties themselves. In my opinion, it also injected significant unfairness into the process.

The prohibition on cross-examination disrespected not only the elders, but also the lawyers for the parties and the panel itself. It inferred that the lawyers were unwilling or unable to cross-examine elders in a respectful manner and that they would not be sensitive to physical limitations, including frailty or fatigue. Most lawyers whom I encountered during my time on the ICC were attuned to the nature of their roles in the process and to the unique challenges and exigencies of the community session. With a few exceptions, I had faith that they would treat all witnesses with respect, including elders. And in those rare instances where my faith was qualified, I had absolute confidence in my own willingness and that of my colleagues to intervene if necessary. We had an obligation to neutrality but also to fairness, and most of us would take steps to ensure that witnesses were accorded both fairness and respect.

Furthermore, the cross-examination rule was unfair because it was directed primarily at Canada's lawyers. That it protected *all* elder witnesses did not make it fair, as virtually every witness to which it applied furnished testimony in support of the claimant. Certainly, had Canada brought forward elders who supported its case, they too would have escaped cross-examination, but no such witness ever appeared before the panels in which I participated. That they could have done so does not render the rule any less unfair or undermine its impact on our process.

Whenever discussion of the rule arose, its justification emphasized not only the need to protect elders, but also that its "small unfairness" offset a much greater one – the conflict of interest in the claims policy and process. Although this logic has some appeal, it is irrelevant as a rationale for introducing bias into our process. No one who sat on the commission or worked in its offices would deny the serious flaws of the claims policy; the dominance of the Crown as both judge and party to claims was (and is) a deep unfairness that cried out for remedy. And though we were certainly not loath to comment on this and other flaws, the integrity of our results depended on the integrity of our process. The purpose of the commission was not to address the lack of fairness in the policy by inserting unfairness into its own process. Its role was to hear all parties, consider their evidence and arguments, and determine whether the record established an outstanding lawful obligation. If policy is defective, it should be reformed. This task is separate from the work of bodies such as the ICC, which operate at arm's length from government and in accordance with the principles of fairness that are integral to administrative law.

Although the rule disproportionately affected Canada's counsel and case, it could harm the claimant's case as well. The value of the ICC process was that it captured as broad an evidentiary record as possible, drawing upon both written records and oral testimony. In my experience, panels were not passive recipients of the evidence or arguments. We were skeptical and, for the most part, immune to superficial arguments and unsubstantiated statements, and hard on outlier or untested evidence. In other words, *we needed to be convinced* of the parties' cases, and the best evidence was that which could withstand our scrutiny and counter challenges to its accuracy. Testimony and evidence not subjected to cross-examination at the community session did not escape analysis by the panel, and unlike in a classic context of examination of evidence, our deliberations did not enable the claimant to redirect. Simply put, the panels I experienced were hard on the evidence, and to me, evidence that went untested in the community session did not remain untested in the final analysis.

It is important to acknowledge that, though legal counsel were not permitted to cross-examine elders, the panel could question all witnesses directly, including elders. As a result, if any of us wished to query an element of testimony, we were certainly within our rights to do so. When it came to elder witnesses, however, I felt that our latitude in questioning was constrained by the same sort of considerations that had originally fostered the rule against cross-examination. I remember feeling considerable pressure not to question elders and sensed the disapproving stares and anxiety of some commission staff when I did. This does not mean that I refrained from posing questions, but I did think long and hard before I asked them. I cannot say whether my fellow commissioners shared my discomfort on this score, though I do recall that direct panel questioning of elders was always done carefully and advisedly, almost always engendering palpable disapproval from some quarters.

There was an additional problematic dimension of the prohibition against cross-examination, as it did not specify how a witness might qualify as an elder. This is not surprising. Clearly, the rule assumed that all elders are old, frail, and vulnerable, and that cross-examination was not only inappropriate given their age and infirmity, but also disrespectful. And if it were disrespectful to cross-examine elders, it was certainly disrespectful for the commission to dictate to communities regarding which of their members qualified as elders. Although there can be little doubt that only communities have the right to confer that designation, I must confess that some individuals who stepped up to offer evidence as elders did not fit the profile imagined by the ICC when the cross-examination rule was conceived. In more than one community session, I encountered elders who were in their late thirties or early forties, and whose testimony was not consistent with either the form or content of knowledge sharing among the elders whom I had met outside the commission processes. At least some of these witnesses seemed to have assumed the mantle of elder, not because they were seen as such by the community, but rather because it conferred a strategic advantage. As a matter of tactics, such an approach is perhaps understandable; witnesses were often under significant pressure to play a meaningful role in the vindication of their community's claim and were prepared to exploit all opportunities to do so. The difficulty, of course, is that though we received all evidence at face value, only that which could stand up to intense scrutiny informed our findings.

Other difficulties arose in elder testimony. Sometimes, claimants took advantage of the prohibition against cross-examination and of elders' vulnerability. In one inquiry, we had reached the second day of the community session. On the day before, we had heard from a number of witnesses, most of whom were not elders and were thus subject to cross-examination. The session had proceeded relatively smoothly, although we had glimpsed tension in the community regarding the claim and the case that had been created around it. It was apparent that not everyone agreed with the version of events that was emerging through the testimony, and despite our efforts to keep our distance, we had heard rumours that the witness list was selective and that we were being given only a partial view of the claim events. In this inquiry, as in many others, the stakes for the community were high, and the stress was tangible.

On the second day of the session, we were to hear evidence from a well-known and well-respected local elder. He began his testimony, telling the story of the claims events clearly and well. After he spoke for a time, we took a brief break. Shortly before the session reconvened, we were approached by a member of our legal staff, who told us that one of the elder's grandchildren had asked to sit with him during the remainder of his testimony. We agreed to this, on the understanding that the elder wished to have his granddaughter beside him and that she must sit quietly while he spoke. These small hurdles cleared, the testimony began; within moments, the elder who had spoken so eloquently began to hesitate as his granddaughter whispered in his ear. It soon became obvious that she was coaching him: his earlier version of events started to change, as did his language, which suddenly became peppered with legal terms. The panel stopped him several times to gently but firmly question him on the discrepancies in his testimony and to politely remind the granddaughter, apparently a first-year law student, not to interrupt him. In the end, we suspended his testimony and directed the young woman to step away from him, as he had become visibly agitated by her interventions. This unfortunate experience, though more the exception than the rule, served as an important reminder that challenges to the inquiry process were not always anticipated by its architects and that unfairness and disrespect can come in many forms and from many places.

Although community sessions and witness testimony could sometimes prove difficult, the content and quality of the evidence could be breathtaking. In my graduate studies at Simon Fraser University, I had conducted extensive research on how non-literate societies retain and transmit historical records, and in the process I had acquired a sound grasp of the intricacies and characteristics of oral history. These entail particular ways of speaking that are designed to aid memory through cadence and mnemonic devices; they have become increasingly unusual in a world dominated by the written word. True oral records are few and far between, and are becoming more so as the elders who carry these records pass away.

The purpose of community sessions was to secure the evidence of the community and, perhaps most importantly, to hear the elders' oral histories of the claim events. We heard from many elders and received a large amount of important and significant knowledge pertinent to many claims, but one occasion stands out in my mind. In 2002, the ICC accepted a request for an inquiry into the rejected claim of the Taku River Tlingit First Nation, located in the northwestern corner of British Columbia. The claim concerned Wenah, the primary Taku village on the shore of Atlin Lake, where the Taku were residing long before gold was discovered there in 1898.[7] As miners and speculators pushed in, the Taku relocated to a small area of their original village on the southern edge of what had become the Atlin townsite. When the BC government sent in a surveyor to complete a survey of Atlin in 1899, he marked out an "Indian Village,"[8] but when a second survey was completed a year later, the village was not recorded. As a result, no reserve was set aside at Atlin when the McKenna-McBride Commission visited the area in 1915. Despite this oversight, the Taku continued to live in Wenah and consistently pressed the Crown for clarity regarding the status of their land. In 1945, the Indian agent for Atlin confirmed that the village site should have been reserved for the Taku, and the department attempted negotiations with the BC government to have the land transferred to it to be set aside as a reserve. The provincial government refused (the good citizens of Atlin reportedly did not want an Indian reserve within their townsite), and for more than a decade it consistently blocked any attempt to create a reserve for the Taku. In the end, the department managed to obtain three lots in Atlin for the Taku, in exchange for a parcel of land at a nearby lake.[9] The inquiry into the loss of much of the land at Wenah focused on three issues: whether Canada had a fiduciary, statutory obligation or duty of care to the Taku regarding the selection of reserve lands by the McKenna-McBride Commission; the loss of much of Wenah to private interests; and, the surrender of the lake lands.[10]

We went to Atlin in May of 2004 for a community session and site visit, and we heard testimony from five elders, all of whom spoke at length about the loss of their lands at Wenah during their own lifetimes and those of their parents. I vividly remember walking along Atlin Lake on a bright, sunny day and listening as an elder recited a very clear oral historical account regarding the Taku use of the lake and shore. It was a mesmerizing experience – the cadence and phrasing of his recitation corresponded with everything I had read about pure oral traditions. In this remote village, surrounded by his traditional territory and encased within the community that had resided there since time immemorial, this man had inherited the oral history of the Taku River Tlingit, which had survived intact. That record and those provided by other witnesses who spoke at the community session were important in our analysis, which focused on that history and the documented actions of the provincial and federal government, to find an outstanding lawful obligation on the part of the Crown to the Taku. We completed our report, which we submitted to the minister in March 2006; the commission closed three years later without any response to our recommendations in the Taku inquiry.

Community sessions were remarkable experiences that furnished us with a rich and deep understanding of how the claims and the events behind them affected Indigenous people across Canada. They taught a profound lesson in the importance of the land to First Nations and the connections to the earth that persist and, in many cases, transcend treaties, surrenders, and the boundaries of reserves. Our time in the community often gave shape and context to an inquiry that the mountains of documents and records could never have provided. Sessions were a crucial element of the inquiry process, one that reflected the unique approach of the commission to the resolution of specific claims. They brought us into greater acquaintance with the claim and its impact, and often constituted the first time that Canada's representatives had set foot in the community. And though they presented some difficulties, their benefits greatly outweighed the potential problems raised by challenging witnesses, peregrinating commissioners, and the necessity of preserving the panel bubble. Time spent in the community brought the claim to life and rendered very real the consequences of treaties, surrenders, and all that came in their wake. During my years as a commissioner, the community sessions and walking the grounds of the claim provided some of my strongest and most memorable experiences.

The community session was followed by the presentation of the legal arguments, which usually occurred within a few weeks or months in the urban centre that lay closest to the claimant. If, for the community, the sessions were about justice, the orals were very much and only about the law.

6

By Law or In Justice
Legal Arguments, Panel Deliberations, and the Murky Waters of the Mediation Unit

The community session was followed by oral legal arguments – the "orals," as we called them – in which the parties and their counsel appeared before the panel to argue the merits of the claim. The orals provided many important insights into the parties' respective understanding of claims, and when added to the lessons of the community session, they often exposed the thin, strained line between law and justice.

As public hearings that were often attended by members of the claimant community and by other people who were likely to be affected by the outcome of the claim, the orals were usually uneventful and tended to proceed in an orderly fashion. There is little to be said about them and even less that can be said about the deliberations that followed. Restricted to the panel, legal counsel, and occasionally, where appropriate, researchers, deliberations were confidential. As a result, I can say little about the content of our discussions around the table in the commission's Ottawa offices. What I can and will share, however, is a basic discussion of how deliberations proceeded and of the tensions and issues that could arise within them. Our deliberations were important, as the decisions made in this setting shaped our contribution to the resolution of specific claims and the legacy of the Indian Claims Commission (ICC).

In this chapter, I will also speak briefly about the ICC's Mediation Unit, which completed reports on seventeen mediations over the commission's lifespan.[1] The unit, its functions, and the involvement of commissioners in mediation were often discussed during my time with the ICC and until the commission closed following the passage of the Specific Claims Tribunal Act.

First Thing We Do, Let's Kill All the Lawyers:
Legal Arguments and Panel Deliberations

As a general rule, the evidence-gathering phase of the inquiry ended once the community session concluded, and we then moved towards closing the record that contained the documents, history, and other related materials regarding the inquiry. However, one or both parties sometimes applied to the panel to bring in experts to speak to key issues. Where the panel granted these requests, the evidentiary record remained open to accommodate not only the expert report, but also in some cases a session at which the expert testified before the panel and could be questioned and cross-examined by the parties. Such a full hearing was not inevitable, however. In some instances, the report would be circulated, and the opposing party could respond with an expert report of its own; in other cases, the panel might allow the party to question the expert about the report before a court reporter and in the presence of the other party's lawyer. Regardless of how the expert input was managed, the record of the inquiry remained open to permit the inclusion of any reports or transcripts that emerged from it.

If no expert involvement was required, the days following the community session were devoted to reviewing the transcripts for accuracy and making any necessary revisions. Once finalized, the transcripts were added to the record as an exhibit, and the evidentiary record was closed. In the later days of the commission, the record was collated and put on a CD-ROM, which was shared with the panel, the parties, and the ICC staff who were connected with the inquiry. Next, we moved to the orals, the penultimate stage in our process.

The orals enabled the parties to present their final arguments, which were based on the evidence provided by the historical research and community testimony. Respecting that the community session could furnish additional evidence that might affect the parties' positions, the inquiry schedule gave them time to revise their legal submissions. Although the timelines had some flexibility, we normally expected to receive the First

Nation's finalized submission within six to eight weeks after the record was closed, and Canada's responding submission would follow within a similar period. The claimants then had a final two weeks in which to respond to Canada's submission. The gap between the closure of the record and the commencement of the orals varied from inquiry to inquiry, but the shift from community session to orals normally took four to five months.

Once all the submissions were in, the commission's legal counsel compiled a decision tree, which outlined the "factual description of the claim based upon the legal arguments put forward by the parties."[2] This document summarized the cases that the parties would present at the orals, and it was a critical component of the briefing kit that commissioners received and studied. Having reflected upon this material, we often formed at least tentative opinions regarding the issues before we arrived at the orals. Though it would be naive to suggest that these opinions did not affect our views of the claim, most of us were conscious of the importance of keeping an open mind and thus resisted firm positions until after the orals were complete.

As noted earlier, orals were commonly held in a city that was near the claimant community, typically in the meeting room of a hotel. The panel usually flew into town the day before the orals, to be rested and ready to hear the submissions. As a first task, we met with the associate on the file and commission counsel, who briefed us in preparation for the orals. They summarized the evidence and arguments, and linked this with the issues. In some cases, despite their best efforts to present the information as neutrally as possible, counsel's views of the correct outcome seeped into the briefing. Such seepage could be quite problematic.

Briefings could afford the first opportunity for the panel and the lawyers to exchange their views on the evidence and arguments. Given this, contention between panel members, or between panel members and legal counsel, could begin to crystallize at this point. More than once, I felt that my emergent understanding of the claim did not entirely match the overview being given by the associate at the briefing. In some cases, this tension was cleared up at the orals; in others, it persisted to the deliberations and beyond, and not always to a satisfactory resolution between commissioners and counsel. I will return to this matter below.

The process at the orals was quite straightforward. The claimant opened the session by presenting its arguments, after which Canada took its turn. Both parties were permitted to question and redirect. The panel could interrupt submissions to ask questions or seek clarification from legal counsel for the parties, and commission counsel or the associate could ask questions with leave from the chair of the panel. Like the community sessions, orals were recorded and the transcripts were given to the panel and the parties once the session ended.

Orals were attended by the panel, our legal counsel, and the researcher, who was on hand to field questions regarding the history of the claim. The Indian Affairs representative was accompanied by legal counsel, and the claimant's lawyer was often buoyed by the support of at least a few band councillors and/or community members. In some cases, the latter attendance would be quite strong; for example, many community members came every day to hear the arguments at the Cowessess First Nation orals.[3] There was also a good turnout for Lower Similkameen.

There were usually few surprises at the orals. Organized by Liaison staff and overseen by commission lawyers, consisting almost entirely of the arguments and responses of lawyers, they tended to be relatively well scripted and tightly run. The sole sources of controversy were commissioners who might slip over the line into too zealous questioning of counsel or who pressed too hard on a question that proved difficult to answer. We sometimes also felt uncomfortable in witnessing the harshness of legal language and argument, which could fail to capture the full experience of the parties or could seem disrespectful of them. There was rarely much to be done in such situations; the law is often a blunt instrument, one that resists compromise or genuine conflict resolution. If either party became disrespectful of the other or of the panel, the chair responded carefully and in a manner that did not create perceptions of bias or undermine our neutrality. In my experience, incidents of controversy, other than those entailed in a conflict of legal opinions, rarely occurred at orals and never amounted to more than a few moments of discomfort, whether due to the fractious nature of the conflicts or the usually minor foibles of panel members.

Orals were usually completed within a day, though they could require more time if an inquiry were exceptionally complex. Next, the panel again convened with our legal counsel to share our first impressions. In this confidential setting, with the assistance and oversight of commission counsel and the associate, we discussed our perceptions of the quality, strength, and soundness of the presented arguments. This meeting was followed by a much more detailed and protracted period of deliberations once the panel returned to Ottawa. These deliberations were common satellites revolving around our regularly scheduled commission meetings. If panel members could not meet face-to-face, some parts of the deliberations could proceed through conference call.

If orals were unremarkable in structure and content, panel deliberations could be quite the opposite. I cannot speak to those in which I did not participate, but I can confirm that a few were delayed not only by disagreements between commissioners, but also between panel members and associates and commission counsel. In my experience, these disagreements were typically grounded in differences regarding the application of case law or in very divergent views on the motives, competencies, and choices of Canada and the claimant with regard to the events that preceded the claim.

My first inquiry concerned the Lower Similkameen Band and its railway right-of-way claim. The BC claims were complex at many levels and were made so by the long and acrimonious relationship between the federal and provincial governments over Indigenous land rights and title, and by the Province's chronic flouting of those rights.

British Columbia joined Confederation in 1871, and the details of its inclusion are spelled out in the British Columbia Terms of Union, article 13 of which provided for federal-provincial co-operation in the creation of Indian reserves.[4] Such collaboration was necessary because, though the Constitution Act, 1867, granted Ottawa authority over "Indians and lands reserved for Indians," the Crown land on which the reserves would stand belonged to the Province.[5] Thus, neither government could create reserves without the assistance of the other. Canada had begun to map out and set aside reserves in northeastern British Columbia after much of that region was included in Treaty 8 in 1899, but the Province often thwarted its efforts to protect Indigenous lands. Victoria seemed to take little heed of reserves or Indigenous rights and had no compunction about selling the land to white settlers. Between 1871 and 1938, the two levels of government frequently clashed over the question of Indigenous rights and reserve creation.

The findings of three royal commissions (1875 Reserve Commission, 1912 McKenna-McBride Commission, and 1920 Ditchburn-Clark Commission) failed to resolve the matter. It was not until July 29, 1938, that the BC government appeared to sign on to the reserve creation process, when it passed an Order in Council by which it conveyed a series of reserves to the federal government.[6]

The Lower Similkameen inquiry drew the panel into this complicated history, which was made no less so by the 2002 Supreme Court of Canada decision in *Wewaykum*. We were in the early stages of Lower Similkameen when the court handed down this decision, which determined that, in effect, no Indian reserves existed in British Columbia before the 1938 Order in Council secured provincial co-operation in their creation. This had a direct impact on the Lower Similkameen inquiry. As will be recalled, the Similkameen had sold a portion of their reserves in 1905, which became a VVandE right-of-way. The status of this land would determine the nature of the Crown's fiduciary obligation to the First Nation. In short, according to *Wewaykum*, the Crown's fiduciary depended on whether the events in question occurred before 1938 or afterward. If they predated 1938, the Crown's duty would be "limited to the basic obligations of loyalty, good faith in the discharge of its mandate, providing full disclosure appropriate to the subject matter, and acting with ordinary prudence with a view to the best interest of the aboriginal beneficiaries."[7] This is clearly a lower standard than that which applies after 1938, wherein the fiduciary obligation "expands to include the protection and preservation of the band's quasi-proprietary interest in the reserve from exploitation."[8]

In our deliberations regarding Lower Similkameen, the status of the affected reserves and the fiduciary obligation of the Crown became central and hotly contested issues. The parties both agreed that the Crown had a fiduciary obligation to the band with regard to the taking of the right-of-way. The crux of the matter was the degree of the fiduciary and, based upon that determination, whether the Crown's actions were sufficient. This is where things got fractious.

Relying on the 1938 cut-off as the essential fact, our legal counsel insisted that a finding that went beyond the lesser fiduciary was untenable and wrong in law. In the strict letter of the law, his position had some foundation, but the difficulty here is that the ICC process was not solely about law. It was also about justice, and we were entitled to comment if the law failed to serve justice. Unwilling to accept the *Wewaykum* cut-off but needing to stay within the law, we tried to push the boundaries as far as possible. We focused on the actions of the Crown in creating the Lower Similkameen reserves, including the mapping out of the reserves in 1878, the subsequent survey of 1889, and the addition of the reserves to the federal "Schedule of Indian Reserves" as "confirmed" in 1902 and 1913. Taken together, these acts indicated that Ottawa intended to create reserves for the Lower Similkameen, took clear steps to do so, and treated the lands as reserves in the result. At the time, and indeed, until *Wewaykum* created the 1938 cut-off in 2002, both Canada and the First Nation understood the lands to be reserves. As the inquiry report stated,

> The historical record demonstrates the requisite intention, and clearly the Band had accepted the lands (which they understood as "set apart") and had started to make use of them. However, the difficulty is that, for constitutional reasons, all these steps were without legal effect. The final step was taken only in 1938.[9]

It seemed to me that the effect of *Wewaykum* was to rewrite history, transmuting what the Crown had always treated as reserves into something less and thus reducing its duty to protect them. This seemed unjust. How could reserves that had existed since at least 1902 and been treated as such until 2002 suddenly be retroactively transformed into something else?

Although we could not overcome the lesser fiduciary duty that *Wewaykum* placed on the Crown with regard to reserve creation prior to 1938, we could certainly ensure that the Crown met that standard to the fullest degree possible. Arguing that the facts in Lower Similkameen were such that "it was not possible to conceive of a more certain state of pre-reserve conditions in 1905," we asserted that "the highest level of fiduciary duty obtained in this case short of the duty owed once a reserve is established."[10] In short, although *Wewaykum* clearly placed the reserves in the pre-1938 category of Crown obligations, this status did not vitiate the duty owed to the First Nation by Canada.

Although we tried to push the envelope of *Wewaykum*, I do not think we pushed past it or beyond a legally correct outcome. And yet, our counsel

was so committed to his position that we were unable to finalize our findings and recommendations, and actually produce a report, for *three years.*
The Similkameen orals were completed by the end of January 2005, but
our report was not finished until 2008 and was published in 2009. To his
credit, our counsel was confident in his legal opinion and determined that
our report would not be founded on an incorrect interpretation of *Wewaykum,* which could potentially allow Canada to dismiss it. However, with
all due respect to his diligence, his position reflected a misunderstanding
of our role as commissioners who were responsible for the oversight of
the specific claims policy. Certainly, those of us who had legal training had
no illusions about the centrality of the law in resolving claims, but we all
understood that the resolution of claims once and for all could require
looking beyond the letter of the law to ensure a just result. And in situations, such as Lower Similkameen and Red Earth and Shoal Lake, where
the law did not achieve justice, many of us believed that our proper role
was to remind the Crown of its larger responsibilities to justice and honour
in all its dealings with Aboriginal peoples. We were certainly not alone in
this regard; honour is conspicuous in the jurisprudence that clarifies the
Crown's role and obligations with respect to treaty and Aboriginal rights.

As a concept, the honour of the Crown historically embodied the notion
that the Crown should have good intentions in all its dealings, a position
that enabled the "courts to achieve greater justice by tempering the strictness
of the law."[11] As it has evolved in the context of Aboriginal jurisprudence,
the honour of the Crown has continued this emphasis on fair dealings and
equity. *R. v. Taylor and Williams* (1982) was one of the first cases to raise
the honour of the Crown in relation to Indigenous issues, stressing that it
is always involved in the interpretation of the terms of a treaty and that no
"sharp dealing" would be tolerated.[12] The principle was further shaped by
the Supreme Court of Canada through its decisions in *Sparrow* (1990),
Van der Peet (1996), *Badger* (1999), *Mikisew Cree First Nation* (2005), *Haida
Nation* (2004), and *Taku River* (2004).[13] *Taku River* states,

> In all its dealings with Aboriginal peoples, the Crown must act honour-
> ably, in accordance with its historical and future relationship with the
> Aboriginal peoples in question. The Crown's honour cannot be inter-
> preted narrowly or technically, but must be given full effect in order to

promote the process of reconciliation mandated by s. 35(1) [of the Constitution].[14]

The sum of the jurisprudence is clear: though honour may not offer an independent cause of action, it is nonetheless a defining principle in all the Crown's dealings with the Indigenous people of Canada, one that requires respect for fairness in both process and result. As Thomas Isaac observes, the highest court has "clearly expressed the express duty of the Crown to do the right thing in its dealings with Aboriginal people."[15]

Honour not only encompasses a set of criteria for assessing the past conduct of the Crown but also sets a standard for its behaviour in the present. As a commissioner, I believed strongly that honour should have been foremost in the minds of Canada's representatives and legal counsel with regard to specific claims policy, their involvement with the ICC, and their responses to our recommendations. And yet, in my opinion, "doing the right thing" in connection with claims often seemed conspicuous by its absence. During my time with the ICC, I learned that arguing the honour of the Crown in our reports and recommendations availed us little. Although the Crown should have embraced the concept, it had little traction. If, as in the case of Red Earth and Shoal Lake, we could find no outstanding lawful obligation other than a duty to act honourably and the moral suasion of entreaties to do the right thing, our recommendations would be ignored. For the Crown, what mattered was the force of law. In virtually all cases, this, rather than justice or honour, moved it to resolve outstanding claims.

Much of my skepticism regarding the honour of the Crown was focused on our recommendations. If these did not confirm that Canada had an outstanding lawful obligation, the Crown happily accepted them, but if they deviated from its preferred outcome or if we invoked our supplementary mandate, honour was much thinner on the ground. As will be recalled from Chapter 4, the supplementary mandate enabled us to advocate for fairness where a legally correct result led to unfairness or injustice, as in the case of Red Earth and Shoal Lake. In that inquiry, we determined that the Crown had no outstanding lawful obligation, but we invoked our supplementary mandate to encourage it to enter discussions with the First Nations regarding their unsustainable living conditions. To date, Canada has not responded. This hardly seems consistent with honour and will certainly not encourage the ongoing social and political project of reconciliation. Of course, given the glacial pace at which the claims process moves, it may be too soon to judge Canada's reactions to a report that dates from 2008. If, as Canada's own documents indicate, submissions take an average of thirteen years to process,[16] Red Earth and Shoal Lake may yet receive a response from Canada on our inquiry report and recommendations.

In many of our inquiries, the fiduciary relationship between the Crown and First Nations was a key issue, and I would suggest that our deliberations and approach to the fiduciary made a contribution to the development and understanding of the term. We pressed hard on those obligations and tried to be diligent in ensuring that Canada respected its fiduciary responsibilities to First Nations. At the same time, however, we understood that the Crown has many obligations and that it can never act without considering all of them, including those it owes to non-Indigenous interests. Thus, though the Crown has special obligations in connection with various Indigenous interests, it is also clear that it "can be no ordinary fiduciary."[17] In dealing with claims and a range of other matters, Canada cannot focus solely upon its fiduciary obligations to First Nations but must also always respect that its choices and decisions affect a wide range of other interests as well. The challenge of managing these competing obligations was something we considered in our inquiries, and it could become a source of considerable tension, not only among commissioners, but also between commissioners and counsel. Such was the case in phase II of the Cowessess First Nation inquiry.[18]

The Cowessess First Nation resides in southern Saskatchewan on reserve lands that it secured through adherence to Treaty 4 at Fort Qu'Appelle in September 1874. At the time they took treaty, the predominantly Saulteaux people who followed Chief Cowessess and later took his name lived primarily by the hunt, following the buffalo through their seasonal migrations across the prairies. Although they were promised reserve lands in 1874, the Cowessess were not immediately interested in settling down and becoming farmers.[19]

For the first few years after signing Treaty 4, the Cowessess continued to hunt, and they collected their treaty annuities at Fort Qu'Appelle. However, as the buffalo began to diminish, they moved west, closer to the

Cypress Hills, and in 1878 and 1879 the Crown promised them reserve lands north of Fort Walsh and later at Maple Creek. Although some of the people began to settle at Maple Creek, the promise to survey and set aside the lands was not initially met, and four years later, in 1883, Cowessess and his followers left Maple Creek to join other Saulteaux on established reserves at Crooked Lake. They joined with the community led by Chief Louis O'Soup and took up residence near the lands settled by his people. In 1889, this land was surveyed and confirmed as Cowessess Indian Reserve No. 73. The reserve consisted of 78 square miles, reflecting the treaty entitlement of 128 acres for each of the 390 band members.[20]

Even as the reserve was being surveyed and set aside for the Cowessess, settlers were attempting to acquire its southern portion. As early as 1886, settlers near Moosomin, Saskatchewan, had asked the minister of the interior to relocate the four Crooked Lake reserves away from the Canadian Pacific Railway, which ran along their southern edge, arguing that this was "desirable in the public interest and in the interests of the Indians themselves."[21] Though the minister appeared to favour this move, the resident Indian agent disagreed on the grounds that a surrender and relocation were not in the best interests of the residents, as it would negatively affect their haylands and cattle ranching. His report convinced the Department of Indian Affairs, which refused the settlers' request to open up the land, stating that the surrender "would not be prudent."[22]

The matter lay dormant for a time, but it repeatedly resurfaced in 1891, 1899, and 1900, when the First Nations and the department again rejected a surrender.[23] The issue simmered for a few years, but the communities steadfastly refused to give up their southern haylands, and the department was unwilling to push them. In 1904, the question of a surrender was again raised, this time during a meeting when all four communities had assembled to receive their treaty annuities. The leadership informed the government that settlers who lived on the borders of the reserve continually allowed their livestock to graze on the reserve's hay fields. Indian Commissioner David Laird seized the opportunity to argue for surrendering a portion of the reserve, the proceeds of which could be used to fence off the remainder, thereby solving the problem of settler trespass.[24] The bands asked for time to consider the question, and Laird relented, admitting that the issue required "very careful handling."[25]

Between 1906 and 1907, the possibility of surrender was again mooted, and the matter was pressed by William Graham, the inspector of Indian agencies for the Qu'Appelle inspectorate. Many of our Prairie inquiries showed that his approach to Indigenous lands and surrenders was questionable at best. This time, the surrender went through, but the Cowessess vote proved contentious, and the surrender was passed by just one ballot.[26]

In 1981, the Cowessess First Nation submitted a claim to the Specific Claims Branch (SCB), alleging that the 1907 surrender was invalid because it did not comply with the relevant provisions of the Indian Act. This submission was followed by another in 1984, which challenged the surrender based on breach of treaty, breach of fiduciary duty, fraud, and unconscionability.[27] Further submissions were made in 1985 and 1992. The SCB reviewed the claim and rejected it in 1994. Two years later, the Cowessess approached us, asking that we launch an inquiry into their rejected claim. Their request was accepted, and the resulting inquiry was divided into phase I and phase II. The former, heard by Commissioners Carole Corcoran and Roger Augustine, was concerned with the interpretation of the surrender provisions in the Indian Act, the factual questions of voter eligibility, and the number of ballots cast in favour of the surrender.[28] The inquiry proceeded in October 1996, with the first of two planning conferences, and was concluded with the findings and recommendations of Augustine in March 2001. Regrettably, Carole Corcoran passed away during the inquiry, leaving Augustine alone to communicate the panel's findings.

According to the inquiry report, the validity of the surrender was based upon votes taken at two meetings in January 1907. It was unclear whether a vote actually did occur at the first meeting, held on January 21, but the history compiled for the inquiry contended that it had. A paragraph in the minutes for the January 21 meeting summarizes Inspector Graham's explanation of the surrender and its implications, and of the vote that would determine the issue. Immediately below, a single word appears to have been inserted and subsequently erased at an unknown date. Our historian suggested that this originally read "refused," which was taken as proof that the band had voted to reject the surrender. Directly following the erased word, the minutes give the remarks of the Cowessess headman, Chief Joe LeRat, who said that the surrender had been well explained and that the Cowessess understood it but would need some time to reflect. The minutes do not refer to a vote having transpired.[29] A later report by Graham stated that no vote was taken at the meeting. However, the panel agreed with the historian's interpretation – that the vote had in fact occurred. Graham's assertion to the contrary was accepted by the panel as evidence of wrongdoing by both him and the department. This was reinforced by the minutes of the second meeting, during which the decision to surrender passed by a single ballot: that of an "Alex Gaddie."

Gaddie is recorded as "one of the most productive farmers in the Cowessess Band."[30] He was also the interpreter at both surrender meetings. At the community session for phase I of the inquiry, testimony indicated that Inspector Graham had brought in a "stranger" – an "extra person," whose job was to break the tie vote and thus secure the surrender. Documents from the surrender include a letter from Gaddie to David Laird, the Indian commissioner, dated July 13, 1908, in which Gaddie confirmed that he was the tie breaker.[31] There was also some question about the number of eligible voters at the second meeting, with much speculation revolving around the identities of one or two. The key question was whether the Indian Act required that majority consent must be obtained from all eligible voters who were present at a surrender meeting, not merely from those who cast their ballots. The panel determined that this calculation must include individuals who attended the meeting but who abstained from voting and that "abstentions must be counted to determine the quorum."[32] Focusing on perceived uncertainties regarding the identities of two abstainers, the panel decided that "on the balance of probabilities, we find that there were not 29 but at least 30 eligible voters in attendance at the surrender meeting on January 29, 1907."[33] Fifteen people had voted in favour of the surrender. This finding, the fact that only fifteen eligible voters had supported the surrender, and the "beliefs of the elders who gave evidence at the community session to the effect that a valid majority vote was not attained" led the panel to conclude that the surrender was invalid.[34] It recommended that Canada accept the Cowessess claim for negotiation. Canada rejected that recommendation on March 27, 2002.[35]

The second phase of the Cowessess inquiry got under way less than a year later. I have no knowledge of the phase I deliberations, but I sat on the panel for phase II. We relied heavily on the history completed for phase I and, at the request of the claimant, did not hold a community session.

Instead, phase II consisted of the review and deliberations of the parties' written legal arguments. At issue were the nature of Canada's pre-surrender fiduciary obligation to the Cowessess First Nation and whether it had breached that obligation. If the answer was yes, the Crown would have an outstanding lawful obligation to the First Nation regarding the 1907 surrender.[36]

At the time of our deliberations, the most relevant legal authority on the Crown's fiduciary obligations to Aboriginal people was the 1995 Supreme Court decision in *Blueberry River Indian Band v. Canada*,[37] also known as *Apsassin*. This provided a test for determining whether a pre-surrender fiduciary duty had been breached. The test turned on four points: whether the band had adequately understood the surrender; whether the Crown's conduct had so tainted the dealings that relying on the band's understanding and intention was unsafe; whether the band had ceded its decision authority to the Crown; and whether the decision was so foolish or improvident as to amount to exploitation.[38] Not surprisingly, our deliberations soon became difficult and prolonged.

Although our deliberations were necessarily affected by the findings of phase I, a majority of the panel refused to be bound by them, myself included. In our view, and with all due respect, the evidence supporting a finding of questionable Crown dealings seemed dangerously slim and in contradiction to the abundant historical record. This clearly established the competence of the Cowessess people, both in assessing and acting upon their own best interests; they were strong and successful farmers who initially refused surrender and whose wishes appear to have been consistently respected by the Crown. When the surrender issue was raised in 1906 and 1907, the community appreciated the importance of the southern haylands and any advantages or disadvantages that could result from giving them up. On the sum total of the evidence, we simply could not find that the band misunderstood the surrender or its implications – Chief LeRat, who was capable and competent, stated that the surrender had been well explained and that the band had a good understanding of it. The Crown may have initiated the final discussions that led to the surrender, but that in itself did not equate with tainted dealings. Nor did the provision of a down payment upon a vote favouring surrender. Successful farmers and ranchers, the Cowessess people were neither vulnerable nor dependent and were perfectly capable of determining what was in their best interest. They made their own decision, based on the knowledge that the loss of the haylands would not diminish their long-term prosperity, and in fact, the record indicates that it had no such ill effects. The Cowessess First Nation surrendered poor land, kept the best for themselves, continued to flourish, and never once in the years following the surrender complained to the Crown regarding it or its consequences, if any.[39]

Although we felt that Canada had passed the *Apsassin* test and had discharged its fiduciary obligations to the Cowessess people in its management of the 1907 surrender, a minority of the panel disagreed, supported by legal counsel. In their dissenting reasons, they relied on the phase I findings that the surrender vote was invalid, arguing that this rendered the question of Crown assent to the surrender "hypothetical." In their opinion, the Crown should have known that parting with the land was "improvident." Although admitting that the band gave up less than half of its reserve, the minority stated that this affected the "agricultural potential and economic future of the Cowessess Band because it was almost 95 percent of the Band's slough hay acres and almost 75 percent of its arable land."[40] These numbers may have been accurate, but there was nothing to indicate that the surrender had adversely affected the Cowessess, a fact that the minority did not address.

In many respects, the crux of these disagreements lay in two matters – the ability of the Cowessess and their leaders, notably Chief LeRat, to understand the surrender and their own best interests, and the nature of the Crown's fiduciary duty to the band. On the former matter, we firmly believed that the Cowessess people and their leaders were entirely qualified to reach their own decisions. They were highly successful farmers and ranchers, and though they may have differed among themselves regarding the fate of the lands in question, they had a right to resolve the issue on their own, without interference from the Crown or anyone else. Certainly, the Crown had duties to ensure that the First Nation understood the terms and implications of the surrender, but once these were met, the band's right to choose had to be respected. The evidence indicated that the Crown did meet its duties and that the Cowessess people made their choice based on knowledge of both the deal and their own best interests.

Although the vote to surrender had passed by a slim margin, nothing gave the appearance that it had been tainted by either the community or the Crown's representatives. Given this, refusing to countenance the surrender would have been high-handed on the part of the Crown. And the fact that no complaints or downturn in the community's agricultural prowess occurred in the wake of the surrender indicates that the Cowessess Band made the best decision in the circumstances, and Canada seems to have respected that fact. Quite simply, the majority believed that the Cowessess people and their leadership were competent to make their own decisions and thus required the Crown's respect more than its protection. In our view, the right of the Cowessess First Nation to be an equal partner in the decision to dispose of the land and the resulting process was unquestioned.

Although much of our deliberation regarding the Crown's fiduciary obligation coalesced around *Apsassin*, the *Wewaykum* decision also resonated. The minority felt that "the Crown had no duty to act on behalf of the local settler population" but had done just that when "new officials and politicians had become involved" and discussion of the band's best interests allegedly ceased.[41] We agreed that the Crown did not have a duty to *act on behalf* of non-Aboriginal interests, but it could not entirely ignore those interests. As *Wewaykum* confirmed, the Crown "can be no ordinary fiduciary; it wears many hats and represents many interests, some of which cannot help but be conflicting."[42] The challenge for the Crown is to manage these conflicts while also respecting its unique relationship with First Nations and the obligations that flow from it. From 1886 through to 1906, the department had clearly respected the Cowessess Band's resistance to the surrender, and nothing shows that it failed in its legal obligations to the band after 1906, when the Cowessess people appeared open to the option of surrender. Furthermore, presenting the possibility of surrender to the band hardly constitutes acting "on behalf" of settler interests, especially as the subject was fully explained and understood by the First Nation, which was then given a week to consider and vote on the matter. In 1907, as with all previous settler requests for a surrender, the Crown respected its obligations to the newcomers when it posed the question to the Cowessess Band. And when it accepted the band's decision, it fulfilled its duty to the First Nation. Thus, it respected the many conflicting interests that animated the question of a surrender while still meeting its fiduciary duties to the First Nation.

In Cowessess, as in some of the inquiries discussed here, our deliberations were amicable and courteous, but they could be trying, frustrating, and difficult. I had expected that there would be heated moments and colourful debates among the commissioners. What I had not foreseen was the degree to which deliberations could be complicated and drawn out by individuals who were not commissioners and who had no power to decide the issues or shape the findings. Too often, I felt pressured by our legal counsel to accept a position with which I disagreed. Certainly, the job of counsel was to provide a full briefing of the relevant law, and they were entitled to share their views of a legally proper outcome when asked to do so, but the ultimate decision lay with the commissioners. Most of our counsel accepted this fact, but some appeared to feel that their role was to convince or even coerce commissioners regarding outcomes. Such was the case with Cowessess and Lower Similkameen in particular, where the deliberations were unnecessarily and inappropriately prolonged and complicated by counsel. No doubt, they believed that their position was the correct one, but they seemed to forget that the power to decide rested with the commissioners alone.

The fraught nature of some of our inquiries and deliberations also speaks to a conundrum at the heart of the specific claims policy and the inquiries themselves. The policy was grounded in the law, and Canada's approach to claims was clearly one in which legal obligations, as opposed to moral or ethical ones, ruled the day. We quickly learned that the Crown was unlikely to hold to anything other than legal obligations – and not always those, as evidenced by its negative responses to our recommendations that it accept and negotiate rejected claims. We ourselves were tasked with overseeing the implementation of the policy, and we had the power to conduct inquiries as a form of second sober thought that could aid in resolving claims. Our role was to *facilitate the resolution of claims*. To many of us, this was a matter of justice, not law, and though our deliberations were invariably guided by legal considerations, we were also prepared to move beyond lawful obligations if the facts warranted. Claims may be largely legal matters, but they also involve questions of justice. To me, the fact that the ICC was composed of both lawyers and others, and of Indigenous and non-Indigenous commissioners, was intended to inject a broader set of experiences and interests into its work. Most of us brought non-legal skills into our deliberations, and this knowledge and experience often ensured that the force of justice was not sacrificed under the weight of law. Although I cannot speak for my fellow commissioners, I can say that my work at the ICC was defined by the need to balance law and justice. Where law seemed to resist justice, the challenge was to find a way of bringing them into balance, thereby moving the relationship between First Nations and Canada one step closer to wellness.

The deliberation phase of an inquiry also entailed reviewing the various drafts of the final report. Commissioners had a direct hand in . the drafts, but the finished product was usually the result of collaboration between the panel and legal counsel. Once the report was finalized, it was sent to the chief of the claimant band, the Indian Affairs and Justice ministers, and the attorney general of Canada. Very occasionally, the First Nation replied to it, and as mentioned above, Canada's reactions were mixed, inconsistent, and, in the last few years of the commission, largely non-existent.

Alternative Approaches: The Mediation Unit

Our empowering Order in Council set out a mediation mandate for the commission, whereby we were to "provide or arrange, at the request of the parties, such mediation services as may in their opinion assist the Government of Canada and an Indian Band to reach an agreement in respect of any matter relating to an Indian specific claim."[43] Within this mandate, our Mediation Unit provided a variety of services. These included mediation and facilitation of claims negotiations, co-ordinating expert reports to assist in claims resolution, overseeing and supporting meetings of the parties, and acting as the "record keeper for the negotiations."[44]

The Mediation Unit supported fourteen claims to a successful resolution.[45] Only in two cases was it unable to assist the parties to resolve the claim.[46] The unit also supported a number of pilot projects that brought a claimant together with Canada at a single table to discuss all outstanding specific claims. This was a unique collaborative approach, whereby the parties dealt with claims co-operatively and with the oversight and support of ICC mediators. It was applied to three claims, which involved the Michipicoten, Fort William, and Cote First Nations.

The Michipicoten had two claims under review in 1996, when their chief contacted the Indian Affairs minister, seeking a different approach to the researching and review of the claims. The chief envisaged a more collaborative strategy and hoped to apply this not only to the two claims then in review, but to the eleven other claims that the First Nation expected to submit. The minister proved amenable, and both Canada and the Michipicoten asked the ICC to assist their efforts by facilitating their collaboration. The ICC agreed to do so and worked with the parties for eleven years to research, review, and settle six claims and thirteen grievances, leading to a settlement of $64 million, the addition of 3,000 acres of Crown land to the Michipicoten reserve, and the authorization to acquire a further 5,400 acres.[47] Efforts to resolve the Cote and the Fort William claims were less successful. The Cote project was initiated in 1997 and was not completed when the commission closed its Mediation Unit on December 1, 2008.[48] The Fort William pilot project began in 1998 and led to the acceptance for negotiation of three of the band's eight claims, including one that was resolved in 2006. The remainder were still outstanding when the unit closed its doors.[49]

By all indications, the Mediation Unit was remarkably successful in its work, most of which was completed by its staff. Although commissioners received extensive mediation training, and some of us were proficient in that skillset, we had virtually no involvement with the mediation function of the ICC. This struck me as odd. We had been trained in mediation to provide this service to Canada and claimants, and we repeatedly discussed the potential role that we could, and should, play in mediating and facilitating claims negotiations and disputes. We were never able to take up this role, however, as we encountered substantial resistance from a number of senior staffers in a range of ICC departments, including the Mediation Unit itself.

The reluctance to involve commissioners in mediation was very much caught up in concerns about preserving our independence and neutrality, a theme that became a defining and quite constraining aspect of our work. Essentially, the concern was that a conflict of interest could arise if a commissioner sat on a panel and acted as a mediator for the same claim or on claims involving a single community. As both commissioners and staff understood the importance of impartiality and avoiding conflicts of interest, it seemed to me quite unlikely that such an overlap would ever occur. There was no question that a commissioner might sit on a panel and mediate on the same claim or on any matter involving the claimant. Neither commissioners nor staff would permit this to occur, and yet we were consistently barred from using our mediation skills to actually mediate.

This situation was made all the more curious by the emergence of reports of Canada's views regarding ICC involvement in mediation. During an ICC meeting of April 2003, a senior source within the Mediation Unit cautioned the commissioners that Canada had misgivings about accepting the ICC as a mediator between the Crown and First Nations. Canada, the source explained, had little experience with mediation, and its track record had made it leery of the process. The staffer was unable to provide commissioners with any direct evidence of Canada's reluctance, speaking cryptically of government fears that mediation may give the commission too much influence over the process. The implication, however, was clear: if Canada was hesitant about mediation under the current approach, we risked a full withdrawal from the process if commissioners were to become involved in mediation.[50]

It was deeply difficult to secure clear information about activities within the Mediation Unit, which made it hard to assess internal reports of Canada's hesitation. However, expressed concerns about the government's fear of losing control over the process may have had more to do with fears of bias. Though it is impossible to be certain, the fact that a single person from the Mediation Unit chaired all the planning conferences that mapped out mediations and determined the issues central to each mediation may well have aroused concern on the part of Canada. If it were concerned about bias in only one of these conferences, the fact that the same person chaired all of them may have affected its view of mediation generally. If Canada's concerns about mediation partially arose from the control exerted by a single member of the Mediation Unit, the decision to exclude commissioners seems even more strange. Setting aside the fairness of burdening just one staffer with the responsibility for chairing all the

planning conferences, bringing commissioners into even the early phase
of the process might have alleviated Canada's uneasiness about the monopoly control of a single individual. Of course, this person had a responsibility to be neutral, both as a staffer and as a mediator. However, the
scrupulous attention paid to ensuring commissioner neutrality might have
assuaged some of Canada's fears. One wonders how the government would
have responded if commissioners had chaired planning conferences or
acted as mediators. As it is, we will never know, since they were generally
barred from both roles during my time with the ICC.

This exclusion was reinforced by the Mediation Unit's unwillingness
to reveal its inner workings to the commission. For most of my time with
the ICC, the unit remained largely a mystery to me. Reports on its active
files that were given at our regular meetings contained little to no information, and the oral presentations that were intended to expand on the
sparse written reports typically failed to achieve this to any significant
degree. That we knew so little about the unit's activities struck me as problematic. Although the unit seemed to have good success in mediation,
most of its successes were exceedingly slow to come, and from one year to
the next seemed to gain little traction in the direction of resolution or an
agreement.

Although admittedly we knew little about the unit, it seemed to have
no timeline that might introduce discipline into the process and no logical
progression through the expected phases of mediation. Rather, the unit's
role seemed largely to provide the support services that enabled Canada
and claimants to discuss the conflict or claim at hand. Perhaps the unit
did aid in facilitating these discussions, but its reports often indicated that
it concentrated primarily on co-ordinating meetings and managing and
paying for research and studies requested by the parties. All of this was
obviously helpful, and if the unit's success rates were anything to go by, it
led to positive mediations. The challenge at the time, however, was that we
had no real sense that progress was being made. In retrospect, it appears
that the range for the completion of mediations ran from as few as two
years to as many as eleven. The Kahkewistahaw mediation/facilitation
(the report in the *Indian Claims Commission Proceedings* uses both terms)
required four years from the "beginning of substantive negotiations" to
ratification of an agreement.[51] The Fishing Lake mediation took five years

to reach resolution.[52] As mentioned above, the Cote and Fishing Lake pilot projects did not succeed despite more than six years of ICC support, co-ordination, and facilitation. Admittedly, a range of factors could slow the pace, some of which were beyond the control of the mediators. However, my concern is not that the mediations took too long, but that we simply never had a firm grasp of what was transpiring in the unit or how mediations were progressing. To a unit that was determined to keep its distance from us, withholding information may have seemed appropriate, but we were accountable for the ICC's activities and thus had a right to receive clear, systematic, and sufficient information to understand how mediations were unfolding. Regrettably, in my seven years as a commissioner, I never once had any sense of those things.

To some extent, our concerns on this front were overshadowed by the arrival of Bill C-6 in 2002, which heralded the demise of the ICC and the rise of the Specific Claims Tribunal. As will be seen, this development initially consumed a significant amount of our time and energy but soon took second place as we struggled to complete inquiries before our formal closure in March of 2009.

7

Beyond Lawful Obligation
The Closure of the ICC and the Rise
of the Specific Claims Tribunal

The choice is clear. Justice, respect, honour. Oka. Ipperwash.
Caledonia. Canada is a great nation in the world but Canada
will only achieve true greatness when it has fulfilled its legal
obligations to First Nations.

– CANADA, "NEGOTIATION OR CONFRONTATION: IT'S CANADA'S CHOICE"

In 1948, a special joint committee of the Senate and House of Commons
recommended the immediate creation of a "claims commission" that would
be responsible for assessing and settling "in a just and equitable manner
any claims or grievances" of First Nations against the Crown.[1] The committee made this recommendation a full three years before amendments
to the Indian Act permitted First Nations to raise funds or retain legal
counsel to pursue their claims. The recommendation is portentous, but it
also reflects the deep perversity of Canada's approach to claims. Today,
more than half a century after the act was amended, Canada's approach to
its outstanding obligations to Indigenous nations and communities is still
conflicted. Successive ministers of Indian, then Aboriginal, and now
Indigenous Affairs have fiddled with the edges of a specific claims policy
whose core principles and approach have remained virtually unchanged
since 1973.[2] And like the rebranding of Indian Affairs, the tinkering with
policy appears neither to have altered the approach of the Specific Claims
Branch (SCB) nor to have encouraged greater justice or fairness.

A short-lived commission surfaced briefly in 1969 under Lloyd Barber, only to dissolve about eight years later, leaving a limited impact on the claims landscape. Repeated calls from Aboriginal people, their allies, and other stakeholders for the creation of a truly independent claims resolution body were ignored until the 1990 Oka Crisis highlighted the failings of the claims policy. Unable to shrug off the violence and loss of life at Kahnesatake, Ottawa created the Indian Claims Commission (ICC). Although the ICC was permitted to define its own processes within a relatively robust mandate, Canada was typically judicious in policing its own interests: the commission could review rejected claims and oversee the implementation of the policy, but it had no binding authority. It was limited to making recommendations, which prompted some observers to dismiss it as "a toothless tiger [that] cannot enforce or bind its decisions on any of the parties, especially the Crown."[3]

Calls persisted for the creation of an independent body that *could* bind the parties. They were endorsed by the 1996 final report of the Royal Commission on Aboriginal Peoples and in the reports of two successive joint working groups in 1992 and 1996, comprised of representatives from the Assembly of First Nations (AFN) and Canada.[4] Six years later, Ottawa finally acted, introducing Bill C-6, the Specific Claims Resolution Act, in 2002. The bill received Royal Assent on November 7, 2003, but was so reviled by Aboriginal people and their allies that it was never proclaimed into effect. Its initial effort abandoned, Canada persisted, and on November 27, 2007, handed down Bill C-30, the Specific Claims Tribunal Act. This achieved better traction; it received Royal Assent in June 2008 and was proclaimed into force on October 17, 2008. Although it failed to alter the 1973 specific claims policy in any meaningful regard, it nonetheless fundamentally changed the claims landscape in Canada in at least two ways: it signalled the demise of the ICC and the rise of an independent, quasi-judicial body for the resolution of claims – namely, the Specific Claims Tribunal.

Sophistry in Specific Claims: The Rise and Fall of Bill C-6

The claim of the Kahnesatake Mohawks regarding their land at the Pines was rejected in 1986, setting in motion a series of events that would ignite the Oka Crisis and national Indigenous protests over land rights and claims throughout the summer of 1990. The state's response consisted primarily of creating the Indian Claims Commission and striking joint working groups with the AFN.[5] The ICC was to be an interim measure that would attend to some of the policy's deficiencies, whereas the working groups studied it with a view to crafting a viable alternative. Probably no one anticipated how long this journey would be: even limited policy change required nearly eighteen years of research, recommendations and ensuing debate, and more research and recommendations. The path to the tribunal began with the efforts of the joint working groups.

When the first AFN-Canada Joint Working Group was struck in 1992, it was given just one year to complete its review of the specific claims policy. This rather unrealistic deadline expired before the parties could achieve consensus on many of the issues under study save one: like many other committees, stakeholders, and their reports beforehand, the working group agreed on the need for an *independent claims body* to implement an *independent* claims process.[6]

The review process was resumed in 1996, with the creation of the Joint First Nations–Canada Task Force (JTF), which consisted of the AFN Chiefs Committee on Claims and its advisors, as well as officials from Indian Affairs and Justice. The group faced "many difficult legal, political and financial questions," only some of which could be addressed by those at the table. Conspicuous by their absence were any federal bureaucrats who could speak to the funding issues that had dogged the implementation and effectiveness of the specific claims policy.[7]

The JTF published its findings in a 1998 report.[8] This focused on a series of key challenges, including the inherent conflict of interest in the claims policy and the government's approach to the funding and compensation that flowed from claims. To many Indigenous groups and their allies, the SCB approach reflected a fundamental disconnect between First Nations and the Crown regarding the substance and obligations implicit in claims. To them, the wrongdoing and errors that had given rise to most claims comprised both moral and monetary debts that were best seen as a product of Canadian nation building. They should have been respected and treated as a portion of the "national debt." Canada viewed claims quite differently.

As evidenced by the behaviour of Indian and Northern Affairs Canada (INAC) and the SCB, it appeared to cast claims as just another government program for which a budget existed and compensation was simply part of "program spending."[9] This basic incongruity was one of many such conflicts rooted in very different understandings of claims and how best to rectify them, all of which fed into a single overriding tension: how much would it cost for Canada to repay its many debts to First Nations?

In 2006, "the outstanding contingent liability" was estimated to be a "minimum of $6 billion dollars,"[10] and the cost of unresolved claims continues to rise almost daily as Canada demurs and equivocates. Given the magnitude of the bill, Canada's need to exert control is as understandable as it is counterproductive. But dancing around a debt hardly makes it go away. In the realm of specific claims, it has simply compounded the economic and social costs. And though the size of the debt is frightening, so too are its legacies for Indigenous people. As the Senate Standing Committee on Aboriginal Peoples points out, there is no debate about the "direct connection between alleged federal wrongdoing in the past, including Canada's failure to live up to the promise in the Constitution of honouring Aboriginal and treaty rights, and First Nations' poverty, unemployment, and substance abuse today."[11]

There is no question that Canada's historic approach to treaties, surrenders, and the management of Indigenous lands and resources is directly responsible for the poverty and hopelessness that have encouraged Indigenous underdevelopment and undermined Indigenous success at virtually every turn. As Indigenous leaders and their allies have argued many times, the resolution of specific claims is not only about turning the page on an unedifying history; it is also about the payment of a debt that will permit First Nations to return to prosperity.

Canada's anxieties regarding cost were on clear display in the JTF talks of 1992, and shaping the fiscal framework for claims resolution proved the most contentious aspect of the JTF's work. In the end, the AFN agreed to a fiscal framework for claims consisting of a "budgetary allocation of settlement funds over the initial five year period" of the new tribunal's life. If the allocated funds were exhausted before the five years concluded, this "would trigger a pause in the Tribunal caseload until the next budgetary allocation is determined."[12] And if the framework did become part of a new claims policy, the budgetary allocation would be reviewed and renewed every five years.

The AFN's compromise on the fiscal framework was an important concession, as it was leery of setting financial caps on claims settlements. Indeed, its membership had mandated it to avoid caps. In the words of the JTF,

> It was with great difficulty that the Task Force managed to reach agreement on a fiscal framework that would not prejudice or exclude claims. The Task Force firmly believes that its proposal will provide the best means by which to settle claims. It is important to begin addressing these outstanding matters in a significant way, as the costs for First Nations and Canada can only rise with further delay. The costs of not settling these matters in a fair and timely fashion will be far greater.[13]

Although agreement on a claims compensation structure was fraught and hard-won, the JTF managed to reach some consensus on a number of other key issues, all of which were evident in its proposed model for a new approach to claims.[14] Cutting across these issues and central to the JTF's suggested framework was the conflict of interest in the claims policy. The JTF understood that resolving this conflict was vital to the credibility and viability of the new approach, especially for First Nations, and it envisaged a process that would operate almost entirely at arm's length from the Crown.

The new approach would transfer responsibility for claims policy implementation from the SCB to an expanded First Nations Specific Claims Commission (FNSCC). It would also create a Specific Claims Tribunal to resolve legal disputes that could not be resolved by the commission.[15] The tribunal would be a fully independent quasi-judicial body and would have the power to rule on the validity of claims, the compensation criteria to be used in negotiating reparations for accepted claims, and on compensation awards themselves. Importantly, it would also consider the role and responsibility of provincial governments in the events leading to a claim and could adjust Crown liability accordingly.[16]

The FNSCC was to consist of a full-time chief commissioner and between three and five commissioners, who could be either full- or part-time;

the tribunal would include a chief adjudicator, an associate adjudicator, and an unspecified number of "other members."[17] Appointments to both bodies were to ensure regional representation from across Canada and would be made through a joint process in which both the AFN and the Indian Affairs minister chose all candidates. Those who were selected would join the FNSCC or tribunal as Governor in Council appointments and would stay in their positions for no more than five years at the pleasure of the governor. They could be removed for cause only, upon the recommendation of the AFN and the minister.

This approach to appointments was integral to ensuring the perceived independence of both the FNSCC and the tribunal, and of the claims policy and processes they were to oversee. Although not everyone would agree that the AFN was capable of representing all Indigenous people and interests, injecting Canada's largest Indigenous political organization into the appointments process added a measure of balance that had been conspicuously absent to date. For example, though the ICC had both Indigenous and non-Indigenous members and a predominantly Aboriginal staff, its commissioners received their Governor in Council appointments through nominations by government and, in my case, through the Prime Minister's Office. The background and experiences of prospective commissioners were always scrutinized, but Indigenous organizations had no direct involvement in their nomination. In its early years, the ICC had equal numbers of Indigenous and non-Indigenous commissioners, but this equilibrium shifted over time. During its last decade, and especially after the passage of Bill C-6 signalled its imminent closure, most of the five commissioners were non-Indigenous, which was probably not lost on the claimants who became involved with our processes. All commissioners worked assiduously to be unbiased, balanced, and independent, but the appearance of impartiality was not enhanced by the appearance of either most commissioners or the one-sided process that selected them. Although the FNSCC and the tribunal could potentially have both Indigenous and non-Indigenous commissioners and decision-makers, their presumed neutrality would be enhanced by the involvement of both the AFN and the minister in the appointments process.

Whereas the tribunal was to be the arbiter of issues that eluded resolution through negotiations, the FNSCC would operate as a fully independent and neutral third party, separate from both government and First Nations. It would receive claims submissions and would provide oversight and support of negotiations regarding accepted claims. To this end, it would offer mediation, facilitation, and arbitration services, and would manage and disperse funding to support research and preparation of claims, a task previously under the authority of the SCB.[18] Like the ICC, the FNSCC would structure the claims process, which the JTF foresaw as retaining planning conferences and community sessions. It would also coordinate the necessary research and training to assist in resolving outstanding claims.[19]

Within those processes, the FNSCC would receive claim submissions based on a revised understanding of the specific claims policy. As visualized by the JTF, the new policy moved beyond the narrow approach enshrined in *Outstanding Business*. In this 1982 policy statement, as discussed in Chapter 2, claims were limited to the non-fulfillment of a treaty or agreement, breaches of obligations arising from the Indian Act or other statutes, government administration of Indian funds or other assets, or an illegal disposition of Indian land.[20] Under the new policy, claims could arise from

a) a breach by, or non-fulfillment on the part of, the Crown of a legal obligation, including a fiduciary obligation, that arises from a treaty, under any law of Canada pertaining to Indians or lands reserved for Indians, from a unilateral undertaking or under an agreement between a band and the Crown;

b) a breach by the Crown of a legal obligation, including a fiduciary obligation, that arises out of the Crown's administration of Indian moneys or other assets;

c) failure to provide compensation for reserve lands taken by the Crown or any of its agencies under legal authority, and

d) fraud by employees or agents of the Crown in connection with the acquisition or disposition of reserve lands.[21]

The JTF's proposed policy significantly revised claims liabilities as expressed in *Outstanding Business*. It expanded the focus on "non-fulfillment of a treaty or agreement" to include a much larger range of lawful obligations and, most importantly, non-fulfillment of Crown fiduciary obligations.

Equally vital was the inclusion of a number of actions and inactions previously characterized as "beyond lawful obligation." Among these were the
Crown's failure to provide compensation for lands that it or its agencies
had taken or damaged, or for clearly demonstrated acts of fraud by Crown
officials in their dealings with Indigenous people.[22]

Ottawa released a proposal for a revamped claims policy in May 2000,
which retained some elements of the JTF model but also revealed much
disagreement with the AFN on the shape of the policy.[23] For example, it
did not include sharing power with the AFN regarding appointments, and
it took advantage of the concessions made by the AFN on the fiscal framework of the JTF proposal by placing a $5 million cap on tribunal awards.[24]
In the fall of 2001, Canada took its policy on the road to present information on the new independent claims body pictured in the federal plan.
Those consultations revealed widespread dissatisfaction with this latest version of the policy, including serious concerns about the cap and an almost
complete failure to respect the work of the JTF in any other than the least
consequential ways. In the wake of the consultations, Bill C-6, the Specific
Claims Resolution Act, was introduced in the House of Commons.

Review of the bill revealed not only the lack of respect for the views
expressed by Indigenous stakeholders, but also a series of new measures
that were unlikely to achieve anything other than simply entrenching the
worst elements of the status quo. For example, its grounds for claims were
based on *Outstanding Business,* and the JTF's inclusion of the fiduciary,
through claims arising from specific treaty provisions, would be limited
to "land and assets." Reasons for this shift were unclear, though the intent
was probably to protect the government from any future claims that were
not related to treaty land or assets.[25] The bill also retained the basic structure
of a commission and tribunal composed of Governor in Council appointees, but it denied the AFN any input into their selection and eschewed
any attention to regional representation in either body. Claimants would
be permitted to make representation regarding appointments, but there
was nothing in the bill requiring the minister to respond or to revise the
appointments.[26]

Overseen by a chief executive officer, the commission and tribunal
were to be housed in a Canadian Centre for the Independent Resolution
of First Nations Specific Claims.[27] The CEO, who could also sit as the chief

commissioner of the commission, would "supervise and direct the Centre's work and staff."[28] Under Bill C-6, the commission was the location of efforts to resolve claims by negotiation, and commissioners would oversee the provision of funding to support claims research and development. Although these duties remained true to the JTF vision, little else about the commission did so. For example, there was no mention of the use of planning conferences or the community sessions historically valued by the parties. The bill did refer to "preparatory meetings," but there was little to indicate that these would be modelled on the ICC planning conferences, which, though imperfect, were integral to setting the tone and structure of inquiries. The conferences, like the community sessions, reflected the ICC focus on facilitating face-to-face communication between the parties; the community session in particular was designed not only to enhance communication, but also to balance the process by ensuring that neither party consistently enjoyed the home field advantage. Taking the inquiry to the community and the orals to a nearby town broke the long-established practice of requiring claimants to come to Ottawa and thus undermined one of the more obvious manifestations of the conflict of interest. It also ensured that elders, some of whom were too frail to travel, could be heard in the relative comfort of their own community. Claimants often stressed the value of the sessions, and Canada commonly benefitted as well, acquiring important additional knowledge through elder testimony and visits to the claim site. That this would now be discarded was unfortunate, and it suggested a return to the old practice of requiring First Nations to come to Ottawa, cap in hand, to present their claims.

The commission also lost the role of reviewing conflicts over the validity of claims. Along with compensation, this became a matter for the tribunal, should the commission prove unable to resolve it. In such cases, upon request from the First Nation, the commission could refer the claim to the tribunal, which would have the power to decide it. Though this option does not initially appear problematic, deeper scrutiny reveals at least one large devil in the details, especially with regard to validity. According to clause 32(1) of the bill, the claim would be forwarded to the tribunal if it met a series of criteria.[29] The submission must be complete and must have been reviewed by the minister, and all efforts at dispute resolution must have been exhausted. These requirements were harmless enough, but the fourth and final hurdle promised to be insurmountable for many claimants: they would be compelled to waive any compensation in excess of the bill's stated threshold of $7 million.[30] The Senate would later recommend raising this limit to $10 million, but the boost did not fundamentally alter the unfairness or arbitrariness of the cap.

By 2002, the ICC had inquired into roughly 120 claims, only 3 of which involved compensation amounts that would fall under the $7 million cap.[31] Given that claims often ask for compensation well in excess of even $10 million, the tribunal was likely to prove unviable for many claimants, who would be left with no recourse other than going to court. As some commentators noted, this rendered the process proposed in Bill C-6 even worse than the previous one, which at least included the independent review process offered by the Indian Claims Commission.[32] Should Bill C-6 become law, the cap would force many claimants to jump from the commission to the courts – precisely the outcome the policy was putatively intended to avoid.

Bill C-6 also appeared to encourage greater accountability on the part of the minister for delay in the claims process, but this too did not hold up to serious scrutiny. Although the bill did not prescribe time limits on the review and decision process, it did require the minister to produce regular status reports on claims every six months, estimate a date for decision, and justify delays.[33] This clause was interesting in at least two respects. First, nowhere did the bill make provision for the injection of greater resources into the process. As a result, the number of legal counsel assigned to claims would not be increased, and the SCB personnel or processes to expedite claims review would not be expanded. If, as many commentators believe, much of the claims backlog is due to chronic underfunding of the resolution processes, the bill would arguably achieve nothing more than furnishing a better picture of the snail's pace. Furthermore, as no consequences would arise from the minister's reports, it is unclear what this accountability was intended to accomplish other than creating the appearance that something was being done – even if that something was no more than tracking and explaining delays every six months or so.[34]

The apprehension that Bill C-6 had no intention of doing anything other than institutionalizing delay was heightened by its statement that "no passage of time in relation to the decision on whether to negotiate a claim may be considered as constituting a decision not to negotiate the claim."[35] This clause appears to be a direct response to the ICC's constructive rejection policy, discussed in Chapter 4, in which unreasonable delay was a key factor in accepting claims that had not yet been formally rejected. The creation of a statutory bar to exclude delay as a ground for constructive rejection would further constrain the ability of claimants to hold Canada to account for the mismanagement endemic to the SCB and the claims policy generally.

On all fronts, Bill C-6 utterly failed to eradicate the flaws of the claims process. The removal of delay and mismanagement as grounds for constructive rejection, combined with the failure to allocate much needed additional funds to resolution, did not inspire confidence that the government had any real intention of addressing either delay or the backlog. As discussed in the preface to this book, the situation remains virtually unchanged to this day.

From the first moments of my appointment to the ICC, Bill C-6 consumed a remarkable amount of our time and energy at meetings. Chief Commissioner Phil Fontaine, who had served as grand chief of the AFN prior to taking up his role at the ICC, knew only too well the implications of the bill not only for claimants and the process, but also for the incremental improvements the ICC had introduced. Its proposed reforms promised to set back claims resolution, institutionalize poor practices at the SCB, and pave the way to court for claimants. Because we were a neutral body, our contribution to the debate on Bill C-6 was necessarily limited. At the same time, our mandate tasked us with overseeing the implementation of claims policy, and by all indications Bill C-6 was poised to worsen, rather than improve, the situation. After considerable discussion about the bill and its implications, Phil Fontaine met with the minister of Indian Affairs' liaison, INAC staffers who had worked on the bill, and representatives from the AFN, who had tabled no fewer than sixty-seven objections to it.[36] These consultations, combined with our own research and informed by our long history of dealing with claims, crystallized in a number of concerns that we communicated to Parliament on November 26, 2002, through the House Standing Committee on Aboriginal Affairs, Northern Development and Natural Resources.

As we informed the committee, we had no fewer than eight reservations about Bill C-6 and its approach to claims resolution. First and foremost was the proposed tribunal. Although we saw the creation of an independent tribunal with decision-making power as a positive development, there was much in the bill to reduce that independence. Particularly notable were the lack of consultation between Indigenous leadership and Canada regarding appointments to the tribunal and the commission, and the minister's continued control of the claims process. As Phil Fontaine explained,

> It is our view that to be independent a body must be self-governing and not dependent on an outside body, such as the department or minister, for its validity. In the context of the claims body, independence also means impartiality, neutrality, procedural fairness, and objectivity. We believe that if the new centre envisaged by this bill is to have any hope of success, it is vital that the principle of independence and its related concepts must exist in fact and be perceived to exist by the parties involved and by the public. This perception would be greatly enhanced if there were a consultative process involving representatives of First Nations for the appointments to the commission and the tribunal. We are also concerned that the centre's independence is compromised by its lack of authority to compel the involved parties to act ... We know from our own experience how frustrating it can be when one party or the other can impede the process by delays or other unreasonable barriers. There are provisions in the bill that empower the minister to control when and if the commission or tribunal may act. These take away the ability of the centre to control its own process.[37]

The ICC was also deeply troubled about the cap and its implications for access to justice on the part of the claimants:

> First Nations must have reasonable access to the process in order to ensure justice is both done and seen to be done. The gathering of oral evidence and the provision of the necessary funding are important to the First Nations participation in the process. We are concerned that limitations to the tribunal, especially the financial cap on the tribunal and the unknown prescribed limits to the necessary funding, are among

a number of aspects of the new legislation that may seriously interfere with the access to justice principle.[38]

These points were reiterated in a subsequent ICC presentation before the standing committee on June 11, 2003.

Despite the concerns expressed by the ICC and a remarkable number of Indigenous and non-Indigenous stakeholders and their allies both before the House and beyond, Bill C-6 moved quickly through the legislative process to become the Specific Claims Resolution Act (SCRA) on November 7, 2003, when it received Royal Assent.[39] The government's decision to damn the torpedoes did it little good in the long run. Rather than abandoning the fight against the SCRA once it became law, claimants and their allies persisted with their protests against the approach to claims. Roughly two years after the bill became law, Minister of Indian Affairs Andy Scott announced that it would not be implemented.[40] The shelving of the SCRA was greeted with relief and pride by the new chief of the AFN, former ICC chief commissioner Phil Fontaine:

> This decision is a victory for First Nations. It is a direct result of lobbying efforts by the Assembly of First Nations, many of our allied First Nation organizations and citizens like you. This about-face has come after the Minister, in consultation with Cabinet, had considered the submissions made by the AFN regarding the aspects of the legislation that required amendment. We made recommendations regarding policy, regulatory and administrative changes that could strengthen an amended SCRA. Minister Scott has refused to bring the SCRA into force with the AFN's endorsement. We are pleased to see that the Minister has proven once again to be a man of his word and of conscience when it comes to First Nations issues, and hope that he will continue to be an ally in our quest for self-determination and improved quality of life.[41]

Canada returned, once again, to the specific claims drawing board.

Bill C-30, the Specific Claims Tribunal, and the End of the ICC

The closure of Parliament in November 2005 cut short the review of claims policy by the House committee, which was in turn picked up by the Senate

Standing Committee on Aboriginal Peoples. Over the course of that study, the committee received extensive accounts of the frustration and despair of claimants and commentators over the intractable and endemic unfairness, under-resourcing, delays, and backlog in the claims process – none of which was likely to be corrected by the SCRA. The committee wove this testimony and research into a compelling and important condemnation of the approach to claims. The process, its report stated, was fundamentally "flawed" and characterized by "inadequate resources," "untrained researchers," "flawed communication" between the parties, and an inability to deal effectively with "complex and varied claims."[42]

To remedy these deficiencies, the report prescribed the same antidote that had long been seen as necessary to secure an effective and just claims process: establish an independent body that would "ensure fairness and timely resolution of Specific Claims" and that "all parties respect as much as the courts." The report emphasized that "First Nations want an independent body to ensure that claims do not remain in the system for decades without a mechanism to compel the government to make a decision on the claim and to exert pressure on First Nations and the government to reach agreements."[43]

Stakeholders concurred that this body should have the power to make binding decisions and that its decision-makers should be appointed through a collaborative process involving Indigenous and non-Indigenous governments.[44] Many asserted that the Specific Claims Resolution Act could be saved if Canada and First Nations came to the table and worked together openly, ethically, and productively on amendments that would build a better and more transparent claims process.

Attention to specific claims accelerated in 2007, with a series of pivotal developments that dovetailed into Bill C-30, the Specific Claims Tribunal Act, during the fall of that year. On June 12, Minister of Indian Affairs Jim Prentice announced a "new, decisive approach to restore confidence in the integrity and effectiveness of the process to resolve specific claims."[45] That approach was unveiled in "Justice at Last," which professed to prioritize negotiations rather than courts and confrontations, and to consult with First Nations regarding the development of an independent claims tribunal and new legislation. The minister referred to legislation that "we intend to introduce in Fall 2007 following discussions with First Nations over the summer,"[46] a quick turnaround time that belied his professed commitment to meaningful consultation. Given the myriad problems plaguing the process and the importance of claims to the claimants and their future prosperity, it is difficult to imagine that stakeholders could be fully heard in the remaining eleven weeks of the summer or that their views could be integrated into the Conservative government's apparently pre-existing plan for specific claims.

"Justice at Last" articulated the new approach to claims as standing on four independent pillars, the first of which consisted of "impartiality and fairness." They would be effected through the creation of an "independent claims tribunal" that claimants could resort to if Canada's "first choice" of a negotiated approach failed. First Nations could access the tribunal for review if their claim were not accepted for negotiation, if it were accepted but the parties agreed to refer it for a binding decision, or if three years of unsuccessful negotiations had elapsed.[47] The tribunal would thus have jurisdiction over matters of claim validity and compensation, which could not exceed $150 million or include land and resources, punitive damages, cultural or spiritual losses, or any other non-financial compensation.[48] This approach, Prentice declared, would bring "greater fairness to the process while accelerating the settlement of outstanding claims."[49] The second pillar consisted of "transparent and better" funding arrangements. In a rather curious remark, the minister conceded that "finding information about spending on specific claims is not easy the way proposed spending has been presented to Parliament and others." He stated that "substantial and visible funding dedicated to specific claims settlements would address this lack of transparency."[50] Jointly approved claims settlements and tribunal decisions would have an upper limit of $250 million per year or $150 million per settlement. "Justice at Last" also promised to expedite claims processing through a number of measures, including fast tracking small-value claims, bundling similar claims for purposes of research and assessment, and putting measures in place to ensure that "all new claims ... receive a preliminary assessment within six months to identify those that qualify for negotiation and process them faster."[51] Larger claims were to be hived off from the specific claims process to speed up the resolution of the smaller ones. Finally, the work and role of the ICC would be refocused to provide better access to mediation. The commission would no longer conduct inquiries into rejected claims and would concentrate exclusively on "resolution services," which would "help Canada and First Nations in overcoming impasses at all stages of the process."[52]

Roughly six weeks after announcing the Justice at Last policy, Minister Prentice joined with AFN chief Phil Fontaine to launch a joint INAC-AFN task force that was to collaborate on the development of the new specific claims legislation. The brainchild of these two former ICC chief commissioners,[53] the task force was comprised of eight members. Four were drawn from INAC, Justice, and the Prime Minister's Office, and four from the AFN.[54] Despite what appeared to be a rather fully formed legislative proposal that INAC expected to launch in just a few months, the task force was charged with shaping the legislation that would create an independent claims tribunal. It appears to have worked quickly and effectively: on November 27, 2007, Prentice announced that he and the AFN had signed a political agreement on specific claims reform.[55] As he did so, Bill C-30, the Specific Claims Tribunal Act (SCTA), received its first reading in the House of Commons.[56]

The bill moved rapidly through the legislative process and was reportedly little discussed in government or the media;[57] it received Royal Assent on June 18, 2008, and was proclaimed into force on October 17, 2008. The restated grounds for claims that lay at its core revealed how little the government had progressed from its original understanding of claims, first propounded in 1973 and later in *Outstanding Business*. The SCTA narrowed the grounds for compensation arising from a breach or non-fulfillment of the Crown's fiduciary obligations, as outlined in Bill C-6 and the JTF proposal. This reduction was somewhat balanced by the inclusion of grounds for the failure to provide reserve lands and for the inadequate compensation for lands taken, a clear improvement over the previous grounds for a failure to compensate.[58] On the whole, however, little in the new legislation suggested that the government's view of claims had advanced since 1973. The problems were less with the grounds for claims than with the policy and practices adopted by the Canadian state. As with much, if not all, legislation pertaining to Indigenous people, lands, and rights, the lofty goals and aspirations that coloured "Justice at Last" lost much in the trickle down to law and suffered even more in the implementation of the SCTA.

Central to Bill C-30 and Ottawa's new approach was the creation of an independent body that would make binding decisions on claims – the Specific Claims Tribunal. Under the terms of the bill, this would consist of up to six full-time decision makers, all of whom would be Governor in Council appointees from among the ranks of superior court judges across Canada. The tribunal would be overseen by a full-time chairperson, who would supervise and direct its work. He or she would be supported by a roster of additional members who could sit either as full- or part-timers. Appointments would be for three years and would be renewable once. On this front, little changed when the bill became law, though the appointments shifted from three to five years, and the tribunal would consist of no more than six full-time members and any number of part-timers, all of whom must be superior court judges. A member would hold office "so long as he or she remains a superior court judge."[59]

In an important and risky departure from the SCRA and the promises of consultation in "Justice at Last," the SCTA did not require that appointments to the tribunal entail consultation with the AFN or any other First Nations organization. Instead, in what may easily be construed as an attempt to sidestep a major stumbling block in the SCRA, the new act excised AFN input into appointments and relied upon the INAC-AFN political agreement that Prentice had announced on November 27, 2007. This stated that "the National Chief will be engaged in the process for recommending members of the Tribunal."[60] What the chief's engagement might consist of was not clear; nor was there any sense that the minister would solicit consultation beyond the chief, as even the latter's input was limited in the political agreement to "a manner which respects the confidentiality of the process."[61]

This preference for the terms of an agreement rather than for obligatory consultation was problematic in many ways. If history has shown anything about the relationship between Canada and First Nations, it is that Canada's partiality for the handshake approach to its obligations places First Nations at a disadvantage and is almost always instrumental for the Crown. There was little to suggest that consultation regarding tribunal appointments would fare much differently or better than other handshake deals. Should it do better, the approach to consultation itself was also problematic, especially as not all Indigenous stakeholders felt that the AFN spoke for them. For that matter, some AFN members might not necessarily agree with the grand chief concerning appointments. Ultimately, there was small reason to believe that First Nations, who have much to lose in the tribunal process, would have any real say in appointments. Should this apprehension prove correct, Indigenous doubts regarding the independence of the tribunal would probably worsen.

In Bill C-30, provisions for access to the tribunal were largely loyal to the intentions of "Justice at Last." First Nations could go to the tribunal at two points in the claims resolution process – at the pre-negotiation phase following a ministerial decision rejecting all or part of a claim and at the negotiation phase, with the consent of the minister. In both contexts, the right to approach the tribunal was automatic if a claim had not been reviewed or resolved within three years of its submission or acceptance for negotiation. In effect, the SCB had six years in which to review, accept, and negotiate a claim to successful resolution. If this did not occur, the First Nation was entitled to go to the tribunal. The act itself retained this structure and specified that claim submissions would be subject to a "minimum standard" set by INAC. The standard must be satisfied before the SCB accepted the claim as "filed" and the three-year countdown began. In like fashion, the three-year deadline on negotiations began when the SCB informed the First Nation in writing that its claim had been accepted for negotiation.

These timeframes were an improvement over the usual thirteen-year review period, but the SCTA process nonetheless potentially imposed a six-year wait on claimants. According to the act, claims that had already embarked upon either review or negotiation would be deemed filed "on the day in which this Act comes into force."[62] Thus, thanks to the revised filing date, at least three more years could be added to claims that had already spent time in the queue and on review or negotiations. Essentially, they would be penalized for having entered the process before the act became law, and only claims that were submitted afterward would be exempt from this disadvantage. Furthermore, this approach seemed to fly in the face of the SCB's "first in, first out" policy and even institutionalized queue jumping, as newer claims could ostensibly be processed before older ones. This was hardly an auspicious start for the new policy or for the promises of "Justice at Last" to eliminate backlog and delay. As will be seen, the act has proven unable to overcome delay in the process, as the SCB appears to have simply off-loaded the bulk of the queued specific claims onto the tribunal.

The legislation optimistically encouraged an enhanced commitment to mediation and facilitation, which, according to "Justice at Last," would be more collaborative and expeditious. The SCRA and "Justice at Last" anticipated a new or modified Indian Claims Commission's involvement in supporting mediation and facilitation to assist in the negotiation of claims. Importantly, "Justice at Last" provided for a "refocus" of the ICC "exclusively on resolution services."[63] Neither Bill C-30 nor the SCTA assigned this role to the commission. In fact, the legislation was entirely silent with regard to the ICC and the provision of mediation and facilitation services. This responsibility fell to the Specific Claims Branch, which was tasked with oversight and control of access to mediation. To this end, the SCB maintained a roster of mediators who would be made available if both parties agreed to mediation; evidently, the choice of mediator remained with Canada.[64] Situating mediation services within the department was problematic, as it placed control over potential mediators in the hands of Canada, thus entirely undercutting the neutrality that is so vital to the process. Subsequent practice demonstrated the folly of this choice, as Canada took a strict position against participating in voluntary mediation at all.[65]

Nor did the SCTA appear to provide for an infusion of additional resources into the claims process beyond noting that the yearly annual reports submitted by the tribunal chair "may include a statement on whether the Tribunal had sufficient resources, including a sufficient number of members, to address its caseload in the past fiscal year and whether it will have sufficient resources for the following fiscal year."[66] Virtually all commentators agree that most problems encountered in claims resolution are due largely to under-resourcing, so it is strange that the legislation made no move to correct this flaw. It is equally odd that the SCTA would impose three-year timelines on the review and negotiation process without also allocating the necessary resources that would enable both the SCB and Justice to meet this schedule. Instead, as with the political agreement to consult the AFN chief in the appointment of tribunal members, the question of additional resources was to be left to another day and the "further collaborative development of policy and legislation."[67]

We are now some distance from the implementation of the Specific Claims Tribunal, and "another day" is firmly upon us, begging the question: Has the SCTA realized justice at last? The AFN, which seems to have been much involved in the consultations and discussions around Bill C-30, expressed basic support for the new law and cautious optimism regarding the "new approach" that government claimed lay at its foundation. Others were less positive, both about the legislation and the AFN consultations. In responding to the bill, the Mohawk Council of Akwesasne noted that "the AFN is not a First Nation and does not speak for all First Nations peoples in Canada. Akwesasne wishes to make it abundantly clear that support by the AFN does not translate into acceptance of the new Specific Claims Tribunal Act (Bill C-30), by the First Nations who are affected by this Bill."[68] Although there is little published commentary on the bill,[69] the Mohawks voiced clear reservations about the $150 million cap on claims, the policy's exclusion of claims for injury to culture, and the overall lack of consultation leading up to the legislation. They also suggested that the "new Tribunal will be seen as Canada's attempt to replace an impartial body with one that will be more favourable to the federal government's positions."[70] The Canadian Bar Association echoed concerns about the cap and expressed fears that, should Canada not keep to the promises of "Justice at Last," the new approach "could give the superficial impression that problems with specific claims have been addressed without actually dealing with the underlying problems of INAC internal processes and policies that have led to the current problems."[71] This comment would prove prophetic.

The New Approach to Claims, or, Business as Usual at the Specific Claims Branch

Many First Nations across the country have been waiting for
years to get action on their claims. If the government doesn't
deliver justice regarding First Nations claims, then the expectation is that the Tribunal will indeed deliver justice at last.

– SHAWN ATLEO, AFN CHIEF, 2011

The sweeping promises of "Justice at Last" and the SCTA had been made many times before and with little to no follow-through. The creation of the tribunal, despite the small stumbles that plagued its first moments of life, was significant. It not only honoured an important promise, but suggested that we could be witnessing an *actual* new approach to the resolution of claims. Unfortunately, despite the best efforts of the tribunal, what has emerged in the wake of "Justice at Last" indicates that the new approach taken by the SCB is even more obstructionist and mean-spirited than its predecessor. Whatever First Nations may hope to receive from the SCB in the handling of their claims, it will almost certainly not be justice.

After the SCTA was passed and the tribunal was set up, the approach to claims was divided into two stages. In Stage One, a First Nation prepared and filed its claim with Canada, which reviewed it to determine whether it constituted a valid and outstanding lawful obligation on the part of the Crown. If the claim was accepted, negotiations ensued. If agreement could not be reached within the three-year timeframe, the claim moved to Stage Two, review by the tribunal.[72] Stage One was to be characterized by transparency, efficiency, and speed, and was to provide access to mediation to aid negotiation. In Stage Two, the tribunal's six full-time members offered binding resolution on the validity of the claim and the nature of compensation, with a final appeal to the Federal Court of Canada. This approach looked promising, but as so often occurs with policies in relation to Indigenous people, the problem was less in the policy than in its realization.

The dangers implicit in the trickle down were evident early in the history of the SCTA, most notably with regard to the struggles over the implementation of the tribunal. The first appointments were made in November 2009 and included one full-time member, BC justice Harry Slade, who also assumed the role of chairperson, and two part-time members, Justices Patrick Smith from Ontario and Johanne Mainville from Quebec. Under the steady hand of Harry Slade, the tribunal spent much of its initial years establishing its processes and putting in place the necessary structures to support its work. On July 4, 2012, it handed down its first decision, in *Re Osoyoos Indian Band,* and by the time Slade produced its submission for its five-year review on May 15, 2015, it had ruled in over forty cases.[73] Given the obstacles that mitigated against such success, this record is remarkable.

As early as 2011, Slade pointed out that the tribunal's resources would prove inadequate if its caseload were to increase. Within a year, his annual report indicated that the caseload was rising significantly and that additional staff and more appointments would soon be necessary.[74] A year later, a single additional part-timer was appointed to the tribunal, bringing its membership to the equivalent of 2.5 judges rather than the 6.0 specified in the SCTA. This did little to alleviate the pressures on the tribunal, especially as it had just one member from British Columbia, where the majority of claims currently originate. By 2014, and on the eve of the tribunal's five-year review, under-resourcing had reached a crisis point. In his annual report in that year, Slade stressed that

> the Tribunal has neither a sufficient number of members to address its present and future case load in a timely manner, if at all. Nor is it, due to the imminent coming into force of s. 376 of the Economic Action Plan 2014 Act, No. 1, which provides for the creation of the Administrative Tribunal Support Services Canada (ATSSC), assured of its ability to continue to function with adequate protection of its independence. These concerns have been raised with the Minister of Justice and the Minister of Aboriginal Affairs and Northern Development. There has been no adequate response from Government.
>
> Without the appointment of at least one additional full time member and several part time members, there will be unacceptable delays in servicing the current case load, much less any new claims.
>
> I am the only full time member, and the Chairperson of the Tribunal. My term expires in December 2015. Without the appointment of one or more full time members in the interim there will be no ability to implement a succession plan or service the case load. The Tribunal will fail.[75]

The lack of government support for the tribunal was central in the five-year review, which was completed in 2015. Virtually everyone who participated in the review criticized the ongoing under-resourcing, not only of the tribunal, but also of the claims process generally.[76] Canada's commitment to "further collaborative development of policy" plainly did not extend to adequately staffing and supporting either the tribunal or claims resolution.[77] In fact, in its submissions to the AFN Independent Expert Panel hearings on the SCTA, the Federation of Saskatchewan Indian Nations stated that its ability to conduct research and support claims submissions had been diminished by funding cuts.[78] This complaint was echoed by the Neskonlith Band and others.[79] The federation noted that the Specific Claims Branch, which retained control over funds for claims development, now approached funding based on what "Canada believes the claim is worth before the claim has even been negotiated."[80] If the government believed that a claim could be resolved for under $3 million, the First Nation would receive no funding to support negotiation, and those whose claims went to the tribunal were consistently under-funded in that process. Other commentators concurred and expressed serious concerns about the impact of under-resourcing:

> With funding cut-backs it has been difficult for First Nations to access adequate funding to advance claims through the claims and tribunal process. This includes inadequate financial and, consequently, inadequate personnel resources to efficiently and effectively process claims through the Specific Claims branch as well as through Justice. With fewer resources available to First Nations to submit and validate claims, the entire objective of the Policy and government's Action Plan is subverted.[81]

The AFN expert panel summarized these issues in its final report:

> The primary consistent concern regarding the entire specific claims process was the lack of appropriate funding at all stages – from claims research to preparing a submission, to engaging in negotiations, to the Tribunal process and judicial review. The claims process is involved and protracted and it is very difficult for a First Nation to advance a claim with inadequate resources.[82]

Resource limitations also applied directly to departmental practice, as funds for travel and in-person meetings between claimants and federal negotiators were severely constrained, leaving negotiations to proceed via conference call, email, and letters. In many cases, this penny pinching simply mirrored the SCB's miserly approach to the claims themselves. First Nations in British Columbia, the province with the largest number of outstanding claims against the Crown, spoke of being notified in letters from Canada that their claims had been accepted for negotiation, only to discover that this applied solely to a small portion of the claim. The acceptance was accompanied by a one-time "take-it-or-leave-it" offer of compensation. If the First Nation took the offer, it was required to release Canada from any liability for the remaining – usually larger – part of the claim.[83] The offer was time-limited; if the claimant did not accept or reject it within ninety days, the SCB closed and shelved the claim. If the band entered negotiations with the Crown, it would soon realize that

> Canada has moved from negotiating claims to using an insurance adjuster model whereby Canada tells a First Nation what they believe the claim is worth. The First Nation can either accept the offer or make a case for the higher compensation amount which Canada may or may not take into account, and if the First Nation does not agree, they can go to a different process which in this case is the Tribunal. There are no real negotiations.[84]

The Algonquin Nation Secretariat echoed this concern and mentioned its own experience with the churlishness of Canada's approach to claims:

> Instead of working cooperatively and engaging First Nations, SCB has become increasingly remote and unresponsive. SCB appears unwilling or unable to deal in a meaningful way with Claims Research Units. Before 2007, we used to know who the analyst was who was dealing with our claims, and we could engage them. Now, we're not permitted to engage. We do not know who is reviewing our claims submissions, and there is no opportunity to deal at the staff level as claims are being processed. We have concerns about federal capacity to assess our claims. In some claims it appears that SCB staff are unfamiliar with basic factual issues related to the claims being submitted. This must affect their ability to assess incoming claims. But we are effectively prevented from engaging SCB to address any concerns we might have.[85]

The lack of accountability that emerged in the SCB's new approach to claims and claimants also masked a series of other practices that undermined the resolution of claims. Among these practices was the approach to implementing the minimum standards that a submitted claim is required to meet before it is filed with the SCB. The SCTA provided for the development of these standards, specifying only that they should be "reasonable" with regard to the information, form, and manner in which a claim was presented.[86] Their formulation was left to the minister. According to the AFN expert panel, the standards that the SCB adopted were extreme, inflexible, and patently *unreasonable*. First Nations reported that their submissions had been returned due to "unclear photocopies or incomplete documents, even where the missing portions of the document were not relevant to the claim."[87] This created untold additional work for the claimants, whose funding for submissions had been cut and who had precious little money to pay for recopying or retyping documents. The expert panel heard that the SCB's adoption of "unnecessarily strenuous minimum standards waste[s] time and costs have been very significant – sometimes hundreds of hours and thousands of dollars – with no funding available to support these."[88]

By the time of the five-year review in 2015, despite ongoing problems with under-resourcing and a shortage of members, the tribunal had rendered decisions in more than forty cases, more than a few of which spoke to the sharp dealings and bad faith of the SCB's "new approach." The claim of the Aundeck Omni Kaning First Nation (AOKFN), submitted to the SCB in 2008, is illustrative.[89] The SCB decided that this was a small-value claim and thus eligible for expedited review. Like First Nations in British Columbia and Saskatchewan, the AOKFN received a letter from Canada, proposing to settle its claim. The AOKFN was given ninety days to submit a band council resolution accepting the offer; if this were not forthcoming before the deadline date, the file would be closed. The band chose to reject the offer and was duly informed in July 2012 that its file had been closed. When it took its claim to the tribunal, Canada quickly moved to block its access. In an ironic and self-serving twist of logic, Canada argued that the AOKFN claim was ineligible for tribunal review because it had not been in the SCB queue for three years.[90] As originally conceived, the three-year timeline was intended to encourage the resolution of claims, but in the hands of the SCB it became a punitive measure with which to frustrate resolution. Observing the complete lack of transparency in the SCB handling of the AOKFN claim and the time-limited "take-it-or-leave-it" offer that precluded any real possibility of negotiation, Justice Patrick Smith declared that

> the process employed by the Specific Claims Branch for small value claims in relation to this Claim, and perhaps many others, is, frankly, paternalistic, self-serving, arbitrary and disrespectful of First Nations. It falls short of upholding the honour of the Crown, and its implied principles of "good faith" required in all negotiations Canada undertakes with First Nations. Such a position affords no room for the principles of reconciliation, accommodation and consultation that the Supreme Court, in many decisions, has described as being the foundation of Canada's relationship with First Nations.[91]

With Canada's new approach to specific claims laid bare, its application to keep the AOKFN out of the tribunal was denied.

The SCB's "paternalistic, self-serving, arbitrary and disrespectful" approach extended to mediation as well. "Justice at Last" emphasized the importance of mediation and facilitation in supporting claims negotiations, asserting that "mediation is an excellent tool that can help parties in a dispute to reach mutually beneficial agreements."[92] It had foreseen that mediation services would be provided by a revamped Indian Claims Commission, which would undertake this task as its sole purpose. However, although the AFN and Canada worked together briefly with a view to creating a framework for mediation and an Alternative Dispute Resolution Centre, Canada

> subsequently closed off discussions with the AFN on this matter and unilaterally announced mediation services will be housed in the Department of Indian Affairs offices, administered by INAC staff and will only be available while negotiations on a specific claim are active. Mediators will be chosen by INAC. In a letter dated November 15, 2010, Canada indicated it will not participate in any mediation it deems inappropriate. In effect, mediation will be available only when Canada wants it and Canada

controls it. The practice of independent mediation does not exist in the current specific claims process.[93]

The Indian Claims Commission was closed, and mediation became a rarity in Canada's specific claims process. The 2015 five-year review of the SCTA confirmed that Canada was unwilling to make mediation available to claimants and that it consistently refused to participate voluntarily in it.[94] As one claimant told the expert panel,

the fourth pillar of the [Justice at Last] Action Plan, better access to mediation, is not being achieved. In our experience, when our First Nations have proposed mediation at the negotiation table, the response from Canada has been that Canada does not intend to change its position, so mediation will not be helpful.[95]

As mentioned above, Canada's declaration that it had reduced the backlog by nearly 90 percent is more illusory than real, as the reduction consists almost entirely of claims that were "resolved" by rejection or file closure, whereas a mere 10 percent were resolved by administrative remedy or through actual settlement.[96] Reflecting on these realities, the expert panel concluded that

Stage One [of the claims process] has become a forum for rejecting and delaying claims, not resolving them. The backlog of specific claims is effectively moving to Stage Two, the Tribunal, rather than being resolved at Stage One. This means Canada has altered the Tribunal from that of a final arbiter of justice, to an inevitable part of the process.[97]

As the AFN observes, "the Tribunal was not created to be the new home of the massive backlog of claims that are considered 'unresolved' by First Nations."[98] Yet, this is precisely what has happened.

At every point, from conception through legislation to implementation, the vision enshrined in "Justice at Last" has dimmed and narrowed. The ICC was erased from the landscape, along with its almost two decades of experience in both inquiries and mediation. The conflict of interest in claims policy remains well entrenched. Indeed, it is increasingly obvious in Canada's approach to claims resolution, which treats the tribunal with no more respect than it shows to claimants. The chronic under-resourcing of the tribunal has not been addressed, and what is perceived as Canada's war of attrition against claimants merely persists, via the mechanism of "moving the backlog of claims from Stage One to Stage Two, and then starving Stage Two." As the AFN points out, this is "a disastrous result and a complete betrayal of the promise of Justice at Last."[99]

Yet, despite Canada's efforts to hobble the tribunal, it emerged as worthy of considerable respect. First Nations see it as independent and have respect for the calibre of its members and its flexibility and cultural sensitivity.[100] Despite the incredible push-back from Canada, the tribunal has persevered with its mandate and has become a source of some hope to claimants. In the same way that they once looked to the ICC, they can now look to the tribunal, not only for a thoughtful and neutral reconsideration of their claim, but one that can bind the government, which must be forced to attend to claims by law, rather than as a matter of justice.

8

The Legacy of the ICC and Lessons
for the Future of Specific Claims

The tabling of Bill C-30 and the passage of the Specific Claims Tribunal Act marked the beginning of the end for the Indian Claims Commission (ICC). Our nearly two-decade tenure as an "interim measure" was formally brought to a close through an Order in Council that directed us to cease all inquiry and mediation work by 2009.[1] We received the order in 2007, which gave us two years to wrap up our inquiries and shut down the commission. The end, when it came, was bittersweet. Most of us knew that the ICC could not, and indeed should not, persist. To truly resolve claims and mitigate the myriad problems with the process would require that the neutral ICC be endowed with the power to make binding decisions. We had done our best, and as much as we could, but it was clear that much more was needed if true "justice at last" were to be achieved. At the same time, the closure of the ICC was the end of an era and of our roles as commissioners. I cannot speak for my colleagues, but I knew I would miss our work, which, for me, was central to the reconciliation process and integral to the pursuit of social justice in Canada. I would miss the thrust and parry of deliberations, and the knowledge that each claim carried of cultures, communities, and histories. I would also miss the many people and places that had defined my time at the commission and had taught me so much.

The impending closure also led us to ponder our legacy. What had we actually accomplished? Had we advanced claims justice or simply been another cog in the slow-grinding wheel of the status quo? A glance at the official record shows that we certainly appear to have achieved a great deal: as of March 2009, we had accepted 129 requests for inquiries leading to

88 reports, and our mediation services had facilitated settlement of 14 claims.[2] Of course, our ability to actually affect claims resolution depended greatly on how Canada chose to respond to our recommendations. As has now become apparent, we ended with a split decision on this front: Canada accepted our recommendations in 19 inquiries and rejected them in a further 19.[3] However, the balance tips when reports that the government seems simply to have ignored are placed on the scale. If no response essentially amounts to a rejection – a fair assumption from the point of view of actually resolving claims – our impact is radically diminished, with 19 accepted reports and 43 rejected or ignored reports. Although these numbers suggest that the commission's eighteen years of hard work had a rather diluted impact, it seems to me that they say more about the attitude of the successive Canadian governments who received our reports than about the commissioners who laboured diligently and in good faith to produce them. And nowhere was the disregard for their work more apparent than in the closing moments of the ICC.

As soon as we were informed of our two-year deadline, we redoubled our efforts to complete the inquiries before us. At the time, we had thirty-seven claims in active inquiry. Records indicate that twenty-three of these were simply closed and that any documents and records were returned to the parties. Over the ensuing two years, we completed as many of the remainder as possible and issued reports. The *Indian Claims Commission Proceedings* for 2008–09 contains sixteen of these reports, and to my knowledge most never received a single response from Canada. In the end, as noted above, a full twenty-four were simply ignored. As mentioned elsewhere, our final report excuses this figure as resulting from the submission of most of those reports on the eve of our closure, which seems to rely on an assumption that our work became irrelevant once our doors closed. To me, this seems a generous qualification, as these inquiries involved claims that were live issues for the claimants and, based on our findings in many of them, potentially also in law. It seems a small thing for Canada to pick up those reports, review our findings and recommendations, and communicate a position to the claimants – this would be both respectful and consistent with the notion that the point of specific claims policy is to resolve claims. However, this seems not to have occurred, a situation that is unlikely to change, given the approach to claims taken by the Specific

Claims Branch (SCB) in the wake of the new legislation. This is disappointing, not only because it entails a complete waste of the work done by the parties and the commission in producing the reports and the wealth of historical research and legal analysis they contain, but also for what it reveals about Canada's commitment to resolving claims. The reports we completed during the commission's final year may have provided information that would have assisted in the resolution of these claims, thus removing them from the process and perhaps achieving some justice for the parties. As it is, we will never know what became of our reports or whether they aided the claimants and Canada in dealing with the claims.

The evident disregard for our reports after 2007 was accompanied by a more general disrespect for the ICC. Although our inquiry and mediation work continued, the government chipped away at our structure and supports. We would arrive for meetings only to discover that chunks of our office space had simply been walled off to make way for the Oliphant Inquiry into the questionable dealings between former prime minister Brian Mulroney and his business associate Karlheinz Schreiber.[4] Our staff would find themselves without office or workspace, which must have added to the stress of impending job loss and the sheer magnitude of the work to be done before our final day – March 31, 2009. To me, this seemed disrespectful to both the commission and the parties, and to our determination to complete as much of the remaining work as possible. Surely, the government could wait until our mandate actually expired before picking at our bones?

Although many of our last efforts seem to have achieved little in terms of actual claims resolution, there can be no question that the cumulative impact of our work was significant. I believe that it contributed to important developments in the approach to claims, both in terms of Canada's process and some of the legal principles that are integral to claims resolution. With regard to process, our constructive rejection policy was a significant development that endeavoured to make parties accountable for their conduct. It was a direct response to deficiencies in the process, and it attempted to hold Canada accountable for the ambivalence in much of its treatment of claims. Although Indigenous claimants could sometimes delay the process, the simple fact was that most delays and difficulties were generated by the government. Readers should not perceive this remark as proof of bias on my part: it simply acknowledges the reality that Canada controls the bulk of the claims process and is thus predominantly responsible for the flaws in its administration. We worked assiduously to achieve balance in applying our constructive rejection policy and were attentive to actions by both the claimants and the Crown. For example, if a claimant alleged that unreasonable delay had occurred, we scrutinized the behaviour of both parties to determine who was responsible, but we typically discovered that the fault lay in Canada's approach to both claims and claimants. I believe that the government's tendency to insert unreasonable, often unexplained delays into claims reviews, especially of relatively simple, straightforward ones, or to renege on undertakings, is tied to the conflict of interest in the process. As both party and judge, Canada holds virtually all the cards. Where power is unequal, mishandling can arise, and the actions of the Crown displayed a lack of respect for its own policy and processes, and for the First Nations who submitted their claims in good faith.

We invoked our constructive rejection policy as frequently as seemed necessary, and the response from Justice and the SCB was fairly consistent: intolerant of any challenge to its monopoly or questioning of its approach or motives, the SCB usually reacted with petulance, refusing to participate in the inquiry or threatening litigation. It rarely acknowledged that it might be at fault (the closest it came to a mea culpa was to blame Justice) and typically showed no real openness to rectifying the failings of the process. Instead, Canada and the SCB seemed determined to retain their grip and were unwilling to entertain any challenge that could set a precedent they might later regret. During my time as a commissioner, this seemed an ongoing feature of our interactions with the SCB, and though I cannot speak to the inner workings of the SCB today, the concerns expressed by Indigenous stakeholders about its current approach to claims certainly suggest that things did not improve after 2009 and may even have worsened.

Whereas I am hopeful that we had some impact on the specific claims process, I am convinced that we contributed to the advancement of some key legal principles integral to claims, both in terms of compensation and the obligations that arise in resolution. For example, we pushed the boundaries on the compensation criteria enumerated in *Outstanding Business* in our report on the Long Plain First Nation inquiry.[5] Under the terms of

Treaty 1, the Long Plain Band was entitled to receive thirty-two acres of reserve land for each of its 223-odd members. However, the Crown set aside enough land for only 165 people. Many years later, Long Plain sought compensation for this shortfall in acreage, the Crown accepted its claim, and the two parties reached a settlement in 1994. Our inquiry turned on whether the band was also entitled to receive compensation for *loss of use* of the land. The ICC panel found that payment for loss of use was consistent with the current specific claims compensation criteria, which provided that compensation "will be based on legal principles."[6] This was the first time that the ICC had considered and accepted loss of use as a component of treaty land entitlement compensation, and it was later accepted as a head of damage in other treaty land entitlement negotiations.[7]

Central among our accomplishments was the greater elucidation of Canada's fiduciary obligations to First Nations. These obligations form the historic core of the First Nations–Crown relationship and are integral to understanding both it and the honour of the Crown.

The principle that Canada's obligations to Indigenous people are shaped by its historic, trust-like relationship with them received its first substantive consideration in *Guerin v. The Queen,* a 1984 Supreme Court case in which the court described the relationship as a fiduciary duty.[8] Should the Crown breach the relationship, it would become "liable to the Indians in the same way and to the same extent as if such a trust were in effect."[9] Since *Guerin,* the nature and extent of the fiduciary have been developed in a series of cases. The concept continues to evolve, but the jurisprudence establishes that the Crown's duties to First Nations will vary depending on the differing circumstances in which they arise and that not all obligations flowing between the Crown and Indigenous people are themselves fiduciary in nature. Where such obligations do exist, they must be balanced with the interests of Canada as a whole.[10] Of course, the Crown can be "no ordinary fiduciary."[11] However, Canada must be mindful that "the honour of the Crown is always at stake in its dealings with Aboriginal peoples" and that

in all its dealings with Aboriginal peoples, from the assertion of sovereignty to the resolution of claims and the implementation of treaties, the Crown must act honourably. Nothing less is required if we are to achieve the reconciliation of the pre-existence of Aboriginal societies with the sovereignty of the Crown.[12]

The ICC dealt with the fiduciary relationship in a range of contexts, including those of reserve creation; protection of reserves from encroachment, alienation, and trespass; and in surrenders and the post-surrender fiduciary duty.[13] We consistently understood the obligations and duties arising in the fiduciary relationship as falling within the scope of lawful obligations, the breach of which led to outstanding lawful obligations on the part of Canada. It is significant that the Specific Claims Tribunal Act contains, for the first time, the explicit acknowledgment of fiduciary obligations as grounds for claims. Although the policy limits these grounds to "unilateral undertakings [by the Crown] that give rise to a fiduciary obligation" and thus entertains a narrow understanding of the fiduciary, this inclusion is an important step in the right direction.[14]

It is, of course, impossible to speak of the fiduciary without referring to the honour of the Crown, which is most clearly expressed through the fiduciary obligations to Indigenous people. A "fiduciary duty may arise as a result of the Crown assuming discretionary control over specific Aboriginal interests," especially in regard to lands historically used and occupied by Indigenous nations.[15] In managing this duty, the Crown must ensure that its actions are consistent with the "ultimate purpose" of its honour, which is the "reconciliation of pre-existing Aboriginal societies with the assertion of Canadian sovereignty."[16] As the Supreme Court explained in its 2013 *Manitoba Metis Federation* decision,

> The honour of the Crown speaks to how obligations that attract it must be fulfilled, so the duties that flow from it vary with the situation. In the context of the implementation of a constitutional obligation to an Aboriginal people, the honour of the Crown requires that the Crown: (1) take a broad purposive approach to the interpretation of the promise; and (2) act diligently to fulfill it. The question is whether, viewing the Crown's conduct as a whole in the context of a case, it acted with diligence to pursue the fulfillment of the purposes of the obligation. The duty to act diligently is a narrow and circumscribed duty. Not every mistake or

negligent act in implementing a constitutional obligation to an Aboriginal people brings dishonour to the Crown, and there is no guarantee
that the purposes of the promise will be achieved. However, a persistent
pattern of errors and indifference that substantially frustrates the purposes of solemn promise may amount to a betrayal of the Crown's duty
to act honourably in fulfilling its promise.[17]

In making this statement, the court meaningfully addressed the "conceptual
nexus between Crown honour accountability and Crown fiduciary accountability" for the first time and significantly advanced the elevation of
honour above the fiduciary as the "new core of Aboriginal law."[18] Here, the
honour of the Crown is directly linked with the obligations that flow from
the Constitution's recognition and affirmation of existing Aboriginal and
treaty rights, including a range of cultural, social, political, and economic
rights such as the right to land, to hunt, fish, practise culture, and enter
into treaties. Where an obligation lies, the expectation is that the Crown
will act diligently to meet it. The determination whether it does so will
depend upon its "actual conduct, as opposed to the results of its conduct,
and should be seen with reference to what was known at the time as opposed to hindsight."[19]

The duty to act diligently is "narrow and circumscribed," and "not every
mistake or negligent act" will reflect negatively on the Crown or, evidently,
require remedy. Indeed, the jurisprudence sets a rather high bar for dishonourable conduct, asserting that it "may" occur if there is a "persistent
pattern of errors and indifference that substantially frustrate the purposes
of solemn promise." If a persistent pattern of bad behaviour does not equate
with dishonourable conduct, one is left to wonder what does.

To me, the honour of the Crown is both a legal principle and an ethical
one, and throughout my time at the ICC I believed – and continue to
believe – that honour matters. I often raised this point in our discussions,
not only of individual inquiries, but also more generally with regard to
Canada's administration of the claims policy and process. Although my
commission colleagues agreed to some extent that honour mattered, they
greeted my position with disdain and were doubtful that the principle
could motivate Canada to take positive action. In my early years at the
ICC, they saw invoking Crown honour as a Hail Mary pass that had

little chance of moving us farther down the field or closer to justice. As a result, if our inquiry determined that the government had no outstanding lawful obligation to the claimant but that remedial action was nonetheless required, appealing to the honour of the Crown was futile. Honour did not appear to register with the SCB and Canada, and it certainly could not propel them to positive action. This view seemed rather cynical to me, but I came to realize that it was simply realistic – a lesson that was reinforced in many ways, including, for example, by Canada's silence in connection with the Red Earth and Shoal Lake inquiry.

That the honour of the Crown should play no role in its administration of claims policy seemed wrong at the time, and since *Haida Nation,* it may also be questionable in law. In this case, the Supreme Court stressed the importance of the Crown's honour "in all its dealings with Aboriginal peoples, from the assertion of sovereignty to *the resolution of claims* and the implementation of treaties."[20] Claims resolution is inextricably bound up with policy and processes, and it does not seem much of a stretch to state that *Haida Nation* requires these to be implemented in a manner consistent with the honour of the Crown, diligently and with an absence of sharp dealings. And yet, in my experience both as a commissioner and a researcher inquiring into the state of claims since the advent of the Specific Claims Tribunal Act and the closure of the ICC, the resolution process is often markedly deficient in honour. Indeed, it sometimes seems devoid of even the basic trappings of civility. How is the honour of the Crown demonstrated when First Nations can wait an average of thirteen years for their submission to be reviewed?[21] How is it compatible with the climate of "micromanaging" and "bullying" at the SCB, where "needless changes which do not change the substance of agreements but add con-siderable delays to the process" are common?[22] Where is the honour in the sleight of hand that "eliminates" the massive claims backlog simply by shunting the bulk of it to the tribunal? And where, of course, is the honour in participating in ICC inquiries, only to ignore the resulting report, as was the case in twenty-four reports, most of which were produced in the twilight of the commission?

The honour of the Crown is a legal principle, to be sure, but the idea of honour also evokes a set of ethical principles that, in an ideal world, should shape our behaviour. In its original incarnation in pre-Norman

England, the honour of the Crown was firmly attached to the person of the sovereign, and all who swore allegiance to the Crown promised to uphold that honour in all their dealings. As David Arnot notes, "the Crown was not an abstract or imaginary essence in those days, but a real person whose power and prestige were directly dependent on the conduct of his advisors, captains and messengers."[23] Here, the idea of honour embodied a "traditional bedrock of principles of fundamental justice that lay beyond persons and politics," and restrained the Crown from acting with "ignoble intent" or in ways that would harm its subjects.[24]

Today, our world, like the concept of the honour of the Crown, is more complex, and though the principle was always imperfect in practice,[25] it seems especially fraught in the realm of claims. As the courts continue to develop it as a legal principle to guide First Nations–Crown relationships, much seems to become lost in the trickle down from legal pronouncements to the individual actions of those who are responsible for claims. Grand declarations about honour seem to mask a multitude of dishonourable actions: delay and equivocation in claims assessment, misrepresentation regarding the management of the backlog, and a myriad of actions and choices that daily threaten the very existence of honour in the Crown's dealings with claims. The courts should not be required either to iterate the ingredients of honourable behaviour or to force us to behave honourably; indeed, if the law is driven to take this step, it must also be stepping into a void. If we truly are honourable people, behaving in honourable ways should not require the force of the law.

To me, the ascendance of honour as the overarching principle shaping the Crown's dealings with First Nations throws the tension between law and justice most sharply into relief. At the ICC, we spent the largest part of our time focusing on the law and how it defined our understanding of claims and their resolution. Did the oral histories shared by claimants and the written documents retained by the Crown meet the legal threshold that established an outstanding lawful obligation? If they did, would the law provide justice? If they did not, and if legal justice proved elusive, would the honour of the Crown hold a promise that social justice may lie where legal justice did not? For the Crown, the only route to justice seemed to be through the law, and if there were no lawful obligations, it felt no other form of obligation to claimants. Perhaps this was (and is) a rational position for it to take; after all, as *Wewaykum* asserted, "the Crown can be no ordinary fiduciary."[26] It must always be mindful not only of its duties to First Nations but also of the interests of Canada as a whole. In the face of complex claims, histories, and the numerous competing interests that must be managed in a modern Canada, falling back upon the ruthlessly rational rule of law and legal precepts makes the most political sense. It also enables the government to claim that a legally just result has been achieved. The difficulty, of course, is that legal justice is merely one type of justice, and it is often a parsimonious and partial justice that serves only to further divide winners and losers.

If we are to achieve full resolution of claims and further the process of reconciliation between First Nations and newcomers, Canada must commit to acting honourably in its administration and implementation of the claims policy. It must step away from the sharp dealings that, in my opinion, too often characterize the actions of the SCB and that cannot help but reflect badly on the Crown. Since the implementation of the Specific Claims Tribunal Act, Canada has slashed its funding for claims research and development, and has robbed both the SCB and the tribunal of the resources necessary to resolve claims. The SCB has adopted a more tight-fisted and mean-spirited approach, not all of which can be traced to the impoverishment of resources, both there and in the Department of Justice.

Can we take a different path with regard to claims? I believe that we can. It seems to me that much of Canada's worst behaviour occurred within a Conservative federal administration whose reputation for meanness – both in the fiscal and most other senses – is probably unparalleled in our recent history. And yet this bad behaviour is distinguished only by degree from that of the past, which saw the scourge of residential schools, the sixties scoop, and the purposeful underdevelopment and forced marginalization of Indigenous peoples. Today, we talk of reconciliation between our nations, and of healing and moving forward. To achieve these goals, we must commit to a truly new approach to claims, understanding these as lawful obligations arising from debts incurred in the building of Canada. We must honour the treaties and meet our obligations, not only in law, but also in the spirit of justice. To this end, we must provide adequate funding for the research, negotiation, and resolution of claims, and for the tribunal, which, if we truly commit to the just resolution of claims, should find its queue much diminished. The cost will be significant but less so than if we continue on the current path. The time has come to face our debts, account for our history, and build a better future. It is time to start focusing on the achievement, not only of legal justice, but also of social justice for First Nations and all the generations. Only then can we hope to attain justice at last.

Notes

Introduction

1 There are two broad categories of claims in Canada: comprehensive claims and specific claims. The former concern lands that have not been surrendered and to which Aboriginal title remains intact. In British Columbia, most of which remains unceded and is therefore subject to Aboriginal title, the British Columbia Treaty Commission is striking new treaties to address the ongoing claims issues. The comprehensive claims policy was first spelled out in 1973 and was reaffirmed in Department of Indian Affairs and Northern Development (DIAND), *In All Fairness: A Native Claims Policy* (Ottawa: DIAND, 1981). Specific claims arise from unfulfilled treaties or agreements, or unmet obligations under the Indian Act on the part of the Crown toward Aboriginal people. *Indian Act,* RSC 1985, c. 1–5. Specific claims policy was first spelled out in DIAND, *Outstanding Business: A Native Claims Policy* (Ottawa: DIAND, 1982). Whereas the comprehensive claims policy remains relatively true to its 1981 incarnation, specific claims policy was revamped in 2007. Not surprisingly, the overhaul left untouched the most glaring flaws and does not appear to have effected any significant or positive change in the processing of claims.

2 A Red Tory, Bernard Valcourt was the fifth Aboriginal Affairs minister appointed by Stephen Harper after he ascended to power in 1997. The first of these (known by the more dated handle of Indian Affairs minister) was Jim Prentice, a long-time Tory who had served as an Indian claims commissioner from July 1994 to December 2001 and left to pursue a career in politics. Shortly after being elected to federal government in 2004, Prentice was named to Harper's Cabinet and became Indian Affairs minister. He was succeeded by Chuck Strahl, who served from 2007 through 2010 and oversaw the decommissioning of the Indian Specific Claims Commission (ICC). Strahl was replaced by John Duncan in August 2010. James Moore succeeded him as acting minister for a total of seven days between February 15 and 22, 2013. Valcourt, whose

political career spanned almost thirty years, interrupted only briefly by involvement in a drunk-driving incident and the loss of his seat from 1993 to 1995, took up the post on February 22, 2013.

3 Confidential letter leaked to APTN reporter Nigel Newlove, passed to the author on September 20, 2013.

4 Ibid.

5 Ibid.

6 Ibid. The letter claims that when line-level workers at the Specific Claims Branch tried to bring important additional information about claims to senior management, they were often met with exasperation and dismissal. Decisions, once made, were not open to question or challenge ("I've made my decisions and that's it").

7 "Aboriginal Affairs' Poisonous Atmosphere Symptomatic of Failing Relationship with First Nations," Union of BC Indian Chiefs, press release, October 2, 2013, in *Elders Voice* 13 (12) (November 2013), http://www.bcelders.com/Newsletter/November2013.pdf.

8 Indian and Northern Affairs Canada, "Specific Claims: Justice at Last," Ottawa, 2007, http://www.aadnc-aandc.gc.ca/eng/1100100030458/1100100030472.

9 Canada, *House of Commons Debates* (September 25, 1990), 13320.

10 Canada, Senate of Canada, "Evidence of May 27, 2003," in *Proceedings of the Standing Senate Committee on Aboriginal Peoples* 16, http://www.parl.gc.ca/Content/SEN/Committee/372/abor/16eva-e.htm?Language=E&Parl=37&Ses=2&comm_id=1; Canada, Senate of Canada, "Evidence of June 4, 2003," in *Proceedings of the Standing Senate Committee on Aboriginal Peoples* 17, http://www.parl.gc.ca/Content/SEN/Committee/372/abor/17evb-e.htm?Language=E&Parl=37&Ses=2&comm_id=1.

11 Canada, "Negotiation or Confrontation: It's Canada's Choice: Final Report of the Standing Senate Committee on Aboriginal Peoples Special Study on the Federal Specific Claims Process," Ottawa, December 2006, http://www.afn.ca/uploads/files/sc/spec_-_2006_negotiation_or_confrontation_(senate_report).pdf.

12 Assembly of First Nations, "Justice Delayed: Assembly of First Nations Submission to Canada for the Five Year Review of the Specific Claims Action Plan: 'Justice at Last,'" Ottawa, Assembly of First Nations, March 31, 2012, 1–2, http://www.afn.ca/uploads/files/specific_claims_-_5-year_review_submission_(final).pdf.

13 Indian and Northern Affairs Canada, "Specific Claims: Justice at Last."

14 Other than a switch in nomenclature from DIAND (the Department of Indian Affairs and Northern Development) to the apparently more respectful DAAND – Department of Aboriginal Affairs and Northern Development. We now have a further change, as DAAND has become Indigenous and Northern Affairs Canada. Regrettably, it appears that the desire to be more respectful, as demonstrated in the

new title, has not penetrated to the Specific Claims Branch. As will be seen, claims processing remains highly problematic and plagued by conflict of interest.

15 Assembly of First Nations, "Justice Delayed."
16 Ibid., 4–5.
17 Ibid., 4.
18 See Aboriginal Affairs and Northern Development Canada, "Progress Report – Specific Claims, 2012–2013," August 2013, http://www.aadnc-aandc.gc.ca/eng/1339 507365950/1339507443870. It is difficult to obtain exact numbers, but Indian Affairs reported that the backlog of claims awaiting assessment was just under 800 in 2007. This figure was challenged by the Senate Standing Committee on Aboriginal Affairs, which put the backlog at over 900 in 2009 – two years after the release of "Justice at Last" and well into the department's self-professed backlog-reduction campaign.
19 Assembly of First Nations, "Justice Delayed," 8.
20 Ibid.
21 Ibid., 5.
22 Ibid.
23 E. Jane Dickson and Sheila Purdy, "Memorandum to Commissioners: Deemed Rejections – Policy Evolution and Implications," internal document, 2005.
24 "Alexis First Nation: TransAlta Utilities Rights of Way Claim," *Indian Claims Commission Proceedings (ICCP)* 16 (2003): 47–66; "Red Earth and Shoal Lake Cree First Nations: Quality of Reserve Lands Inquiry," *ICCP* 24 (2009): 411–594, both at http://publications.gc.ca/site/eng/263487/publication.html.
25 See Indian Specific Claims Commission, *Final Report, 1991–2009: A Unique Contribution to the Resolution of First Nations' Specific Claims in Canada* (Ottawa: Minister of Public Works and Government Services, 2009).

Chapter 1: Specific Claims in Canada

1 *Indian Act,* RSC 1985, c. I-5.
2 Christa Scholtz, *Negotiating Claims: The Emergence of Indigenous Land Claims Negotiation Policies in Australia, Canada, New Zealand and the United States* (London: Routledge, 2006); Peter A. Cumming and Neil H. Mickenburg, *Native Rights in Canada,* 2nd ed. (Toronto: Indian-Eskimo Association of Canada, 1970); John J. Borrows and Leonard I. Rotman, *Aboriginal Legal Issues: Cases, Materials and Commentary* (Toronto: Butterworths, 1998).
3 Both the French and the British were drawn to Canada by the promise of wealth and, in the case of the French, of souls to be converted to Catholicism. They soon learned that Indigenous nations did not conceive of relationships narrowly or in terms of single goals – allies in economic endeavours were also expected to ally in matters of

war. The British in particular seem to have cracked the code of Indigenous relationships early on and pursued deep connections with Indigenous people. Nowhere was this more obvious than in their dealings with the Mohawks, for whom the matrilineage and clan network were defining elements of virtually every aspect of their lives. Key British officials such as Sir William Johnson were quick to insert themselves into the matrilineage through marriage, an act that conferred clan and standing in Mohawk society. Intermarriage, the importation of European technologies (especially guns), conflicts that accompanied Indigenous involvement in the fur trade, and the arrival of missionaries would fundamentally alter Indigenous nations, communities, and families, although they could not have anticipated these long-term impacts. As historian Francis Jennings observes, "Indian dependency was the outcome of rational decisions by rational persons caught up in an objective situation that limited choice. The Indians simply could not foresee the implications of their initiative for the trade in guns. By the time its effects in dependency became clear, the Indians had lost their power of choice." Francis Jennings, *The Ambiguous Iroquois Empire: The Covenant Chain of Indian Treaties with the English Colonies from Its Beginnings to the Lancaster Treaty of 1744* (London: W.W. Norton, 1984), 81.

4 *Royal Proclamation of 7 October, 1763*, RSC 1985, App. II, No. 1, quoted in Borrows and Rotman, *Aboriginal Legal Issues*, 27.

5 Borrows and Rotman, *Aboriginal Legal Issues*, 28.

6 British Columbia is an interesting and somewhat unique case. By 1850, it was largely common knowledge that before settlement of Indigenous lands could take place, Aboriginal title must be secured, and treaty processes had evolved to the point where it was "considered proper to pay compensation and set aside reserve lands for the Indians' exclusive use, in order that they would not be overrun by advancing settlement." According to Dennis Madill, "In anticipation of increased settlement and to avoid conflict with the natives around Fort Victoria, [Governor James] Douglas initiated the policy of purchasing Indian title to land, and in 1849 wrote to the Hudson's Bay Company in England to arrange for such purchases. In reply, the Company relied upon a report of a House of Commons committee examining the claims of the New Zealand Company, and took the position that Indigenous people had only 'qualified dominion' over their country. The Company authorized Douglas to confirm the Indians in the possession of only those lands that they had cultivated or built homes on by 1846 when they came under the sovereignty of Great Britain. All other land was to be regarded as waste and therefore available to colonization." Dennis Madill, "British Columbia Treaties in Historical Perspective," in Richard C. Daniel, *A History of Native Claims Processes in Canada, 1867–1979* (Ottawa: Research Branch, Department of Indian and Northern Affairs, 1980), 13. Although Douglas's approach seems parsimonious, at least he saw Indigenous people as possessing rights to the land and

took steps to secure those rights prior to colonization. His approach did not penetrate to the BC Mainland and did not extend to the men who assumed control of colony governance after he retired in 1864, especially Chief Commissioner of Land and Works Joseph Trutch. Trutch clearly rejected the idea of Indigenous title, and his views were shared by settlers and local government authorities. The result was a general disregard for Indigenous title and rights for most of the province's history, leading to the current reality that almost all of British Columbia consists of unceded Indigenous lands. See also Olive Patricia Dickason, *Canada's First Nations: A History of Founding Peoples from the Earliest Times,* 3rd ed. (Toronto: McClelland and Stewart, 2002).

7 According to the Yukon government, since the passage of the Umbrella Final Agreement in 1993, fourteen Indigenous nations in the Yukon have signed First Nation Final Agreements with the territorial and federal governments. Eleven of the fourteen have also finalized self-government agreements as part of their claims settlement. Today, Yukon First Nations own 41,439 square kilometres and have received more than $242 million in compensation, as well as guaranteed representation on a variety of boards and councils to do with management of land, water, fish and wildlife, and heritage resources. The Final Agreements can be viewed on the Yukon government's website, at http://www.eco.gov.yk.ca/aboriginalrelations/agreements. html.

   Nunavut was carved out of the eastern and central portions of the Northwest Territories, where Inuit comprise roughly 85 percent of the population, through a claims agreement finalized in 1993. According to Indigenous Affairs and Northern Development (DIAND), "the Nunavut agreement was the largest land claim ever settled in Canadian history. The settlement gives Inuit control of more than 350,000 square kilometres of land, of which 36,000 square kilometres include mineral rights. In addition, the land claim settlement gives Inuit more than $1 billion over 14 years, and guaranteed participation in making decisions for managing lands and resources." Indigenous and Northern Affairs Canada, "Creation of Nunavut," https://www. aadnc-aandc.gc.ca/eng/1100100016496/1100100016497.

8 In British Columbia, the only historic treaties were negotiated by James Douglas, chief factor of the Hudson's Bay Company and governor of Vancouver Island, with the Songhee, Sooke, Saanich, Fort Rupert, and Nanaimo First Nations during the 1850s. These rather simple agreements provided for an outright sale of land in return for a lump sum payment. In some cases, the company and the government made out like bandits: "The Songhees, Klallam and Sooke tribes surrendered their lands in return for a few blankets, small reserves and the freedom to hunt over the unoccupied lands, and to carry on their fisheries" as before. Douglas favoured annuity payments so that the Indians would derive a continuing benefit, but apparently the chiefs

preferred a lump sum. Wilson Duff, "The Fort Victoria Treaties," *BC Studies* 3 (1969): 3–55. In the final analysis, the Songhees sold their title to the District of Victoria for 371 blankets and a cap. Madill, "British Columbia Treaties," 18.

9 Arthur J. Ray, Jim Miller, and Frank Tough, *Bounty and Benevolence: A History of Saskatchewan Treaties* (Montreal and Kingston: McGill-Queen's University Press, 2000), 85.

10 Ibid.

11 Daniel, *A History of Native Claims*, 8–9.

12 Dickason, *Canada's First Nations*.

13 Daniel, *A History of Native Claims*, 7.

14 Ibid., 6.

15 Ibid.

16 Ibid.

17 Peter J. Usher, Frank J. Tough, and Robert M. Galois, "Reclaiming the Land: Aboriginal Title, Treaty Rights and Land Claims in Canada," *Applied Geography* 12 (1992): 109–32.

18 Daniel, *A History of Native Claims*, 9–10.

19 Ibid., 12.

20 Ray, Miller, and Tough, *Bounty and Benevolence*, 81–85.

21 Daniel, *A History of Native Claims*, 11.

22 Ray, Miller, and Tough, *Bounty and Benevolence*, 81.

23 Ibid., 83.

24 Ibid., 12.

25 Michael Coyle, "Addressing Aboriginal Land Rights in Ontario: An Analysis of Past Policies and Options for the Future – Part I," *Queen's Law Journal* 31 (2005): 75–120.

26 Ibid.; John Leslie, Robert Maguire, and Robert G. Moore, *The Historical Development of the Indian Act* (Ottawa: Indian and Northern Affairs Corporate Policy Research Branch, 1978).

27 William B. Henderson and Derek T. Ground, "Survey of Aboriginal Land Claims," *Ottawa Law Review* 26 (1) (1994): 209.

28 *St. Catherine's Milling and Lumber Co. v. R.* (1888), 14 App. Cas. 46 (P.C.).

29 Coyle, "Addressing Aboriginal Land Rights," 90.

30 Olthius, Kleer, Townshend LLP, *Aboriginal Law Handbook*, 4th ed. (Toronto: Carswell, 2012); Borrows and Rotman, *Aboriginal Legal Issues*.

31 *Guerin v. The Queen*, [1984] 2 S.C.R. 335. See also Olthius, Kleer, Townshend, *Aboriginal Law Handbook*; Borrows and Rotman, *Aboriginal Legal Issues*.

32 Olthius, Kleer, Townshend, *Aboriginal Law Handbook*.

33 *Tsilhqot'in Nation v. British Columbia*, 2014 SCC 44 at para. 73.

34 Ibid., para. 74.
35 Scholtz, *Negotiating Claims*.
36 Indian Specific Claims Commission, *Final Report, 1991–2009: A Unique Contribution to the Resolution of First Nations' Specific Claims in Canada* (Ottawa: Minister of Public Works and Government Services, 2009).
37 Scholtz, *Negotiating Claims*, 41; Paul Tennant, *Aboriginal People and Politics: The Indian Land Question in British Columbia, 1849–1989* (Vancouver: UBC Press, 1990), 112; Usher, Tough, and Galois, "Reclaiming the Land"; Daniel Raunet, *Without Surrender, Without Consent: A History of the Nishga Land Claims* (Vancouver: Douglas and MacIntyre, 1984).
38 Indian Specific Claims Commission, *Final Report*; Coyle, "Addressing Aboriginal Land Rights"; "The Indian Act," Indigenous Foundations, http://indigenousfoundations. arts.ubc.ca/the_indian_act/.
39 Dickason, *Canada's First Nations*.
40 Ibid.
41 Madeline Dion Stout and Gregory Kipling, *Aboriginal People, Resilience and the Residential School Legacy* (Ottawa: Aboriginal Healing Foundation, 2002); Deborah Chansonneuve, *Reclaiming Connections: Understanding Residential School Trauma among Aboriginal People* (Ottawa: Aboriginal Healing Foundation, 2005).
42 Scholtz, *Negotiating Claims*.
43 Ibid. The Federation of Saskatchewan Indian Nations altered its name to Federation of Sovereign Indigenous Nations on May 25, 2016. As FSIN chief Bobby Cameron explained, the name change was a "message and a reaffirmation ... to our provincial and federal government that our 74 First Nation communities on our treaty territories do practice their sovereignty, they do have and exercise their own jurisdiction and laws and this work is going to continue." "Dropping the Word 'Indian' FSIN Chiefs Vote to Change Organization's Name," *CBC News*, Saskatoon, May 25, 2016.
44 Ibid.
45 Emma Butt and Mary C. Hurley, *Specific Claims in Canada* (Ottawa: Library of Parliament, 2006); Scholtz, *Negotiating Claims*.
46 Scholtz, *Negotiating Claims*, 43.
47 Coyle, "Addressing Aboriginal Land Rights."
48 William Bradford, "'With a Very Great Blame on Our Hearts': Reparations, Reconciliation, and an American Indian Plea for Peace with Justice," *American Indian Law Review* 27 (2002–03): 111.
49 Margaret Hunter Pierce, "The Work of the Indian Claims Commission," *American Bar Association Journal* 63 (1977): 229–32; *Johnson v. McIntosh*, 8 Wheat. 543 (1823).
50 Bradford, "'With a Very Great Blame,'" 68. Bradford (ibid., 40) notes that, in fact, the US Constitution provides no protection to "Indian Tribes." They are exempted

from the "Takings Clause" of the Fifth Amendment, which should have insulated them from the "nonconsensual taking" (read: theft) of land by the US government. The 1980 case of *United States v. Sioux Nation,* 448 U.S. 371, 416–17, no. 30, confirms the exemption of tribes from this protection, thus reinforcing the historical precedent whereby theft of land from tribes was somehow not theft, even though the sole factor that distinguished it from theft from "whites" was the ethnicity of the title holder.

51 Harvey D. Rosenthal, "A Brief History of the Indian Claims Commission," in *Irredeemable America: The Indians' Estate and Land Claims,* ed. Imre Sutton (Albuquerque: University of Mexico Press, 1985), 38.

52 Russel Lawrence Barsh, "Indian Land Claims Policy in the United States," *North Dakota Law Review* 58 (1982): 7–82; Nell Jessup Newton, "Indian Claims in the Court of the Conqueror," *American University Law Review* 41 (1991): 753–854; Nancy Oestreich Lurie, "The Indian Claims Commission Act," *Annals of the American Academy of Political and Social Science* 311 (1957): 56–70.

53 Glen A. Wilkinson, "Indian Tribal Claims before the Court of Claims," *Georgetown Law Journal* 55 (4) (1966–67): 511–28; United States Department of Justice, "Lead Up to the Indian Claims Commission Act of 1946," 2015, http://www.justice.gov/cnrd/lead-indian-claims-commission-act-1946; Rosenthal, "A Brief History."

54 Rosenthal, "A Brief History."

55 Barsh, "Indian Land Claims Policy," 10.

56 Ibid., 11.

57 Howard M. Friedman, "Interest on Indian Claims: Judicial Protection of the FISC," *Valparaiso University Law Review* 5 (1970): 26–47; Bradford, "'With a Very Great Blame.'"

58 Act of Mar. 3, 1871, ch. 120, 16 Stat. 544, 566, codified as amended at 25 U.S.C., s. 71 (2000).

59 Thomas Le Duc, "The Work of the Indian Claims Commission under the Act of 1946," *Pacific Historical Review* 26 (1) (1957): 1–16.

60 Rosenthal, "A Brief History."

61 Ibid., 42.

62 John T. Vance, "The Congressional Mandate and the Indian Claims Commission," *North Dakota Law Review* 45 (1969): 325–36.

63 Rosenthal, "A Brief History."

64 Ibid.; Vance, "The Congressional Mandate."

65 Rosenthal, "A Brief History," 45.

66 Vance, "The Congressional Mandate," 328.

67 Ibid., 330.

68 United States Department of Justice, "Lead Up to the Indian Claims Commission."

69 Vance, "The Congressional Mandate," 329. A number of factors conspired in the successful passage of the legislation. Significant Indigenous American involvement in the Second World War, followed by their increasing participation in the labour market, led Congress to believe the time was ripe to resolve the question of Indigenous claims against the government. Alison R. Bernstein, *American Indians and World War II: Toward a New Era in Indian Affairs* (Norman: University of Oklahoma Press, 1991), 58; Pamela S. Wallace, "Indian Claims Commission: Political Complexity and Contrasting Concepts of Identity," *Ethnohistory* 49 (4) (Fall 2002): 743–67.

70 *Indian Claims Commission Act,* Pub. L. No. 79–726; Lurie, "The Indian Claims Commission Act."

71 Rosenthal, "A Brief History," 47.

72 Newton, "Indian Claims in the Court."

73 Rosenthal, "A Brief History," 47.

74 Vance, "The Congressional Mandate," 328–29.

75 Ibid., 329.

76 Rosenthal, "A Brief History," 47.

77 Ibid.; Wilkinson, "Indian Tribal Claims."

78 Rosenthal, "A Brief History."

79 Wilkinson, "Indian Tribal Claims."

80 Le Duc, "The Work of the Indian Claims."

81 Barsh, "Indian Land Claims Policy."

82 Le Duc, "The Work of the Indian Claims," 15.

83 Senate Subcommittee on Indian Affairs, hearing on S. 2408, 92nd Cong., 1st Sess., 1971, 46, quoted in Rosenthal, "A Brief History," 64.

84 Rosenthal, "A Brief History," 62–63.

85 *Pueblo of San Ildefonso v. United States,* No. 354; United States Department of Justice, "Lead Up to the Indian Claims Commission."

86 *Indian Claims Commission Act,* 60 Stat. 1049 (1946), s. 22(a), para. 2.

87 Rosenthal, "A Brief History," 67–68.

88 A member of the Blood tribe of Alberta, Gladstone was appointed to the Senate in 1958 and made part of his opening remarks to the Senate in Blackfoot. He became a strong advocate for Indigenous education, respect for treaty rights, and Indigenous rights to self-government. His story has been chronicled in Hugh A. Dempsey, *The Gentle Persuader: A Biography of James Gladstone, Indian Senator* (Saskatoon: Western Producer Prairie Books, 1986).

89 Scholtz, *Negotiating Claims,* 48.

90 Ibid.

91 NAC, MG 32, series B1, vol. 100, file 1A-653, 1961–62, quoted in Scholtz, *Negotiating Claims,* 48.

92　Scholtz, *Negotiating Claims,* 48–49.

93　Ibid., 49; Henderson and Ground, "Survey of Aboriginal Land."

94　Scholtz, *Negotiating Claims,* 50.

95　Indian Affairs Branch memo, May 30, 1963, quoted in Sally M. Weaver, *Making Canadian Indian Policy: The Hidden Agenda, 1968–1970* (Toronto: University of Toronto Press, 1981), 39; also in Scholtz, *Negotiating Claims,* 51.

96　Scholtz, *Negotiating Claims.*

97　Weaver, *Making Canadian Indian Policy;* Scholtz, *Negotiating Claims.*

98　Lloyd Barber, "Symposium on Amerindians: Indian Land Claims and Rights," *Saskatchewan Indian,* February 28, 1975, http://www.sicc.sk.ca/archive/saskindian/a75feb2807.htm.

99　Weaver, *Making Canadian Indian Policy.*

100　Ibid., 185.

101　Ibid.

102　Ibid.

103　Scholtz, *Negotiating Claims.*

104　Henderson and Ground, "Survey of Aboriginal Land."

105　*Calder v. British Columbia (Attorney General),* [1973] S.C.R. 313. *Calder* confirmed that historic occupation of traditional territories by Indigenous nations gave rise to legal rights in the land that survived settlement and colonization, and that these rights endured in all regions of Canada where they had not been explicitly surrendered by treaty or other legal means. Mary C. Hurley, *Settling Comprehensive Land Claims* (Ottawa: Library of Parliament, 2009); Patricia Sawchuk, "Introduction: In All Fairness: A Native Claims Policy, Comprehensive Claims," Brandon University, n.d., 2, http://www3.brandonu.ca/cjns/2.1/policy.pdf; Borrows and Rotman, *Aboriginal Legal Issues.*

106　Indian and Northern Affairs, "Statement Made by the Honourable Jean Chrétien, Minister of Indian Affairs and Northern Development, on Claims of Indian and Inuit People," Ottawa, August 8, 1973, http://www.specific-claims-law.com/images/stories/specific_claims_docs/05-Fed_Govt_Docs_INAC_etc/INAC_(IAND)_AINC/StatementChretienClaimsIndianInuitPeople.pdf; DIAND, *In All Fairness: A Native Claims Policy* (Ottawa: DIAND, 1981); Department of Indian and Northern Affairs, "Comprehensive Land Claims Policy," Ottawa, 1987, 5–6.

107　For more information about the James Bay and Northern Quebec Agreement, see Brian Craik and John A. Price, "James Bay and Northern Québec Agreement," *Canadian Encyclopedia,* 2011, http://www.thecanadianencyclopedia.ca/en/article/james-bay-and-northern-quebec-agreement/. The full text of the agreement is at *The James Bay and Northern Quebec Agreement,* http://www.gcc.ca/pdf/LEG000000006.pdf.

For the Nisga'a Treaty, see Nisga'a Lisims Government, "Nisga'a Treaty," http://www. nisgaanation.ca/about-accomplishments-and-benefits-nisgaa-treaty.

108 Butt and Hurley, *Specific Claims,* 3.

109 Sally M. Weaver, "After Oka: 'The Native Agenda' and Specific Land Claims Policy in Canada," *Proactive* 11 (1992): 3; Henderson and Ground, "Survey of Aboriginal Land."

110 Henderson and Ground, "Survey of Aboriginal Land," 215; Weaver, "After Oka."

111 DIAND, *Outstanding Business: A Native Claims Policy* (Ottawa: DIAND, 1982), 1.

112 Ibid.; Sawchuk, "Introduction: Outstanding Business: A Native Claims Policy, Specific Claims," *Policy/Discussion,* n.d., http://www3.brandonu.ca/cjns/2.2/Outstanding. pdf.

Chapter 2: Dependent on the Good Will of the Sovereign

1 Mary Ellen Turpel, "A Fair, Expeditious, and Fully Accountable Land Claims Process," in "Special Issue on Land Claims Reform," *Indian Claims Commission Proceedings* (hereafter *ICCP*) 2 (1995): 61–115, http://publications.gc.ca/site/eng/263487/ publication.html.

2 Department of Indian Affairs and Northern Development (DIAND), *Outstanding Business: A Native Claims Policy* (Ottawa: DIAND, 1982), 20.

3 Ibid.

4 Ibid.

5 Ibid., 25.

6 Ibid., 15.

7 Ibid., 21.

8 Ibid.

9 For example, the court in *Guerin* dealt with specific facts pertaining to the Crown's obligations to "Indians" and "Indian Bands," which left some question about the application and content of the fiduciary with regard to Inuit and Metis. "A Fair and Equitable Process: A Discussion Paper on Land Claim Reform," *ICCP* 2 (1995): 3–24.

10 *Guerin v. The Queen,* [1984] 2 S.C.R. 335.

11 *R. v. Sparrow,* [1990] 1 S.C.R. 1075 at 1117.

12 William B. Henderson and Derek T. Ground, "Survey of Aboriginal Land Claims," *Ottawa Law Review* 26 (1) (1994): 216.

13 Indian Commission of Ontario, "Discussion Paper regarding First Nation Land Claims, September 24, 1990," *ICCP* 1 (1994): 187.

14 Ibid.

15 Ibid., 188.

16 Assembly of First Nations, "AFN's Critique of Land Claims Policies," Ottawa, 1990, 17.

17 Indian Commission of Ontario, "Discussion Paper," *ICCP,* 189.

18 Turpel, "A Fair, Expeditious, and Fully Accountable," *ICCP,* 9.

19 Ibid.

20 James R. Miller, "Great White Father Knows Best: Oka and the Land Claims Process," *Native Studies Review* 7 (1) (1991): 23–51; Geoffrey York and Loreen Pindera, *People of the Pines: The Warriors and the Legacy of Oka* (Toronto: Little Brown, 1991); Linda Pertusati, *In Defense of Mohawk Land: Ethnopolitical Conflict in Native North America* (Albany: State University of New York Press, 1997).

21 Although the Mohawks submitted their claim in 1977, there is nothing to indicate that the SCB dealt with it until nearly a decade later. It was rejected in 1986. As the federal government had no formal specific claims policy before 1982, it is safe to assume that *Outstanding Business* formed the foundation upon which the SCB evaluated the Oka claim. Indeed, one might postulate that the Oka claim, a live issue for DIAND for decades, inspired such practices as "special value to owner" (discussed below).

22 Miller, "Great White Father."

23 Indian Commission of Ontario, "Discussion Paper," *ICCP,* 193–94.

24 Turpel, "A Fair, Expeditious, and Fully Accountable," *ICCP,* 78.

25 Indian Commission of Ontario, "Discussion Paper," *ICCP.*

26 Assembly of First Nations, "AFN's Critique."

27 Ibid.

28 DIAND, *Outstanding Business,* 31.

29 Assembly of First Nations, "AFN's Critique."

30 "The High Cost of Oka," *Edmonton Journal,* May 6, 1991.

31 *The Indian Act, 1876,* SC, c. 18, s. 3(1), https://www.aadnc-aandc.gc.ca/DAM/DAM -INTER-HQ/STAGING/texte-text/1876c18_1100100010253_eng.pdf.

32 Jane Dickson-Gilmore and Carol LaPrairie, *Will the Circle Be Unbroken? Aboriginal Communities, Restorative Justice and the Challenges of Conflict and Change* (Toronto: University of Toronto Press, 2005), 17.

33 Order in Council PC 1151, May 17, 1889; "Friends of the Michel Society Inquiry: 1958 Enfranchisement Claim," *ICCP* 10 (1998): 89–90, http://publications.gc.ca/ site/eng/263487/publication.html.

34 "Friends of the Michel Society Inquiry," 88. It is important to note that having Indian status does not automatically confer band membership and thus, for example, access to residence on reserve and the rights associated with membership. Band councils that have secured control over membership under section 11 of the Indian Act may, through their by-laws, refuse band membership to any persons who re-acquire their Indian status.

35 Ibid., 89–90.

36 Ibid., 74.

37 Ibid., 89–90.

38 E. Jane Dickson and Sheila Purdy, "Memorandum to Commissioners: Deemed Rejections – Policy Evolution and Implications," internal document, 2005.

39 William N. Fenton and Elisabeth Tooker, "Mohawk," in *Northeast,* vol. 15 of *Handbook of North American Indians,* ed. Bruce G. Trigger (Washington: Smithsonian Institution, 1978), 466–80.

40 Miller, "Great White Father."

41 Fenton and Tooker, "Mohawk."

42 Ibid.

43 Assembly of First Nations, "AFN's Critique."

44 Miller, "Great White Father."

45 Ibid.; York and Pindera, *People of the Pines;* Pertusati, *In Defense of Mohawk Land.*

46 Miller, "Great White Father," 27.

47 Ibid.

48 Ibid., 28.

49 Ibid., 30.

50 York and Pindera, *People of the Pines;* Pertusati, *In Defense of Mohawk Land.*

51 Miller, "Great White Father"; York and Pindera, *People of the Pines;* Pertusati, *In Defense of Mohawk Land.*

52 Miller, "Great White Father," 37.

53 Paul Olliver, Assistant Deputy Minister, Department of Justice, to P.F. Girard, Office of Claims Negotiation, Indian and Northern Affairs Canada, February 26, 1975, quoted in ibid., 42 (communication secured through access to information, original in possession of J.R. Miller).

54 Ibid., 43.

55 Indian Specific Claims Commission, *Final Report, 1991–2009: A Unique Contribution to the Resolution of First Nations' Specific Claims in Canada* (Ottawa: Minister of Public Works and Government Services, 2009).

56 Chiefs Committee on Claims, "First Nations Submission on Claims," Ottawa, December 14, 1990, reprinted in *ICCP* 1 (1994): 187.

Chapter 3: The Indian Specific Claims Commission

1 House of Commons, Minutes of Proceedings and Evidence of the Standing Committee on Aboriginal Affairs Respecting: Study on Indian Specific Claims Commission, Issue No. 7, December 10, 1991, 3rd Session of the 34th Parliament, 1991–92, 7.

2 Order in Council PC 1991–1329, July 15, 1991.

3 Ibid.

4 Indian Specific Claims Commission, *Final Report, 1991–2009: A Unique Contribution to the Resolution of First Nations' Specific Claims in Canada* (Ottawa: Minister of Public Works and Government Services, 2009), 11.

5 House of Commons, Minutes of Proceedings and Evidence of the Standing Committee on Aboriginal Affairs Respecting: Study on Indian Specific Claims Commission, Issue No. 9, December 12, 1991, 3rd Session of the 34th Parliament, 1991–92, 6.

6 According to the Ontario Court of Appeal website, Justice Harry S. LaForme has received numerous awards and honours, including the 1997 National Aboriginal Achievement Award in the area of law and justice. Aboriginal elders have on three occasions presented him with an Eagle Feather, symbolizing the virtues of honesty, integrity, and respect; the most recent being at his swearing in as a judge of the Ontario Court of Appeal. He has many publications and articles on issues related to Aboriginal law and justice. In 1989, he was appointed commissioner of the Indian Commission of Ontario. In 1991, he was appointed chair of the Royal Commission on Aboriginal land claims, and in January 1994 he was appointed a judge of the Ontario Court of Justice (General Division), now the Superior Court of Justice, Ontario. At the time, he was one of only three Aboriginal judges ever appointed to this level of trial court in Canada. In November 2004, he was appointed to the Ontario Court of Appeal. He is the first Aboriginal person to be appointed to sit on any appellate court in the history of Canada. Court of Appeal for Ontario, "Brief Biographical Note of Justice Harry S. LaForme," http://www.ontariocourts.ca/coa/en/judges/laforme.htm.

7 House of Commons, Minutes of Proceedings and Evidence of the Standing Committee on Aboriginal Affairs Respecting: Study on Indian Specific Claims Commission, Issue No. 7, December 10, 1991, 3rd Session of the 34th Parliament, 1991–92, 12.

8 Ibid., 8, 17.

9 House of Commons, Minutes of Proceedings and Evidence of the Standing Committee on Aboriginal Affairs Respecting: Study on Indian Specific Claims Commission, Issue No. 9, December 12, 1991, 3rd Session of the 34th Parliament, 1991–92, 7.

10 House of Commons, Minutes of Proceedings and Evidence of the Standing Committee on Aboriginal Affairs Respecting: Study on Indian Specific Claims Commission, Issue No. 7, December 10, 1991, 3rd Session of the 34th Parliament, 1991–92, 10.

11 Indian Specific Claims Commission, *Final Report*.

12 Commission issued September 1, 1992, pursuant to Order in Council PC 1992–1730, July 27, 1992, amending the commission issued to Chief Commissioner Harry S. LaForme on August 12, 1991, pursuant to Order in Council PC 1991–1329, July 15,

1991. Indian Specific Claims Commission, *Final Report*, "Consolidated Terms of Reference," Appendix A, 45–46.

13 The First Nations Summit (FNS) website states, "The FNS is comprised of a majority of First Nations and Tribal Councils in BC and provides a forum for First Nations in British Columbia to address issues related to Treaty negotiations as well as other issues of common concern. As one of the principals of the treaty negotiation process along with Canada and BC, the First Nations Summit plays an important and ongoing role in ensuring that the process for conducting Treaty negotiations is accessible to all First Nations. However, the Summit does not participate in negotiations at individual treaty tables. Each treaty table is autonomous in its negotiations." First Nations Summit, "About the First Nations Summit," http://www.fns.bc.ca/about.

14 For more information about Harper's contribution to First Nations and Canadian politics, see Tabitha Marshall, "Elijah Harper," *Canadian Encyclopedia*, 2013, http://www.thecanadianencyclopedia.ca/en/article/elijah-harper/.

15 "Peepeekisis First Nation Inquiry: File Hills Colony Claim," *Indian Claims Commission Proceedings* (hereafter *ICCP*) 18 (2007): 19–24.

16 Ibid., 348.

17 "Canupawakpa Dakota First Nation Inquiry Turtle Mountain Surrender Claim," *ICCP* 17 (2004): 348.

18 "Re: Canupawakpa Dakota First Nation Turtle Mountain Surrender Claim, Jim Prentice, Minister of Indian Affairs and Northern Development, to Daniel J. Bellegarde and Sheila G. Purdy, Indian Claims Commission, June 7, 2007," *ICCP* 18 (2007): 349.

19 See Tabitha Marshall, "Phil Fontaine," *Canadian Encyclopedia*, 2013, http://www.thecanadianencyclopedia.ca/en/article/phil-fontaine/.

20 Commission issued September 1, 1992, pursuant to Order in Council PC 1992–1730, July 27, 1992, amending the commission issued to Chief Commissioner Harry S. LaForme on August 12, 1991, pursuant to Order in Council PC 1991–1329, July 15, 1991.

21 Tom Siddon, Minister of Indian Affairs and Northern Development, to Ovide Mercredi, Chief, Assembly of First Nations, November 22, 1991, in Indian Specific Claims Commission, *Final Report*, 16 (emphasis added).

22 Order in Council PC 1992–1730, July 27, 1992.

23 "Betsiamites Band: Highway 138 and Rivière Betsiamites Bridge Inquiries," *ICCP* 18 (2007): 277–335, http://publications.gc.ca/site/eng/263487/publication.html.

24 "The Commission Mandate," *ICCP* 3 (1995): 258, http://publications.gc.ca/site/eng/263487/publication.html.

25 Order in Council PC 1991–1329, July 15, 1991.

Chapter 4: Challenges to the Process

1 Most commissions have lifespans of three to four years, which makes the ICC's tenure rather remarkable.

2 Indian Claims Commission, *Annual Report 2008–2009* (Ottawa: Minister of Public Works and Government Services, 2009), 27.

3 Ibid.; Order in Council PC 2007–1789, November 22, 2007.

4 Indian Specific Claims Commission, *Final Report, 1991–2009: A Unique Contribution to the Resolution of First Nations' Specific Claims in Canada* (Ottawa: Minister of Public Works and Government Services, 2009), 32.

5 Ibid., 28.

6 Ibid. The ICC final annual report categorizes the government response to an additional seven inquiries as "other" but does not elaborate.

7 Indian Affairs and Northern Development, "Specific Claims: Justice at Last," Ottawa, 2007, 3, http://www.aadnc-aandc.gc.ca/eng/1100100030458/1100100030472.

8 Confidential letter from staff at the Treaties and Aboriginal Government division of the Specific Claims Branch to Minister of Indian Affairs Bernard Valcourt, leaked to the Aboriginal Peoples Television Network and passed to the author on September 20, 2013.

9 The ICC ceased accepting requests for inquiries in 2007, due to its impending closure.

10 Union of BC Indian Chiefs, "Open Letter to Prime Minister Stephen Harper: In Bad Faith Justice at Last and Canada's Failure to Resolve Specific Claims," March 9, 2015, https://www.ubcic.bc.ca/harperjusticespecificclaims.

11 Indian Affairs and Northern Development, "Specific Claims: Justice at Last," 4.

12 Department of Indian Affairs and Northern Development (DIAND), *Outstanding Business: A Native Claims Policy* (Ottawa: DIAND, 1982), 14.

13 Aboriginal Affairs and Northern Development Canada, "Final Report: Summative Evaluation of the Specific Claims Action Plan," April 2013, 18n17, https://www.aadnc-aandc.gc.ca/DAM/DAM-INTER-HQ-AEV/STAGING/texte-text/ev_spcap_1385136300660_eng.pdf.

14 Ibid., iv.

15 Union of BC Indian Chiefs, "Open Letter to Prime Minister Harper," 13.

16 "Mikisew Cree First Nation Inquiry," *Indian Claims Commission Proceedings* (hereafter *ICCP*) 6 (1998): 192, http://publications.gc.ca/site/eng/263487/publication.html.

17 The Alberta office of DIAND, Specific Claims West deals with the claims of Alberta First Nations, especially as these arise in the Treaties 6, 7, and 8 regions of the province. There are two such offices in Alberta, in Edmonton and Tsuu T'ina First Nation.

18 "Mikisew Cree First Nation Inquiry," *ICCP*, 199.

19 Ibid., 206.

20 Among these were Mikisew Cree (AB); Nekaneet (SK); Alexis (AB); Stanjikoming (ON); Peepeekisis (SK); Siksika (AB); Blood Tribe (AB); One Arrow (SK); Blueberry River and Doig River (BC); Saulteau (BC); Doig River (BC); Dene Tsaa Tsa K'Nai/ Prophet River (BC); Treaty 8 (BC); Red Earth and Shoal Lake (SK); and Makwa Sahgaiehcan (SK). J.B. Edmonds, "Constructive Rejections," memorandum to commissioners, Indian Claims Commission, December 7, 2004.

21 Commission issued September 1, 1992, pursuant to Order in Council PC 1992–1730, July 27, 1992, amending the commission issued to Chief Commissioner Harry S. LaForme on August 12, 1991, pursuant to Order in Council PC 1991–1329, July 15, 1991. Indian Specific Claims Commission, *Final Report*, "Consolidated Terms of Reference," Appendix A.

22 "Interim Ruling: Alexis First Nation Inquiry: TransAlta Utilities Rights of Way Claim Ruling on Government of Canada Objections," *ICCP* 16 (2003): 47–66, http://publications.gc.ca/site/eng/263487/publication.html.

23 "Alexis First Nation Inquiry: TransAlta Utilities Rights of Way Claim," *ICCP* 17 (2004), 21–186 at 98.

24 Ibid., 129–49.

25 *ICCP* 16 (2003): 52–55.

26 Ibid., 6.

27 Ibid.

28 In the interests of closure, I would add that on January 29, 2001, roughly six years after the Alexis Band submitted its claim to the SCB, and five years after Canada's own lawyers supported its acceptance and fast tracking, the minister rejected it. The ICC inquiry proceeded and recommended that DIAND accept the claim for negotiation. Predictably, in July 2005, Canada rejected this recommendation. Indian Claims Commission, *Annual Report 2008–2009*, 69.

29 "Interim Ruling: Athabasca Denesuline Treaty Harvesting Rights Inquiry," *ICCP* 1 (1994): 159, http://publications.gc.ca/site/eng/263487/publication.html; "Lac La Ronge Indian Band Inquiries: Candle Lake and School Lands Claims," *ICCP* 16 (2003): 13–21; "Mikisew Cree First Nation Inquiry," *ICCP*, 209; "Sandy Bay First Nation Inquiry: Treaty Land Entitlement Claim (Interim Ruling)," *ICCP* 12 (2003): 39–46, http://publications.gc.ca/site/eng/263487/publication.html.

30 *ICCP* 16 (2003): 59–60.

31 Ibid., 60.

32 "Red Earth and Shoal Lake Cree Nations: Quality of Reserve Lands Inquiry," *ICCP* 24 (2009): 569.

33 Indian Affairs and Northern Development, "Specific Claims: Justice at Last," 4.

34 ICC transcript, cross-examination of Veda Westlake, director of Research and Policy Directorate, Specific Claims Branch, Indian and Northern Affairs Canada, Saskatoon, August 19, 2005, 118–21, quoted in "Red Earth and Shoal Lake Cree Nations," *ICCP,* 569.

35 Ibid.

36 "Red Earth and Shoal Lake Cree Nations," *ICCP,* 570.

37 Ibid.

38 Ibid., 569.

39 Edmonds, "Constructive Rejections," memo, December 7, 2004, 3.

40 "Red Earth and Shoal Lake Cree Nations," *ICCP,* 570.
The history of this claim and inquiry are from ibid., 427–38. I provide only a brief summary here. For a complete history and a detailed elaboration of the inquiry process and outcome, see the *ICCP* volume.

42 Ibid., 428.

43 Ibid., 431.

44 Ibid., 433.

45 Ibid.

46 Ibid., 433–34.

47 Ibid., 435.

48 Ibid., 436.

49 Ibid.

50 Ibid., 438.

51 Ibid., 547.

52 Ibid., 553.

53 Ibid., 571.

54 Ibid.

55 Ibid., 563.

56 Ibid., 574.

57 Ibid., 580.

58 Ibid., 581–82.

59 Ibid., 582.

60 Ibid., 584.

61 Ibid.

62 Ibid., 585.

63 Federal Court of Canada, file no. T-1864-06.

64 "Red Earth and Shoal Lake Cree Nations," *ICCP,* 416.

65 Indian Specific Claims Commission, *Final Report,* 32.

66 Ibid., 475.

67 Ibid., 478.

Chapter 5: On the Road Again

1 Lower Similkameen Indian Band, https://www.lsib.net/about-us/. The community's population statistic varies slightly from that provided by Indian Affairs, which suggests that the band consists of 515 *registered* members, of whom 226 reside on-reserve. For the department's profile of the band, see Indigenous and Northern Affairs Canada, "Registered Population," http://fnp-ppn.aandc-aadnc.gc.ca/fnp/Main/Search/FNRegPopulation.aspx?BAND_NUMBER=598&lang=eng.

2 "Lower Similkameen Indian Band: Vancouver, Victoria and Eastern Railway Right of Way Inquiry," *Indian Claims Commission Proceedings* (hereafter *ICCP*) 23 (2009): 148, http://publications.gc.ca/site/eng/263487/publication.html.

3 Ibid.

4 "Sandy Bay Ojibway First Nation: Treaty Land Entitlement Inquiry," *ICCP* 22 (2009): 507, http://publications.gc.ca/collections/collection_2009/indianclaims/RC12-1-2009-22E.pdf.

5 "James Smith Cree Nation: Chakastaypasin IR 98 Inquiry," *ICCP* 20 (2008): 502, http://publications.gc.ca/collections/collection_2008/indianclaims/RC12-1-2008-20E.pdf.

6 "James Smith Cree Nation: IR 100A Inquiry," *ICCP* 20 (2008): 179, http://publications.gc.ca/collections/collection_2008/indianclaims/RC12-1-2008-20E.pdf.

7 "Taku River Tlingit First Nation: Wenah Specific Claim Inquiry," *ICCP* 21 (2008): 97–199, http://publications.gc.ca/collections/collection_2009/indianclaims/RC12-1-2008-21E.pdf.

8 Ibid., 102.

9 Ibid.

10 Ibid.

Chapter 6: By Law or In Justice

1 Indian Specific Claims Commission, *Final Report, 1991–2009: A Unique Contribution to the Resolution of First Nations' Specific Claims in Canada* (Ottawa: Minister of Public Works and Government Services, 2009), 66–74.

2 Indian Claims Commission, "Inquiry Process Procedures Manual for the Legal and Research Units," Ottawa, April 2007 (unpublished internal document in author's possession).

3 "Cowessess First Nation: 1907 Surrender Phase II Inquiry," *Indian Claims Commission Proceedings* (hereafter *ICCP*) 21 (2008): 349–533, http://publications.gc.ca/site/eng/263487/publication.html.

4 *British Columbia Terms of Union,* RSC 1985, App. II, No. 10.

5 *Constitution Act, 1867,* 30 & 31 Vict., c. 3, s. 91(24).

6 BC Order in Council 1036, July 29, 1938.

7 *Wewaykum Indian Band v. Canada*, [2002] 4 S.C.R. 245 at 289–90.

8 Ibid., 290.

9 "Lower Similkameen Indian Band: Vancouver, Victoria and Eastern Railway Right of Way Inquiry," *ICCP* 23 (2009): 143, http://publications.gc.ca/collections/collection_2009/indianclaims/RC12-1-2009-23E.pdf.

10 Ibid., 181.

11 Thomas Isaac, *Aboriginal Law: Commentary and Analysis* (Saskatoon: Purich, 2012), 313.

12 *R. v. Taylor and Williams* (1982), 34 O.R. (2d) 360.

13 *R. v. Sparrow*, [1990] 1 S.C.R. 1075; *R. v. Van der Peet*, [1996] 2 S.C.R. 507; *R. v. Badger*, [1999] 1 S.C.R. 771; *Mikisew Cree First Nation v. Canada (Minister of Canadian Heritage)*, [2005] 3 S.C.R. 388; *Haida Nation v. British Columbia (Minister of Forests)*, [2004] 3 S.C.R. 511; *Taku River Tlingit First Nation v. British Columbia (Project Assessment Director)*, [2004] 3 S.C.R. 550.

14 *Taku River* at 564.

15 Isaac, *Aboriginal Law*, 326.

16 Indian Affairs and Northern Development, "Specific Claims: Justice at Last," Ottawa, 2007, 4, http://www.aadnc-aandc.gc.ca/eng/1100100030458/1100100030472.

17 *Samson Indian Nation and Band v. Canada*, [1995] 2 F.C. 762 (C.A.) in *Wewaykum* at 293–94.

18 "Cowessess First Nation: 1907 Surrender Phase II Inquiry," *ICCP*, 349.

19 "Cowessess First Nation Inquiry: 1907 Surrender Claim," *ICCP* 14 (2001): 233, http://publications.gc.ca/collections/collection_2012/gtrpc-rsctc/RC12-1-2001-14-eng.pdf.

20 Ibid., 234.

21 Ibid., 235.

22 Ibid., 236.

23 Ibid.

24 Ibid., 241–42.

25 Ibid., 242.

26 Ibid., 246–47.

27 Ibid., 229.

28 *Indian Act*, RSC 1906, c. 81, s. 49(1); "Cowessess First Nation Inquiry: 1907 Surrender Claim," *ICCP*, 230.

29 "Cowessess First Nation Inquiry: 1907 Surrender Claim," *ICCP*, 246.

30 Ibid., 248.

31 Ibid., 249–50.

32 Ibid., 272.

33 Ibid.

34 Ibid., 272, 273.
35 "Response to Cowessess Inquiry," *ICCP* 15 (2002): 376.
36 "Cowessess First Nation: 1907 Surrender Phase II Inquiry," *ICCP,* 355.
37 *Blueberry River Indian Band v. Canada,* [1995] 4 S.C.R. 344.
38 "Cowessess First Nation: 1907 Surrender Phase II Inquiry," *ICCP,* 390.
39 Ibid., 356.
40 Ibid., 357.
41 Ibid.
42 *Wewaykum* at 293–94.
43 Order in Council PC 1992–1730, July 27, 1992.
44 Indian Specific Claims Commission, *Final Report,* 33.
45 The claims were Blood Tribe/Kainaiwa, Alberta, Akers surrender, settled in 2003 for $3.5 million; Chippewas of the Thames, Ontario, Clench defalcation, settled in November 2004 for $15 million; Fishing Lake, Saskatchewan, 1907 surrender, settled in August 2001 for $34.5 million; Fort Pelly Agency, Saskatchewan, Pelly haylands claim, settled in November 2008 for $78.3 million; George Gordon, Saskatchewan, treaty land entitlement claim, settled in 2008 for $26.6 million; Kahkewistahaw First Nation, Saskatchewan, 1907 surrender, settled in November 2002 for $94.65 million; Keeseekoowen, Manitoba, 1906 land claim, settled in March 2005 for $6,999,900; Metepenagiag Mi'kmaq, New Brunswick, Hosford Lot and Indian Reserve No. 7, settled for $1.4 million; Michipicoten Pilot Project, settled for $52.3 million; Moosomin, Saskatchewan, 1909 reserve land surrender, settled in September 2003 for $41 million; Muskoday, Saskatchewan, treaty land entitlement, settled for $10.25 million; Roseau River Anishinabe, Manitoba, settled in March 1996 for $14 million; Standing Buffalo, Saskatchewan, settled in March 2003 for $3.6 million; Sturgeon Lake, Saskatchewan, treaty land entitlement, settled for $10.4 million. Indian Claims Commission, *Annual Report 2008–2009.*
46 These were Qu'Appelle Valley Indian Development Authority, Saskatchewan, flooding claim, parties unable to come to agreement; Touchwood Agency, Saskatchewan, mismanagement (1920–24) claim, parties unable to come to an agreement, requested an ICC inquiry.
47 "Michipicoten First Nation Pilot Project (Mediation)," *ICCP* 24 (2009): 717, http://publications.gc.ca/site/eng/263487/publication.html.
48 Indian Claims Commission, *Annual Report 2008–2009,* 49.
49 Ibid., 51.
50 This information is from private commissioner notes taken during a presentation by the Mediation Unit in April 2003.
51 "Kahkewistahaw First Nation 1907 Surrender Claim (Mediation)," *ICCP* 17 (2004): 3, http://publications.gc.ca/collections/Collection/RC12-1-2004-17E.pdf.

52 "Fishing Lake First Nation 1907 Surrender Claim (Mediation)," *ICCP* 15 (2002): 291, http://publications.gc.ca/collections/collection_2012/gtrpc-rsctc/RC12-1-2002 -15-eng.pdf.

Chapter 7: Beyond Lawful Obligation

 1 Canada, "Negotiation or Confrontation: It's Canada's Choice: Final Report of the Standing Senate Committee on Aboriginal Peoples Special Study on the Federal Specific Claims Process," Ottawa, December 2006, Appendix C, http://www.afn.ca/ uploads/files/sc/spec_-_2006_negotiation_or_confrontation_(senate_report).pdf.
 2 Outstanding Business: A Native Claims Policy was announced by Minister of Indian and Northern Affairs John Munro on May 13, 1982.
 3 Canada, "Negotiation or Confrontation," 29.
 4 Specific Claims Tribunal Canada, "A Brief History of Specific Claims Prior to the Passage of Bill C-30: *The Specific Claims Tribunal Act*," http://www.sct-trp.ca/hist/ hist_e.htm.
 5 Mary C. Hurley, *Bill C-6: The Specific Claims Resolution Act* (Ottawa: Library of Parliament, Parliamentary Research Branch, 2002), 7.
 6 Ibid.
 7 Assembly of First Nations, "Report of the Joint First Nations–Canada Task Force on Specific Claims Policy Reform," Ottawa, November 25, 1998, http://www.afn.ca/ uploads/files/sc/spec_-_report_on_joint_first_nations_-_canada_task_force_on_ specific_claims_policy_reform.pdf.
 8 Ibid.
 9 Ibid., 9; Canada, "Negotiation or Confrontation," 33.
10 Canada, "Negotiation or Confrontation," 21.
11 Ibid., 20.
12 Assembly of First Nations, "Report of the Joint First Nations–Canada Task Force," 11.
13 Ibid., 14.
14 Ibid., 9; Hurley, *Bill C-6*, 7.
15 Assembly of First Nations, "Report of the Joint First Nations–Canada Task Force," 9.
16 Ibid., 19.
17 Ibid., 13.
18 Ibid., 9.
19 Ibid.
20 Department of Indian Affairs and Northern Development (DIAND), *Outstanding Business: A Native Claims Policy* (Ottawa: DIAND, 1982).

21 Assembly of First Nations, "Report of the Joint First Nations–Canada Task Force," 7.

22 DIAND, *Outstanding Business;* Assembly of First Nations, "Report of the Joint First Nations–Canada Task Force," 6–7.

23 Hurley, *Bill C-6,* 8.

24 Ibid.

25 Ibid., 14.

26 Ibid., 12.

27 Ibid., 10.

28 Ibid.

29 Parliament of Canada, *Bill C-6,* http://www.parl.ca/DocumentViewer/en/37-2/bill/C-6/royal-assent.

30 Hurley, *Bill C-6,* 16–17.

31 Indian Claims Commission presentation to the House Standing Committee on Aboriginal Affairs, Northern Development and Natural Resources, Ottawa, November 26, 2002.

32 First Nations Summit, "Bill C-6 – Proposed Specific Claims Resolution Act," memorandum prepared for the Standing Committee on Aboriginal Affairs, Northern Development and Natural Resources, Ottawa, November 27, 2002, 6; Paul Barnsley, "Government Has Change of Heart on Claims Bill," *Windspeaker* 23 (8) (2005): 11.

33 Hurley, *Bill C-6.*

34 First Nations Summit, "Bill C-6," 5.

35 Hurley, *Bill C-6,* 16.

36 Indian Claims Commission presentation to the House Standing Committee on Aboriginal Affairs, Northern Development and Natural Resources, Ottawa, November 26, 2002.

37 Ibid.

38 Ibid.

39 Mary Hurley, "Legislative History of Bill C-6," in Mary Hurley, *Bill C-6: The Specific Claims Resolution Act* (Ottawa: Parliament of Canada, Law and Government Division, October 10, 2002; revised November 5, 2003), https://lop.parl.ca/About/Parliament/LegislativeSummaries/bills_ls.asp?Language=E&ls=C6&Parl=37&Ses=2&source=library_prb.

40 Phil Fontaine, "Specific Claims Resolution Act Will Not Be Implemented: A Victory for First Nations," *Assembly of First Nations Bulletin,* November 21, 2005, http://www.turtleisland.org/discussion/viewtopic.php?p=6349.

41 Ibid.

42 Canada, "Negotiation or Confrontation."

43 Ibid., 24.

44 Ibid.

45 Indian Affairs and Northern Development, "Specific Claims: Justice at Last," Ottawa, 2007, 1, http://www.aadnc-aandc.gc.ca/eng/1100100030458/1100100030472.

46 Ibid.

47 Ibid., 9.

48 Ibid.

49 Ibid.

50 Ibid.

51 Ibid., 10.

52 Ibid.

53 Jim Prentice had shared the chief commissioner position with Dan Bellegarde for seven years, from 1994 to 2001; Phil Fontaine was chief commissioner from 2001 to 2003.

54 Indigenous and Northern Affairs Canada, "Political Agreement between the Minister of Indian Affairs and Northern Development and the National Chief of the Assembly of First Nations in Relation to Specific Claims Reform," Ottawa, 2007, https://www. aadnc-aandc.gc.ca/eng/1100100030315/1100100030316.

55 Ibid.

56 Mary C. Hurley, *Bill C-30: The Specific Claims Tribunal Act* (Ottawa: Library of Parliament, Parliamentary Research Branch, 2008), i.

57 Ibid., 25.

58 Ibid., 14.

59 *Specific Claims Tribunal Act*, SC 2008, c. 22, s. 7(1), http://laws-lois.justice.gc.ca/eng/acts/S-15.36/page-1.html?wbdisable=true.

60 Indigenous and Northern Affairs Canada, "Political Agreement between the Minister of Indian Affairs and Northern Development and the National Chief of the Assembly of First Nations in Relation to Specific Claims Reform," Ottawa, 2007.

61 Ibid.

62 *Specific Claims Tribunal Act*, s. 42(1).

63 Indian Affairs and Northern Development, "Specific Claims: Justice at Last," 10.

64 Union of BC Indian Chiefs, "Open Letter to Prime Minister Harper: In Bad Faith Justice at Last and Canada's Failure to Resolve Specific Claims," March 9, 2015, 3, https://www.ubcic.bc.ca/harperjusticespecificclaims.

65 Assembly of First Nations, "Specific Claims Review: Expert Based – Peoples Driven," Ottawa, Assembly of First Nations Independent Expert Panel Report, May 15, 2015, 13, http://www.afn.ca/uploads/files/specific_claims/expert_panel_report.pdf.

66 *Specific Claims Tribunal Act*, s. 40(2).

67 Hurley, *Bill C-30,* 24.

68 Mohawk Council of Akwesasne, "Mohawk Council of Akwesasne Presentation to the Standing Committee on Aboriginal Affairs and Northern Development on the Specific Claims Tribunal Act (Bill C30) and the Political Agreement," Ottawa, press release, April 14, 2008, http://akwesasne.ca/pressrelease?q=node/244.

69 Hurley, *Bill C-30*, 23.

70 Mohawk Council of Akwesasne, "Mohawk Council of Akwesasne Presentation," 2.

71 Canadian Bar Association, National Aboriginal Law Section, *Bill C-30 Specific Claims Tribunal Act* (Ottawa: Canadian Bar Association, 2008), 4.

72 Assembly of First Nations, "Specific Claims Review," 4.

73 The decisions and rulings of the tribunal can be found at Specific Claims Tribunal Canada, "Decisions List," http://www.sct-trp.ca/judg/index_e.asp?claimFileNumber=&claimant=&decisionDateFrom=&decisionDateTo=&province=0&pageNumber=2&filterBy=&filterOrder=.

74 Specific Claims Tribunal Canada, "Annual Report," Ottawa, 2012, http://www.sct-trp.ca/pdf/AnnualReport-09302012_eng.pdf.

75 Specific Claims Tribunal Canada, "Annual Report," Ottawa, 2014, 2 (emphasis in original), http://www.sct-trp.ca/pdf/Annual%20Report%202014.pdf.

76 Assembly of First Nations, "Specific Claims Review," 11–12; Algonquin Nation Secretariat, "Specific Claims and the Specific Claims Tribunal Act: Five Years Later: A Presentation by the Algonquin Nation Secretariat on Behalf of the First Nations of Timiskaming, Wolf Lake, Barriere Lake and Eagle Village," March 10, 2015, 3, http://new-wordpress.algonquinnation.ca/wp-content/uploads/2015/09/2015-03-09-ANS-to-AFN-re-SCTA-kit.pdf; Federation of Saskatchewan Indian Nations, "Five Year Review: Specific Claims Tribunal Act (SCTA)" (presentation to the Expert Panel, AFN Forum, Toronto, March 10, 2015); David Knoll, "AFN-Specific Claims Review," n.d., 5, http://www.afn.ca/uploads/files/specific_claims/david_knoll-afn_specific_claims_process_review-_(vancouver_presenter).pdf.

77 Hurley, *Bill C-30*, 24.

78 Federation of Saskatchewan Indian Nations, "Five Year Review," 10. The federation has since become the Federation of Sovereign Indigenous Nations.

79 Assembly of First Nations, "Specific Claims Review."

80 Federation of Saskatchewan Indian Nations, "Five Year Review," 11.

81 Knoll, "AFN-Specific Claims Review," 5. For the action plan, see Indian and Northern Affairs Canada, "Specific Claims Action Plan," https://www.aadnc-aandc.gc.ca/eng/1100100030455/1100100030456.

82 Assembly of First Nations, "Specific Claims Review," 11.

83 Union of BC Indian Chiefs, "Open Letter to Prime Minister Harper," 10.

84 Federation of Saskatchewan Indian Nations, "Five Year Review," 18.

85 Algonquin Nation Secretariat, "Specific Claims," 4.

86 *Specific Claims Tribunal Act,* s. 16(2)(a).

87 Assembly of First Nations, "Specific Claims Review," 13.

88 Ibid., 14.

89 *Aundeck Omni Kaning v. Her Majesty the Queen in Right of Canada,* 2014 SCTC 1, https://decisia.lexum.com/sct/roa/en/item/182275/index.do.

90 Ibid., 3.

91 Ibid., 24.

92 Indian Affairs and Northern Development, "Specific Claims: Justice at Last," 10, https://www.aadnc-aandc.gc.ca/eng/1100100030516/1100100030517.

93 Union of BC Indian Chiefs, "Open Letter to Prime Minister Harper," 24.

94 Assembly of First Nations, "Specific Claims Review," 13.

95 Ibid.

96 Assembly of First Nations, "Justice Delayed: Assembly of First Nations Submission to Canada for the Five Year Review of the Specific Claims Action Plan: 'Justice at Last,'" Ottawa, Assembly of First Nations, March 31, 2012, 7, http://www.afn.ca/uploads/files/specific_claims_-_5-year_review_submission_(final).pdf.

97 Assembly of First Nations, "Specific Claims Review," 10.

98 Assembly of First Nations, "Justice Delayed," 5.

99 Assembly of First Nations, "Specific Claims Review," 6.

100 Ibid.

Chapter 8: The Legacy of the ICC

1 Order in Council PC 2007–1789, November 22, 2007.

2 As noted in Chapter 4, the ICC's *Annual Report 2008–2009* indicates that forty-one inquiries were ended prior to completion; of those, six were concluded at the request of the First Nation, eleven were terminated by the ICC for lack of file activity, and twenty-four were ended by the Order in Council that closed the commission. Indian Claims Commission, *Annual Report 2008–2009,* 25, 30.

3 Ibid., 32.

4 See Daniel Leblanc and Greg McArthur, "Mulroney-Schreiber Relationship 'Inappropriate,' Probe Finds," *Toronto Globe and Mail,* May 31, 2010, https://www.theglobe andmail.com/news/politics/mulroney-schreiber-relationship-inappropriate-probe-finds/article4321310/.

5 "Long Plain First Nation Inquiry: Loss of Use," *Indian Claims Commission Proceedings* 12 (2000): 269–342, http://publications.gc.ca/site/eng/263487/publication.html.

6 Indian Specific Claims Commission, *Final Report, 1991–2009: A Unique Contribution to the Resolution of First Nations' Specific Claims in Canada* (Ottawa: Minister of Public Works and Government Services, 2009), 32.

7 Ibid.

8   *Guerin v. The Queen,* [1984] 2 S.C.R. 335.

9   Ibid., 376.

10 For example, *Guerin; R. v. Sparrow,* [1990] 1 S.C.R. 1075; *R. v. Badger,* [1996] 1 S.C.R. 771; *R. v. Marshall No. 1,* [1999] 3 S.C.R. 456; *Haida Nation v. British Columbia (Minister of Forests),* [2004] 3 S.C.R. 511; *Manitoba Metis Federation v. Canada (A.G.) et al,* [2013] 1 S.C.R. 623.

11 *Wewaykum Indian Band v. Canada,* [2002] 4 S.C.R. 245 at 293–94.

12 *Haida Nation* at 522.

13 Indian Specific Claims Commission, *Final Report,* 31.

14 *Specific Claims Tribunal Act,* SC 2008, c. 22, s. 14(1)(c), http://laws-lois.justice.gc.ca/eng/acts/S-15.36/page-1.html?wbdisable=true.

15 *Manitoba Metis Federation* at 630.

16 Ibid., 631.

17 Ibid., 632.

18 Thomas Isaac, *Aboriginal Law: Commentary and Analysis* (Saskatoon: Purich, 2012), 47, 46.

19 Ibid., 219.

20 *Haida Nation* at 522–23 (emphasis added).

21 Indian Affairs and Northern Development, "Specific Claims: Justice at Last," Ottawa, 2007, 4, http://www.aadnc-aandc.gc.ca/eng/1100100030458/1100100030472.

22 Confidential letter leaked to APTN reporter Nigel Newlove, passed to the author on September 20, 2013.

23 David Arnot, "The Honour of First Nations – The Honour of the Crown: The Unique Relationship of First Nations with the Crown" (paper presented at "The Crown in Canada: Present Realities and Future Options," Ottawa, June 10, 2010).

24 Ibid.; Isaac, *Aboriginal Law,* 313.

25 Isaac, *Aboriginal Law,* 313.

26 *Wewaykum* at 293–94.

Index

Notes: AFN stands for Assembly of First Nations; DIAND, for Department of Indian Affairs and Northern Development; ICC, for Indian Specific Claims Commission; JTF, for Joint First Nations–Canada Task Force; SCB, for Specific Claims Branch; SCC, for Supreme Court of Canada; SCTA, for Specific Claims Tribunal Act.

Aboriginal Peoples Television
    Network, 4–5, 188n6
AFN–Canada Joint Working Group
    (1992), 150, 151–52
Akwesasne reserve, 48, 57
Alexis First Nation inquiry, 11, 89–90,
    203n28
Algonquin Nation Secretariat, 171
Apsassin case (*Blueberry River Indian*
    Band) case (SCC, 1995), 139,
    140–41
Arnot, David, 184
Assembly of First Nations (AFN)
    advice re independent review body
      after Oka Crisis, 6, 149
    AFN Independent Expert Panel
      hearings on SCTA, 170, 172
    on backlog of claims shifted to
      SCT, 174

    calls to replace ICC with permanent
      body, 6, 149
    claims policy's denial of AFN input
      in claims bodies (2000), 155
    on conflict of interest in claims
      process, 42–43
    opposition to Specific Claims
      Resolution Act (Bill C-6), 7, 158
    regret at ICC's demise, 9
    SCTA betrayal of *Justice at Last*
      promise, 175
    support for the SCTA (2007), 167
    "value" of land seen as just monetary
      by government, 47
    See also Joint First Nations–Canada
      Task Force (1992)
Athabaska Denesuline inquiry, 90
Atleo, Shawn, 167
Augustine, Roger, 66, 137

Aundeck Omni Kaning First Nation
claim, 172–73

Badger case (1996) and honour prin-
ciple, 133–34
Bagot, Charles, 18
Barber, Lloyd, 33–35, 149
Bell, Robert C., 29
Bellegarde, Dan, 66, 67, 73
Betsiamites Band inquiry, 77
Bill C-6. *See* Specific Claims Resolution
Act (Bill C-6, 2002)
Bill C-30. *See* Specific Claims Tribunal
Act (Bill C-30, 2007)
Bill C-31 on enfranchisement and
marrying-out *vs.* Indian status, 50
Blueberry River Indian Band (Apsassin)
case (SCC, 1995) on test for fidu-
ciary duty, 139, 140–41
British Columbia
BC Terms of Union, creation of
reserves, 130–31
disagreements with federal govern-
ment re Indigenous rights and
reserves, 130–31
land claims commission endorsed
by, 15
Nisga'a Final Agreement (2000), 36
territory predominantly unceded,
15, 190n6, 191n8
Burlington Northern Railway
Company, 111–12

Calder case (SCC, 1973) on Indigenous
land rights, 20, 35, 196n105
Callihoo, Michael, 49
Canadian Bar Association, on SCTA
(2007), 167

Canadian Centre for the Independent
Resolution of First Nations
Specific Claims, 155–56
Canupawakpa First Nation inquiry, 70
Cardinal, Harold, 34
Chiefs Committee on Claims (1990),
58, 60–61, 64, 150. *See also* Indian
Specific Claims Commission
(ICC), creation; Joint First Nations–
Canada Task Force (JTF)
Chrétien, Jean, 33
claims, comprehensive, 35–36, 187n1
claims, specific. *See* specific claims
claims commission (1969–77), 33, 149
community sessions of ICC
author's experience as commissioner,
9
cross-examination of elders, views
on, 11, 118–21
elder testimony, other difficulties,
122–23
elders, qualifying as, 121–22
elders' oral histories of claim events,
123–24
ensuring integrity of decision
making, 113–14, 116–17, 153
evidentiary record, closing of, 127
integrity of results dependent on
integrity of process, 120
interactions between ICC and
claimants, 75, 77, 108–9
located in claimant's territory, 78–79
not included in government's 2000
policy proposal, 156
panel able to question all witnesses,
121
value to commissioners and claimants, 123–25, 156

comprehensive claims, 35–36, 187n1
conflict of interest
JTF's report dealing with (1998),
150–51
in *Justice at Last* (2007 policy statement), 4–5, 174, 179
in Office of Native Claims (comprehensive claims), 36
in *Outstanding Business* (1982 policy
statement), 4–5, 40, 42–43, 58, 93,
120, 179
remains in claims policy after SCTA,
174–75
constructive rejection policy (ICC)
aim to uphold the "honour of the
Crown," 88, 106–7
in Alexis First Nation claim, 11, 90
criteria determining de facto rejection, 88, 90–91, 93
delay by SCB central factor, 10–11, 83
disallowed in Bill C-6 (2000) as
ground for inquiry, 158
"formal rejection" not defined, 89
formal rejection only ground for
inquiry (view of government), 89,
90–91
in Mikisew Cree claim, 87–88
no pressure on DIAND to determine
claims in timely manner, 100
"queue jumping" argument of government, 91–93
reaction of SCB to, 179
Red Earth and Shoal Lake inquiry
(*see* Red Earth and Shoal Lake
Cree First Nations inquiry)
restricting ICC mandate could lead
to unfairness, 90–91
significant development in accountability, 178–79

Corcoran, Carole, 66, 137
Cote First Nation mediation, 144, 147
Court of Claims (US, 1855), 24, 26
Cowessess First Nation claim
attendance at oral sessions, 129
basis of claim to SCB, 135–37
disagreement between panel and
legal counsel on fiduciary duty,
135, 140–42
ICC inquiry initiated (1996), 137
phase I's key issue the validity of
land surrender, 137–38
phase II's key issue nature of Crown's
fiduciary obligations, 138–42
Coyle, Michael, 19
Crown
ambivalent approach to extreme
poverty on reserves, 18
disinclination to enforce legislation
protecting Indigenous land, 18
enfranchisement of Indigenous
people goal of state (after 1857),
49–50
fundamental flaw in approach to
specific claims, 4–5
honour of (*see* Crown, honour of)
"outstanding contingent liability" re
claims (2006), 151
See also Department of Indian Affairs
and Northern Development
(DIAND); government policies on
land and treaty claims; Indigenous
and Northern Affairs Canada
(INAC)
Crown, honour of
appeals by ICC to honour of Crown
futile, 134, 183
author's skepticism re, 134–35
author's understanding of, 182–83

Crown encouraged by ICC to act
honourably, 71, 106–7, 133
defining principle in dealings with
Indigenous people, 134, 180–82
disregarded in Aundeck Omni
Kaning claim, 172–73
Haida First Nation (2004) on, 133–
34, 183
lawful obligation only ground for
settlement (government view), 7,
73, 108, 134, 184–85
legal and ethical principle, 182–84
Manitoba Metis Federation decision
(SCC, 2013) on, 181–82
reconciliation and need for honourable dealing by government, 185
SCB's failure to uphold honour,
173
SCC jurisprudence on, 133–34
unwritten promises honoured in
Treaty 1, 17
upheld by ICC's constructive rejection policy, 88, 106–7
See also fiduciary obligations of
federal government

Delgamuukw decision (SCC, 1998) re
Indigenous land rights, 20
Department of Aboriginal Affairs and
Northern Development (DAAND).
See Department of Indian Affairs and
Northern Development (DIAND);
Indigenous and Northern Affairs
Canada (INAC)
Department of Indian Affairs and
Northern Development (DIAND)
adversarial approach to claims as-
sessment (after 2007), 7–8, 85,
150–51, 170–75

appeals by ICC to uphold honour of
the Crown futile, 134, 183
claims resolved through rejection or
"file closure," 7–8, 85–86
climate of control and micromanaging, 5
conflict of interest in claims policy
(*see* conflict of interest)
control over claims review and outcomes, 40, 42, 60
disappointing response to ICC
reports, 68–71, 106–7
encouraged by ICC to uphold
honour of the Crown, 71, 106–7,
133
fiduciary obligations not respected,
16, 41–42, 45, 47–48, 86
Indigenous use of courts prohibited
(1927–51), 21, 148
lawful obligation of Crown only
ground for settlement, 7, 73, 108,
134
no pressure to determine claims in
timely manner, 100
Office of Native Claims (1974), 36
policies (*see* specific claims policies)
Special Claims Branch (*see* Specific
Claims Branch)
Specific Claims Action Plan (2013),
85
tension between ICC and DIAND,
68–71
See also fiduciary obligation of federal government; Indigenous and
Northern Affairs Canada (INAC);
Specific Claims Branch
Dickson, Jane
appointment to ICC, 72–73
on closure of ICC, 9, 176

community sessions, value to com-
    missioners, 123–25
elder testimony, other difficulties,
    122–23
elders, qualifying as, 121–22
elders' cross-examination, 118–21
elders' oral histories of claim events,
    123–24
experience as ICC commissioner, 9
first planning conference and com-
    munity session, 110–14
government's general disrepect for
    ICC, 177–78
honour of the Crown, skepticism re,
    134–35
honour of the Crown, understanding
    of, 182–83
on impact of ICC, 178–81
importance of the land to First
    Nations, 47, 51, 125
integrity of decision making essential,
    113–14, 116–17
integrity of results dependent on
    integrity of process, 120
lessons learned from elders, 119
on Lower Similkameen Indian Band
    inquiry, 110–14, 117–18
panel responsibility for just (not
    solely legal) results, 133
Taku River Tlingit First Nation
    inquiry, 123–24
travel experience to northern BC,
    109–10
See also entries beginning with Indian
    Specific Claims Commission
Diefenbaker, John, 30–31
Ditchburn-Clark Commission (1920),
    131

Dupuis, Renée, 71–72, 73, 77
Dutcheshen, Carol, 66

Edmonton Journal, on Oka Crisis, 48
enfranchisement of Indigenous people,
    49–50

Federation of Saskatchewan Indian
    Nations, 7, 22, 170
fiduciary obligations of federal
    government
abandoned in negotiation of num-
    bered treaties, 16
basis for claims in SCTA, 181
Blueberry River Indian Band
    (Apsassin) case (SCC, 1995) test
    for fiduciary duty, 139
description, 41
disagreement between commis-
    sioners and counsel (Cowessess
    inquiry), 135, 140–42
greater elucidation through ICC
    work, 180
Guerin case (SCC, 1984) on, 20, 41,
    180
key issue in many ICC inquiries, 135
lawful obligation of Crown only
    grounds for settlement, 7, 73,
    108, 134
limited to "land and assets" in 2000
    policy proposal, 155
Lower Similkameen inquiry, 131–33
multiple interests to be considered,
    141, 185
non-fulfillment as grounds for claims,
    154–55
not respected by DIAND, 16, 41–42,
    45, 47–48, 86

Oka Crisis (1990), government's failure to respect its obligations, 45, 47–48

recognized by ICC in various contexts, 181

Wewaykum decision (SCC, 2002) and, 131–32, 141, 185

File Hills Colony, 10, 51, 68–70, 93

First Nations Specific Claims Commission (FNSCC), 152–54

First Nations Summit, 66, 201n13

Fishing Lake claim (mediation), 146–47

Fontaine, Phil, 71, 158–59, 160

Fort Frances First Nation, 16

Fort William First Nation claim (mediation), 144

Friends of the Michel Society, 50, 198n34

Gaddie, Alex, 138

Gill, Aurélien, 67

Gladstone, James, 30–31, 195n88

Gladstone parliamentary committee studying Indian policy (1959), 30–31

government policies on land and treaty claims

activist Indigenous organizations created (WWII), 22

amendments to Indian Act (1927), 21–22

assimilation and denial of claims (1927–39), 22

assumptions that Indigenous peoples were a dying race, 21–22

Calder decision (1973), impact of, 20, 35, 196n105

claims agreements (post-1973), 35–36

commission proposal unsuccessful (1964), 33

comprehensive claims negotiated (post-*Calder*), 35–36

conflicts of interest (*see* conflict of interest)

core principles and approach same since 1973, 148–49

enfranchisement goal of state (after 1857), 49–50

Gladstone parliamentary committee to study Indian policy (1959), 30–31

JTF's review (1996–98), 150–55

La Forest's review of government approach (1980), 36

law over morality, delays, and attitude of government, 30

modern policies mainly about how to divest Aboriginal communities of lands, 39

Office of Native Claims (1974), 36

perversity between principles and approach to claims, 148–49

Red Paper (1970, reply to White Paper), 34

Senate Standing Committee on Aboriginal Affairs, 59, 62–64

Senate Standing Committee on Aboriginal Peoples, 7, 151, 161

Senate-Commons joint committee on Indian Act and other Indian Affairs matters (1946), 22–23, 30, 148

title vested in individual Indigenous persons (held in trust by Crown), 31

White Paper (1969), 33–35
See also specific claims policies
Gradual Civilization Act (1857), 50
Gradual Enfranchisement Act (1869), 50
Graham, William, 137
Great Northern Railway, 111
Guerin v. The Queen (SCC, 1984), 20, 41, 180
Gwich'in Treaty, 95 (map)

Haida First Nation (SCC, 2004), 133–34, 183
Hamelin, Charles-André, 66
Harper, Elijah, 67
Harper, Stephen, and end of ICC (2009), 6
Holman, Alan, 71, 73
honour of the Crown. *See* Crown, honour of
House Standing Committee on Aboriginal Affairs, Northern Development and Natural Resources, and Bill C-6, 158–60
Howe, Joseph, 16

ICC. *See entries beginning with* Indian Specific Claims Commission (ICC)
Indian Act (1876)
    aim of "civilizing" and assimilating Indigenous people, 21–22
    amendments (1927) to squash Indigenous claims, 21
    definition of "Indian band," 49
    involuntary enfranchisement of Indigenous people, 50
    state regulation of all aspects of lives on reserves, 18

termination proposed in White Paper (1969), 33
Indian and Northern Affairs Canada (INAC). *See* Indigenous and Northern Affairs Canada (INAC)
Indian Association of Alberta, 22
Indian Claims Commission (US, 1946–78), 23, 25–30, 195n69
Indian Claims Commission Act (US, 1946), 27
Indian Commission of Ontario, 42
Indian Residential Schools Settlement, 67, 71
Indian Specific Claims Commission (ICC)
    activism subtle but present, 60
    appeals to honour of Crown futile, 134, 183
    appointment process for commissioners, 65
    balancing law and justice, 99–100, 133, 134–35, 142–43
    Bill C-6, ICC's response to proposed bill, 158–60
    Bill C-6 (2002), omen re ICC's demise, 147
    bound by DIAND's view of legitimate claims, 73
    calls for it to be replaced by permanent body, 6, 149
    closure (2009) and its impact, 6, 9, 174–75
    commission structure, 74–75
    commissioners, 66–67, 71–73, 153
    constructive rejection policy (*see* constructive rejection policy (ICC))
    creation (*see* Indian Specific Claims Commission (ICC), creation)

DIAND's disappointing response to ICC reports, 68–71, 82–83, 106–7

effectiveness in changing government's mind, 68–71, 83, 104

government's disregard for final ICC reports, 177–78

government's general disrepect for, 178

hope given to communities often unfounded, 104

Indian Claims Commission Proceedings (for 2008–09), 11, 177

inquiries (*see* Indian Specific Claims Commission (ICC), inquiries)

legacy of (*see* Indian Specific Claims Commission (ICC), legacy)

mandate, original and revised, 6, 60–62, 64–65, 73, 90–91, 108

mandate, supplemental, 73–74, 99–100, 134

mediation function, 6, 11, 143

power solely to inquire, report, and recommend, 9, 61, 65, 149

Prentice as Indian Affairs minister (2006–07), 67–71

process (*see* Indian Specific Claims Commission (ICC), process)

recommendations accepted by government, 83, 176–77

rules of procedure controversial, 11, 118–21

Indian Specific Claims Commission (ICC), creation

change of name by ICC, purpose, 60

Chiefs Committee on Claims, role of, 58, 60–61, 64

creation (1991) in response to Oka Crisis, 5, 60, 149–50

mandate, 60–62, 64–65

Order in Council (1991), 59, 61–62, 64

Order in Council (1992), 64–65, 75

stalemate until OIC amended, 64

working group formed to amend first OIC, 64

Indian Specific Claims Commission (ICC), inquiries

Alexis First Nation inquiry, 11, 89–90, 203n28

Athabaska Denesuline inquiry, 90

Betsiamites Band inquiry, 77

Canupawakpa First Nation inquiry, 70

Cote First Nation claim (mediation), 144, 147

Cowessess First Nation inquiry (*see* Cowessess First Nation claim)

Fishing Lake claim (mediation), 146–47

Fort William First Nation claim (mediation), 144

Kahkewistahaw First Nation claim (mediation), 146

Lac La Ronge Band inquiry, 90

Long Plain First Nation inquiry, 179–80

Lower Similkameen Indian Band inquiry (*see* Lower Similkameen Indian Band inquiry)

Mikisew Cree inquiry, 87–88, 90, 93

Nekaneet inquiry, 93

number of recommendations accepted by government, 83

Peepeekisis First Nation inquiry, 10, 51, 68–70, 93

Red Earth and Shoal Lake (*see* Red Earth and Shoal Lake Cree First Nations inquiry)

Sandy Bay First Nations inquiry, 90

Siksika First Nation, 10, 51

Taku River Tlingit First Nation
  inquiry, 123–24

See also government policies on land
  claims; Indigenous land rights

Indian Specific Claims Commission
  (ICC), legacy

constructive rejection policy (*see*
  constructive rejection policy (ICC))

cumulative impact of work, 178–81

government's disregard for final ICC
  reports, 177–78

"loss of use" as consideration for
  compensation, 180

number of mediations/inquiries
  carried out, 6, 11, 82–83, 143,
  176–77, 212n2

Indian Specific Claims Commission
  (ICC), process

balance reinserted into history, 108–9

claims' eligibility criteria, 75–76, 83

community sessions (*see* community
  sessions of ICC)

constructive rejection policy (*see*
  constructive rejection policy
  (ICC))

Crown's lawful obligation only
  ground for settlement (per
  DIAND), 73, 134

delays the chief difficulty, 5, 10, 51,
  68, 83

expert testimony, 127

ICC's ability to choose process,
  108–9

importance of the land to First
  Nations, 47, 125

internal politics and protocol,
  114–16

mediation function (*see* mediation)

oral Indigenous histories *vs.* written
  records, 108, 123–24

oral sessions, 79–80, 126, 128–29

panel deliberations and report (*see*
  panel deliberations and report,
  ICC)

panel members and assistants, 76–77

planning conferences, 77–78, 109–
  10, 112–14, 156

report to Parliament through Privy
  Council Office, 81

supplemental mandate, 73–74, 80

Taku River Tlingit First Nation
  inquiry, 123–24

Indigenous and Northern Affairs
  Canada (INAC)

approach to claims assessment (after
  2007), 7–8, 85, 150–51, 170–75

backlog of claims shifted from SCB
  to SCT, 8, 85–86, 166, 174, 189n18

changes in department's name,
  188n14

disregarding ICC's final reports,
  177–78

ICC's concerns re Bill C-6, 158

INAC-AFN task force on independent claims tribunal (2007), 163

letter to television network re
  specific claims' delay, 4–5, 188n6

"outstanding contingent liability"
  re claims (2006), 151

Specific Claims Branch (*see* Specific
  Claims Branch)

See also Department of Indian
  Affairs and Northern Development
  (DIAND); government policies on
  land and treaty claims; specific
  claims policies

Indigenous land and treaty rights
  Aboriginal title a "mere burden" on
    the Crown (*St. Catherine's Milling*,
    1888), 19, 33
  Aboriginal title similar to fee simple
    (*Tsilhqot'in*, 2014), 20
  amendments to Indian Act (1927),
    22
  condemnation of Canadian ap-
    proach in Oka Crisis (1990), 6
  court cases (*see* Indigenous land
    rights, court cases)
  federal *vs.* provincial control over
    lands (1888), 18–19
  government committed to assimila-
    tion and denial of claims (1927–
    39), 22
  government's lack of interest in deal-
    ing with claims, 21
  Indigenous activism, 22–23, 35
  Indigenous use of courts prohibited
    (1927–51), 21, 148
  land and its value to First Nations,
    47, 51, 125
  "outstanding contingent liability" re
    claims (2006), 151
  recognition in 1763 Royal Proclama-
    tion, 14–15
  Royal Proclamation of 1763 as
    "Charter of Indian Rights," 15
  See also Department of Indian
    Affairs and Northern Develop-
    ment (DIAND); government poli-
    cies on land and treaty claims;
    Indian and Northern Affairs
    Canada (INAC); Indigenous land
    rights, court cases
Indigenous land rights, court cases
  Calder case (1973), 20, 35, 196n105

Delgamuukw decision (1998), 20
Guerin case (1984), 20, 41, 180
Sparrow (1990), 41, 133–34
*St. Catherine's Milling and Lumber
  Co. v. R.* (1888), 18–19, 33
Tsilhqot'in case (2014), 20
Inuvialuit Treaty, 95 (map)
Isaac, Thomas, 134

Jackson, Henry M., 26
James Bay and Northern Quebec
    Agreement (1975), 36, 95 (map)
James Smith Cree Nation inquiries,
    113
Joint First Nations–Canada Task Force
    (JTF)
  AFN compromise on fiscal frame-
    work for claims resolution,
    151–52
  conflict of interest, proposals to
    address, 152–53
  on disconnect between First Nations'
    and Canada's view of obligations
    in claims, 150–51
  First Nations Specific Claims Com-
    mission (FNSCC), 152–54
  government anxieties re cost of
    claims resolution, 151
  membership, 150
  recommendation re commission
    and tribunal, 152–54
  recommended claims liabilities
    expanded, 154–55
  report's focus on key challenges of
    policy, 150–51
  review of specific claims policy, 150
  revised claims policy (2000) (*see*
    Specific Claims Resolution Act
    (Bill C-6, 2002))

Judicial Committee of the Privy
    Council, on *St. Catherine's Milling*
    (1888), 18–19
Justice at Last (2007 policy statement)
    AFN on policy and loss of ICC, 9
    as a new approach to claims policy
        (according to the minister), 73,
        161–62
    conflict of interest remains after
        policy overhaul, 4–5, 174, 179
    four pillars of approach, 162–63, 173
    INAC-AFN task force on independ-
        ent claims tribunal, 163
    little changed since 1973, 163
    mediation and its implementation,
        162–63, 173–74
    new Specific Claims Tribunal (*see*
        Specific Claims Tribunal (SCT)
        (2007–present))
    outstanding claims in 2007, 83–84
    promise betrayed by government's
        approach to claims, 175
    promises re transparency, speed,
        and negotiation, 7
    vision of policy "dimmed and
        narrowed," 174
    See also Specific Claims Branch
        (SCB)
Justice Department (Canadian)
    control over claims review and out-
        comes, 40, 42, 60
    delays in assessing claims, 51, 84–85,
        100
    "discounting" settlements, 46, 61
    inconsistent and obstructionist re
        claims, 38, 51
    interpretation of *St. Catherine's
        Milling and Lumber* decision, 33
    legal review of land claims, 84
    legalistic, narrow approach to claims,
        34, 49
    member of joint INAC-AFN task
        force (2007), 163
    reaction to ICC's constructive rejec-
        tion, 90, 179
    role in determining validity of
        Indigenous claims, 40
    under-resourcing for claims reviews,
        166, 169, 170
Justice Department (US), 26, 29

Kahkewistahaw mediation/facilitation,
    146
Kahnawake reserve and Oka Crisis,
    48, 57

La Forest, Gérard, 36
Labrador Inuit Treaty, 95 (map)
Lac La Ronge Band inquiry, 90
LaForme, Harry, 59, 62–64, 67, 200n6
Laird, David, 136, 138
Le Duc, Thomas, 28–29
LeRat, Joe, 137, 139, 140
Leupp, Francis E., 25, 26
Long Plain First Nation inquiry, 179–80
Lower Similkameen Indian Band
    inquiry
    claim description, 110–12, 130–31
    community session, 117–18
    Crown's fiduciary obligations and
        Wewaykum decision, 131–33, 185
    oral session attendance, 129
    oral sessions, 133
    panel/ICC legal counsel disagree-
        ment re Crown's obligation, 131–
        34, 142
    panel's responsibility for justice, not
        just legal interpretation, 133

planning conference with commissioners, 112–14
See also Dickson, Jane

Maa-nulth Treaty, 95 (map)
Mackenzie King, William Lyon, 22-23
Mainville, Johanne, 168
Manitoba Metis Federation case
(SCC, 2013) on honour of Crown,
181–82
Manitoulin Island Treaty, 95 (map)
McKenna-McBride Commission
(1912), 124, 131
mediation
commissioners kept at arm's length,
11, 144–45, 147
contained in OIC (1992), 65, 143
Cote First Nation claim, 144, 147
decommissioning of ICC, 9, 173–74
Fishing Lake mediation, 146–47
Fort William First Nation claim, 144
government's views re ICC media-
tion, 145–46
handled by Mediation Unit, 75
Kahkewistahaw mediation/
facilitation, 146
Mediation Unit's unwillingness to
reveal its process, 146
Michipicoten First Nation claim, 144
SCB's control of mediation (after
2007), 166, 173–74
successful mediations, 11, 143
Mercredi, Ovide, 59, 62, 74
Meriam Report (US, 1928), 25
Metis peoples, 16, 32
Michel Band, 49–51
Michel Indian Reserve No. 132, 50
Michipicoten First Nation mediation,
144

Mikisew Cree First Nation (SCC, 2005),
133–34
Mikisew Cree inquiry, 87–88, 90, 93
Miller, J., 15
Mohawk Council of Akwesasne, 167
Mohawks of Kahnesatake
concerns about SCTA (2007), 167
extensive delays in processing
claims, 51
on government's narrow interpretation of lawful obligations, 44–45
Oka crisis, 45, 47–48, 53–58
three claims to The Pines rejected by
DIAND, 5, 44, 47–48, 56–57, 149–
50, 198n21
Mulroney, Brian, 6, 48, 58

Naskapi Treaty, 95 (map)
Native Brotherhood of British Colum-
bia, 22
Nekaneet inquiry, 93
New Credit First Nation, 46
Nisga'a Final Agreement (2000), 36, 95
(map)
North American Indian Brotherhood,
22
Northeastern Quebec Agreement
(1978), 36
Northwest Territories and land claims,
15
numbered treaties. *See* treaties,
numbered
Nunavik Inuit Treaty, 95 (map),
191n7
Nunavut Treaty, 95 (map)

Oglala Sioux, 35
Oka Crisis (1990)
Akwesasne reserve, 48, 57

catalyst for ICC's creation, 5, 58, 60,
149–50
condemnation of Canadian approach
to Indigenous land rights, 6, 58
cost of, 48–49
description of events, 47–49, 53–58
government initiatives to deal with,
58, 150
government's failure to respect its
fiduciary obligations to Mohawks,
45, 47–48
Indigenous frustration re policy
Outstanding Business, 38
Indigenous history at Oka, 52–53
Kahnawake reserve, 48, 57
Municipality of Oka's involvement,
47–48, 55, 57
The Pines's importance to Mohawks,
47
result of failed specific claims, 5, 44,
47–48, 52, 56–57, 149–50, 198n21
Sulpicians' involvement, 44–45,
53–54
See also Joint First Nations–Canada
Task Force (JTF); Indian Specific
Claims Commission (ICC)
Ontario, ruling re Saulteaux lands
(1888), 19
oral sessions of ICC, 79–80, 126,
128–29
Orders in Council on ICC
1991 OIC, 59, 61–64
1992 OIC, 64–65, 75, 143
2007 OIC on closing ICC, 176
SCB's statement that justice or reasonableness not to be considered
by ICC, 99
Outstanding Business (1982 policy
statement)

assimilation still the focus of policy,
43
compared with claims policy (2000),
155
compensation criteria and "loss of
use," 179–80
conflict of interest as fundamental
flaw, 4–5, 40, 42–43, 58, 93, 120,
179
criticisms and problems, 38, 40, 43
"degree of doubt" interpretation,
45–46, 61
discounting practice re settlements,
46, 51, 61
extent of consultation with Aboriginal leaders, 40
failure to recognize cultural/spiritual
value of land to Indigenous
people, 47
fiduciary obligation of government
not acknowledged, 41–42
"justice" promised to First Nations,
99
laches and limitations, use by government, 40–41
"lawful obligation" narrowly inter-
preted, 40, 43, 44–45, 73, 154,
198n21
process for making a claim, 39–40
"special value to the owner" interpretation, 47–48, 61
specific claims policy, 36–37
type of claims dealt with, 38–40

panel deliberations and report, ICC
after orals, 80, 129–30
panel/ICC counsel disagreements,
131–34, 135, 140–42
report drafts and final report, 143

restricted participants, 126
tensions between commissioners
and ICC counsel, 11, 80, 128, 130
Peepeekisis First Nation inquiry, 10,
51, 68–70, 93
The Pines, 5, 45, 47–48
catalyst for Oka Crisis, 45, 47–48
planning conferences of ICC
experiment involving commissioners, 112–14
not mentioned in policy proposal
(2000), 156
number needed for an inquiry,
112–13
scheduling problems, 77–78, 109–10
Prentice, James (Jim)
criticism in role re specific claims,
68–71
ICC commissioner, 66–67
as Indian Affairs minister (2006–07),
66–67
new approach to claims policy (Bill
C-30), 161–62
number of outstanding claims in
2007, 83–84
praise for some actions as minister,
67
Pueblo of San Ildefonso v. United States
(US, 2006), 29
Purdy, Sheila, 67, 73

Ray, A.J., 15
Re Osoyoos Indian Band (SCT decision,
2012), 168
Red Earth and Shoal Lake Cree First
Nations inquiry
appeal by government of ICC denial
of Canada'a motion, 102–3
claim, basis of, 98

community session (2007), 103–4,
105–6
constructive rejection policy, efforts
to apply, 11, 88, 92, 93, 100–102
Crown challenge to ICC constructive rejection policy, 98, 99–100
E.B. Campbell Dam, impact, 106–7
ICC recommendations ignored by
government, 94, 107
moral and ethical factors in claim, 94
planning conference (2005), 103
reserve alterations requested due to
flooding, 96–98
reserves' early success, 96
supplementary mandate statement,
81, 134
Red Paper (1970), as reply to White
Paper, 34
Red River uprising (1869–70), 16
Reserve Commission (1875), 131
reserves
Akwesasne reserve, 48, 57
all aspects of life regulated by state
(Indian Act), 18
BC Terms of Union, creation of
reserves, 130–31
Crown's ambivalent approach to
extreme poverty on, 18
insufficient and scattered reserves
result of treaty process, 18
Kahnawake reserve, 48, 57
Michel Indian Reserve No. 132, 50
settler encroachment/squatting,
17–18
Wewaykum decision (SCC, 2002) re
BC pre-1938, 131–33, 141, 185
Riel Rebellion (1885), 16
Robinson-Huron Treaty (1850), 16–17,
95 (map)

Robinson-Superior Treaty (1850), 16–17, 95 (map)

Rosenthal, Harvey, 25, 27, 29–30

Royal Commission on Aboriginal Peoples (1996), 6, 149

Royal Proclamation of 1763 ("Charter of Indian Rights"), 14–15

Ryan, Claude, 58

Sah'tu Dene Treaty, 95 (map)

Sandy Bay First Nations inquiry, 90

Sandy Bay Ojibway First Nation, 112

Saulteaux First Nation, 18–19

Scholtz, Christa, 22, 31

Scott, Andy, 160

Senate Standing Committee on Aboriginal Affairs, 59, 62–64

Senate Standing Committee on Aboriginal Peoples, 7, 151, 161

Senate-Commons joint committee on the Indian Act and other Indian Affairs matters (1946), 22–23, 30, 148

Shoal Lake Cree First Nation. *See* Red Earth and Shoal Lake Cree First Nations inquiry

Siddon, Tom, 74

Siksika First Nation, 10, 51

Slade, Harry, 168

Smith, Patrick, 168, 173

Sparrow decision (SCC, 1990), 41, 133–34

"Special Study on the Federal Specific Claims Process" (Senate Standing Committee on Aboriginal Peoples), 7, 161

Specific Claims Action Plan (DIAND, 2013), 85

Specific Claims Branch (SCB)
  approach to claims assessment (after 2007), 7–8, 85, 150–51, 170–75, 177–78
  Aundeck Omni Kaning First Nation claim (2008), 172–73
  backlog of claims off-loaded to SCT, 8, 85–86, 166, 174, 189n18
  claims process, 5, 39–40, 84–85
  claims viewed as just another government program, 151
  conflict of interest in claims process (*see* conflict of interest)
  constructive rejection policy (*see* constructive rejection policy (ICC))
  delays by Crown in processing claims, 10, 51–52, 83–85, 178–79
  discounting practice re settlements, 46, 51, 61
  disregard of ICC's final reports, 177–78
  fiduciary role (*see* fiduciary obligations of federal government)
  general disrepect for ICC, 177–78
  honour of the Crown, failure to uphold, 173
  judicial criticism of, 9
  letter from staff to television network re specific claims' delay, 4–5, 188n6
  mediation under its control (after 2007), 166, 173–74
  "miserly" approach to claims, 170–71
  narrow construction of "lawful obligation," 44–45, 69–70, 73, 134

Red Earth and Shoal Lake inquiry
(*see* Red Earth and Shoal Lake
Cree First Nations inquiry)
"special value to the owner" interpretation, 47–48, 61
stance that ICC not to consider
justice or reasonableness, 99
"take-it-or-leave-it" offers of compensation, 171–73
terminology construed as narrowly
as possible, 43, 44–45, 49
timeframes for review/resolution of
claims (after 2007), 165–66
under-resourcing, 5, 166–67,
185–86
See also Indian Specific Claims
Commission (ICC), inquiries;
Specific Claims Tribunal (SCT)
(2007–present)
specific claims policies
1958 JTF policy review, 150–55
1959 Gladstone parliamentary committee studying Indian policy,
30–31
1960s, support for land claims commission, 31–33
1963 claims commission bill died in
House, 33
1982 policy statement (see *Outstanding Business* (1982 policy
statement))
2000 policy statement (*see* Specific
Claims Resolution Act (Bill C-6,
2002))
2007 policy statement (see *Justice at
Last* (2007 policy statement))
"degree of doubt" interpretation, 45–
46, 61

discounting practice re settlements,
46, 51, 61
existence because of unkept promises, 14
government's narrow construction
of "lawful obligation," 44–45,
69–70, 73, 134, 154
La Forest's call for independent
claims body (1980), 36
"lawful obligation" narrowly inter-
preted, 40, 43, 44–45, 73, 154,
198n21
process with inadequate resources,
delays, and government ambivalence, 5, 166–67, 169–71, 175,
185–86
"special value to the owner" interpretation, 47–48, 61
specific *vs.* comprehensive claims,
187n1
terminology construed as narrowly
as possible, 43, 44–45, 49
See also Department of Indian
Affairs and Northern Development
(DIAND); government policies on
land and treaty claims; Indigenous
and Northern Affairs Canada
(INAC)
Specific Claims Resolution Act (Bill
C-6, 2002)
accountability of minister illusory,
157
bill not proclaimed due to opposition,
6–7, 149, 160
criteria for forwarding claims to the
tribunal, 156–57, 159–60
delays disallowed as ground for constructive rejection, 158

disregard for JTF's recommendations
re claims policy, 155–56, 159
ICC's reservations to proposed bill,
158–60
impact on ICC and SCT, 147
independence of Centre compromised, 159
Specific Claims Tribunal Act (Bill
C-30, 2007)
AFN Independent Expert Panel
hearings on, 170
disappointment, as little changed
since 1973, 163
fiduciary obligations as grounds for
claims, 181
First Nations' on funding cuts for
claims, 170
ICC's demise signalled, 149
INAC-AFN task force on legislation,
163
mediation under control of SCB, and
not used, 166, 173–74
new approach to claims policy, 73,
161–62
new Specific Claims Tribunal created, 7, 149, 163
reactions by AFN, Mohawk Council,
Canadian Bar Association, 167,
172
SCT members appointed without
AFN input, 164
See also *Justice at Last* (2007 policy
statement)
under-resourcing of SCT and SCB,
5, 166–67, 169–71, 175, 185–86
Specific Claims Tribunal (SCT)
(2007–present)
appointment process, without AFN
input, 152–53, 164–65

appointments (2009), 168
backlog of claims shifted to SCT
from SCB, 8, 85–86, 166, 174,
189n18
creation (2007), 7, 163–64
decisions in first five years, 168,
172–73
eligibility of claims for hearing, 7,
165
independence and powers of SCT,
152–53
judicial criticism of SCB, 9
mediation under control of SCB,
166
"new approach" to claims, 7, 73,
162–63
pillar of government's new approach,
7
respected by First Nations and
source of hope, 175
under-resourcing, 166–67, 169–71,
175, 185–86
specific *vs.* comprehensive claims,
187n1
St. Catherine's Milling and Lumber, on
Indigenous land rights (1888), 18–
19, 33
Sulpicians' involvement in Oka Crisis,
44–45, 53–54
Supreme Court of Canada (SCC)
Badger case (1996) and honour principle, 133–34
*Blueberry River Indian Band
(Apsassin)* case (1995) on test for
fiduciary duty, 139, 140–41
Calder case (1973) on Indigenous
land rights, 20, 35, 196n105
Delgamuukw decision (1998) on features of Indigenous land rights, 20

Guerin case (1984) on Indigenous land rights and fiduciary obligations, 20, 41, 180

Haida First Nation (2004) on honour principle, 133–34, 183

Manitoba Metis Federation decision (2013) on honour of Crown, 181–82

Mikisew Cree First Nation (2005) on honour principle, 133–34

Sparrow (1990) on fiduciary responsibility of government, 41, 133–34

Taku River case (2004) on honour principle, 133–34

Tsilhqot'in case (2014) on Indigenous land rights, 20

Van der Peet (1996) and honour principle, 133–34

Wewaykum decision (2002) on Indian reserves in BC pre-1938, 131–33, 141, 185

Taku River case (SCC, 2004), 133–34

Taku River Tlingit First Nation inquiry, 123–24

Taylor and Williams, R. v. (1982), on honour of Crown, 133

Tlicho Treaty, 95 (map)

Tough, F., 15

treaties

British defeat of New France (1760), impact on treaty relationship, 14

first treaties re friendship and commerce, 13–14, 189n3

in Great Lakes Basin, 15

map of, 95

numbered treaties (1871–1921), 15, 16–18, 95 (map)

reasons for existence, 13

Robinson-Huron Treaty (1850), 16–17, 95 (map)

Robinson-Superior Treaty (1850), 16–17, 95 (map)

Royal Proclamation of 1763 ("Charter of Indian Rights"), 14–15

treaties (1763–1850), 15

treaty commissioners (1870), 16

See also Indigenous activism; Indigenous land and treaty rights

treaties, numbered (1871–1921)

consistent in form and content, 16–17

eleven treaties re prairies, 15

failure of government to act on claims could lead to violence, 15–16

map of, 95

negotiations used by Indigenous peoples to protect land and way of life, 15

settler encroachment on reserve lands, 17–18

Treaty 1, 17, 95 (map)

Treaty 2, 95 (map)

Treaty 3, 18–19, 95 (map)

Treaty 6, 17, 49, 95 (map)

Treaty 7, 95 (map)

Treaty 8, 95 (map), 98

Treaty 10, 95 (map)

treaty commissioners (1870), 16, 21

unwritten promises often not honoured, 17

Treaty and Aboriginal Rights Centre of Manitoba, 7

Trudeau, Pierre, 33

Truth and Reconciliation Commission, 71

Tsawwassen Treaty, 95 (map)

Tsilhqot'in case (SCC, 2014) on
  Indigenous land rights, 20

Union of BC Indian Chiefs, 7, 86
United States
  Court of Claims (1855), 24, 26
  efforts to create body to deal with
    Indian claims (early 1900s), 25
  government's goal the assimilation
    of Indigenous people, 25
  Indian Claims Commission (1946–
    78), 23, 25–30, 195n69
  Indigenous peoples not protected
    by Constitution, 24, 193n50
  Meriam Report (1928) on creation
    of Indian Claims Commission,
    25
  treatment of Indigenous treaty
    claims, 23

treaty process terminated (1871),
  24–25
The Unjust Society (Cardinal), 34

Valcourt, Bernard, 4–5, 187n2
Van der Peet (SCC, 1996), 133–34
Vancouver, Victoria and Eastern
  Railway and Navigation Company,
  111, 131

Weaver, Sally, 34
Wewaykum Indian Band v. Canada
  (SCC, 2002), 131–33, 135, 185
White Paper (1969), 33–35
Williams Treaties, 95 (map)
Wounded Knee (1973) and Oglala
  Sioux, 35

Yukon land claims, 15, 191n7